"I'm truly impressed with this remarkable book. While Nicki shares the magic of Sekhmet's power to create healing and transformation in your life, she gifts you with sacred stories and extraordinary photos to illustrate your journey. Nicki's mastery is clear as she guides you through an alchemical process comprised of many initiations and exercises that will change your life."

SANDRA INGERMAN, M.A., AUTHOR OF *SOUL RETRIEVAL*

"Just reading Nicki's fierce and fearless book can begin the process of transformation. Ah, but if you actually *do* the work—if you let Sekhmet devour you, digest you, heal you, change you—*that* is when the magic happens. Let Nicki be your loving and wise guide on this transmutational journey. It will be scary. There will be fire. But oh, it will be worth it."

M. ISIDORA FORREST, AUTHOR OF *ISIS MAGIC: CULTIVATING A RELATIONSHIP WITH THE GODDESS OF 10,000 NAMES*

"*Sekhmet* is a potent amalgamation of Nicki Scully's *Alchemical Healing* and the wisdom of Sekhmet, the transformative goddess of the threshold who arrives when the Great Ages shift. As the most intense Aquarian shift comes—Sekhmet's hour—Nicki Scully's guidance for regenerating our brains and body systems is a lifesaver—an exquisite healing balm."

BARBARA HAND CLOW, AUTHOR OF *AWAKENING THE PLANETARY MIND*

"Nicki Scully has decades of leading tours to the sacred sites of ancient Egypt, in two of which I participated many years ago. In the course of this book, while focused on Sekhmet, the reader will also encounter Thoth the god of wisdom; Ptah the inventor; Ma'at the cosmic truth, justice, and balance; Knum the potter who rebuilds the body; and Khepera, the protector. The reader learns not only about these mythic figures but learns how to access these deities in a ritualistic way for spiritual transformation. Lavishly illustrated with striking photographs, this book is a treasure chest of healing meditations!"

RALPH METZNER, PH.D., AUTHOR OF *ECOLOGY OF CONSCIOUSNESS*

"I have heard many accounts of Sekhmet and her powerful, ongoing manifestations through select individuals. This goddess refuses to be forgotten. She serves as a hierophant or bridge to a world of vast psychic potentialities. She beckons us to visit her small and obscure shrine located amid the magnificent Temple of Karnak. Nicki Scully takes us further into her mysteries as only a daughter of the goddess can do."

JEFFREY MISHLOVE, PH.D., HOST AND PRODUCER OF
NEW THINKING ALLOWED VIDEO CHANNEL

"This is an amazing book, beautiful in both images and words, empowering readers to deal with the profound issues and challenges of our time. Read it to gain knowledge, surrender to its wisdom to heal yourself, and work it to transform your ability to act for the good of all our relations!"

BROOKE MEDICINE EAGLE,
AUTHOR OF *BUFFALO WOMAN COMES SINGING*

"*Sekhmet* enlivens the alchemical fire of transmutation within and offers a pathway to become one's most refined and potent self. All who choose to partake in this primal alchemical process and embrace Sekhmet as ally and friend have an opportunity to self-initiate into an empowered state of grace. What a gift Nicki is giving to readers."

DANIELLE RAMA HOFFMAN AUTHOR OF *THE TABLETS OF LIGHT*

"Are you ready for transformation? If so, this is the book for you. The belly of the goddess is a haven of peace, a cauldron of illumination and ultimate rebirth. Now, more than ever, we need Sekhmet in our lives and she is available at her finest in this book."

KATHRYN W. RAVENWOOD,
AUTHOR OF *HOW TO CREATE SACRED WATER*

"Nicki Scully's latest book, *Sekhmet,* leads the reader to new depths of understanding and connection with the mighty Sekhmet. Sa Sekhem Sahu."

CANDACE ROSS, RESIDENT PRIESTESS AT THE TEMPLE OF
GODDESS SPIRITUALITY, DEDICATED TO SEKHMET

# SEKHMET

Transformation *in the* Belly *of the* Goddess

## Nicki Scully

Bear & Company
Rochester, Vermont • Toronto, Canada

Bear & Company
One Park Street
Rochester, Vermont 05767
www.BearandCompanyBooks.com

Text stock is SFI certified

Bear & Company is a division of Inner Traditions International

**Library of Congress Cataloging-in-Publication Data**
Names: Scully, Nicki, 1943– author.
Title: Sekhmet : transformation in the belly of the goddess / Nicki Scully.
Description: Rochester, Vermont : Bear & Company, 2017. | Includes
  bibliographical references and index.
Identifiers: LCCN 2016047873 (print) | LCCN 2017013386 (e-book) |
  ISBN 9781591432074 (pbk.) | ISBN 9781591437864 (e-book)
Subjects: LCSH: Sekhmet (Egyptian deity) | Rites and ceremonies. | Shamanism.
  | Medicine, Magic, mystic, and spagiric. | Spiritual healing.
Classification: LCC BF1999 (e-book) | LCC BF1999 .S3694 2017 (print) |
  DDC 299/.312114—dc23
LC record available at https://lccn.loc.gov/2016047873

Printed and bound in the United States by Lake Book Manufacturing, Inc.
The text stock is SFI certified. The Sustainable Forestry Initiative® program
promotes sustainable forest management.

10   9   8   7   6   5   4   3   2   1

Text design and layout by Virginia Scott Bowman
This book was typeset in Garamond Premier Pro with Casandra Graphika, Gill
Sans, Garamond Premier Pro, and Avenir used as display typefaces

Fig. 4.1 copyright © 1991, 2001, 2017 by Angela Werneke
Fig. 17.1 adapted by Debbie Clarkin from an illustration in *Herbs for Eastern
Meridians and the Five Element Theory,* by Evelyn Mulders
Fig. 18.2 and color plate 21 copyright © 2007, 2008, 2017 by Kris Waldherr. Used
by permission. All rights reserved. www.kriswaldherr.com
Color plates 1 and 2 copyright © 2015 by Ptahmassu Nofra-Uaa

To send correspondence to the author of this book, mail a first-class letter to the
author c/o Inner Traditions • Bear & Company, One Park Street, Rochester, VT
05767, and we will forward the communication, or contact the author directly at
**www.shamanicjourneys.com.**

*This book is lovingly and gratefully dedicated*
*to my two mothers,*
*Sergee Summer (1918–2015)*
*and the goddess Sekhmet—*
*may she continue to nurture and protect us eternally,*
*and may I reciprocate in lifelong service as*
*a true warrior of Ma'at.*

# Contents

❋

## PART I
### *Who, What, and How—*
### *Beginning the Alchemical Journey*

## PART IV
### *Transformation*

# It's the Feeling You Get
# When You Are Sekhmetized

## Normandi Ellis

Nicki Scully is an inspiration. When she breathes out, she breathes out the Egyptian mysteries. Over the years I've watched her work up close. When the gods and goddesses take hold, her eyes glitter, and she shines with a golden aura. She says humbly that she doesn't see or channel, but I tell you this: she embodies. If you don't believe me just watch her interview with Dr. Jeffrey Mishlove on the New Thinking Allowed series. You can't tell me that's not Thoth inside that body.

Soon after its inception, *The Anubis Oracle* was well received, and many people have been inspired by it. It has earned its place among some of the best of Nicki's oracular mysteries. The book you hold in your hands, *Sekhmet: Transformation in the Belly of the Goddess,* has been in Nicki's repertoire of mystery school teachings for a while—at least in various incarnations. As you will see in the pages of this book, Sekhmet takes her time, and her work with you is thorough. I find this book among Nicki's most powerful works in its initiations into self-healing and exploration of the mysteries.

My own experience with Sekhmet in July 1989 came during my first pilgrimage to Egypt. Alone and fearful as my domestic life was beginning to unravel at the seams, I encountered Sekhmet and her fierce compassion. For three days the boat on which I sailed stopped at temples along the Nile, while I lay semi-comatose in my bed, ill beyond anything I'd ever experienced. In this delirious, hypnagogic state, the black granite lion/woman/goddess that I had recently seen at Karnak grew a tawny coat and found her way to me as I lay sweating and shivering in my bed. Her wild, golden eyes locked onto mine. I lifted my hand to her, and she put her warm, furry, and leather-padded paw above my hand. Not touching me, she simply merged her auric energy with mine.

We lifted off the damp sheets and flew out of the portal window and over the Sahara hills. My astral body and Sekhmet's floated inches above the golden sands. I could feel the heat of the sand dunes and the grit scouring across my belly. Sekhmet showed me how to breathe through my teeth as if I were birthing a child; I was in desperate need of a new life.

When I came back from that desert journey, healed from my bodily distress, it took about two years to fully integrate that healing experience. I began a new life—the result of which has been my work with the pantheon of Egypt. Every subsequent trip to Egypt (and I took many of them with Nicki Scully), whenever I was able, I made my pilgrimage to the dark chamber of Sekhmet and Ptah's temple at Karnak. Entering the darkened room, I am always eager to see my lion goddess mother, to express my gratitude, and to breathe her breath again.

When you encounter Sekhmet in these pages, you will see that this vision quest is an authentic experience. My healing initiation with Sekhmet occurred years before Nicki and I ever met each other over a phone call—a hilarious story in itself. The experience I had on that boat, however, was never told to Nicki. Yet much of it is a replica of the journey she articulates in this book. All I can say is that, from my experience, "This the real deal."

I did encounter Sekhmet's healing energy a few years after my illness through the work of Robert Masters and Jean Houston. Here I learned the specific mind-body connection with Sekhmet as healer, vision initiator, and the lion heart of the goddess herself. I say these things to make a point. Over the last three-thousand-plus years, Sekhmet has been one busy lady. To date there are numerous books of prayers dedicated to her, as well as a number of recently built shrines, temples, and chapels in the United States and around the world. She is making her presence known.

She is making her presence known in fierce compassion for all of us in this world at this time in the midst of planetary and personal transformation of the highest order. Simply put, this is Sekhmet's hour.

Nicki says in her introduction, *"It appears that the world is split, and many of us are being subjected to . . . the madness that is the result of our refusal to take our job as stewards of our precious planet seriously. . . . Many of us are being called and trained to awaken [Sekhmet's] power within ourselves, so that each of us becomes a powerful guardian of Ma'at."*

We can best do this healing of the planet by first healing ourselves. One of the most powerful medicines of Sekhmet is self-forgiveness. One needs that to become a healer of any kind. One needs to be loved, to be accepted, and to be one's own true self—seeing from one's heart rather than through one's eyes. Sekhmet teaches us this fierce compassion. Like a lioness hunting, she asks us to be vigilant—to notice the changes occurring around us, to seek out and eliminate those self-defeating behaviors and patterns of thought that have held us bound in an inert and modified existence. This difficult and important work is designed to give us a new start, to take the remaining energy in the detritus of an old life and to regenerate it and ourselves at a cellular level.

Not only must we be vigilant about our very human errors, we must recognize and accept our broken and abandoned dreams, for in them lies a great healing balm. In truth we have lost not just our hope, but we have lost the energy to transform when our dreams are shattered. Sekhmet's work with us helps us to reclaim this energy.

One of the most powerful experiences in this book is that of finding one's consciousness able to negotiate time and space, moving from the ancient world to the future self and pulling these back into the present.

The shifts into alternate realities prove to be not just any astral journey, but one that is visceral and sensual—made so through the writing of Nicki Scully. Inside and out she places us firmly in the belly of the goddess, feeling ourselves nourishing and nourished.

Through this deep work each one of us is permitted to choose a new reality to carry us forward in life. And in so choosing we find a new joy, a new exuberance that is necessary to co-create a new self—in the new world. We have no more time for false humility and shyness, the sense of not being enough or knowing enough. Nicki tells us: *We don't have time for that anymore.* Besides that, it is not ourselves alone who are working to co-create a new reality. We are working with the entire *neteru.** We are working with the Divine.

I ask you to step fully into this work, to allow it to deepen your vision of yourself and your reality. Sekhmet assures you that she is there to co-create with you and to empower you to do the sacred work. What are you waiting for? Go now.

NORMANDI ELLIS is an award-winning writer, workshop facilitator, clairvoyant, and spiritualist minister. She is the author of thirteen books, including *Awakening Osiris, Invoking the Scribes of Ancient Egypt, Imagining the World into Existence, Dreams of Isis, Feasts of Light,* and *The Union of Isis and Thoth* (coauthored with Nicki Scully).

---

*Neteru* is the term used to refer to the whole pantheon of Egyptian gods and goddesses. It is the plural of *neter* (masculine) and *netert* (feminine).

# My First Encounter
# with Sekhmet

## Hank Wesselman, Ph.D.

By profession I am an anthropologist (Ph.D., UC Berkeley), a former college and university lecturer as well as a field researcher who has worked since 1971 with several international research expeditions to Ethiopia, searching the ancient, eroded landscapes of the Great Rift Valley in search of answers to the mystery of human origins. My discoveries have been published in my many scientific papers and monographs.*

Yet in addition, I have been a shamanic practitioner and teacher for more than thirty-five years, and in response to my continued focus on the inner worlds, certain unusual life experiences have become available to me. These have been recorded in my published metaphysical books and papers.

In January of 2003, I led a travel group to Egypt, an extraordinary adventure guided by Emil Shaker, who is mentioned later in Nicki's book. During this trip we visited the great sites of antiquity in response to which many of the travelers had strong dreams as well as

---

*This foreword was first published as part of a larger essay, "My Encounters with Sekhmet," in *Heart of the Sun: An Anthology in Exaltation of Sekhmet,* by Candace C. Kant and Anne Key (Bloomington, Ind.: iUniverse, 2011), 104–11.

vivid paranormal experiences. The account that follows records some experiences of my own, and although many of my esteemed academic colleagues might regard them as fanciful, even fictional, everything that follows was experienced as real.

# KARNAK

January 9—Our guide and Eygptologist, Emil, picked us up at our hotel in Luxor at 6:00 a.m. It was still pitch dark as we boarded our bus and headed for the famous temple complex known as Karnak. When we arrived at our destination, I could just make out the guards smiling as they recognized our guide, and he suavely tipped them so we could enter the site at this early hour.

The temple of Karnak was and is the heart of Egypt. It is one thing to view photographs of this incredible place in oversized books at our leisure. It is something quite different to actually stand among the silent, massive stone pillars of this site in the darkness before the dawn, surrounded by the soft, warm, earthy scent of the desert and the stones, with the soft whispering winds and the overarching stars as our companions.

This immense temple complex is composed of many shrines and was constructed by its builders across hundreds of years on a monumental scale fit for the gods, the neteru themselves. How it was done continues to invoke a sense of mystery within us today, as it is doubtful that we could replicate it in our own time, even with all our high technology.

For example, one side of the immense roof that stands many stories above the ground is built slightly higher than its opposing side, creating a natural form of air-conditioning in that warm air is drawn upward during the hot time of the day, allowing cooler breezes from the Nile to the west to flow inward and downward. And this was conceived and executed by Egyptian architects and engineers while the peoples of Europe were still living in their barbarian villages far to the north, a thousand years before the Greek civilization arose.

We in the group stood humbled under the desert sky as we tried to take in the site's full immensity and power. Karnak, and its complement, the Temple of Luxor, is one of the wonders of the ancient world.

The light was just beginning to show in the east as our guide took us up the main avenue and into the small shrine that he told us was historically used by the pharaoh to await the rising sun. Having come so early, we were the only visitors in the vast complex on that day, and so this event carried a certain specialness . . . one could almost say "holiness."

As the rising sun cracked the horizon and suddenly shafted across the altar, we felt our connection with eternity affirmed across more than three-and-a-half-thousand years . . . and we felt our unity with the great mystery that spawned us.

After witnessing the eastern light illuminate the altar, our guide led us quickly to the northeastern edge of the huge site, passing a small scrubby sycamore about eight or nine feet tall, which is more than 2,500 years old and is still alive. We then headed toward a small stone building housing the shrine of Ptah.

## THE SHRINE OF PTAH

The word *Egypt* means "the land of Ptah." This deity was (and forever will be) the archetypal force of creation, who came from the stars and who formed the world by thinking it and by speaking it into being with his words. In his blue aspect—his blue skin or blue cap—Ptah ruled Egypt for 8,000 years, according to myth. His consort (or complement) during this age was (and is) Sekhmet, the great transformational lion-headed goddess.

After our guide greeted the guards and crossed their palms with a modest wad of Egyptian pounds, the iron grate across the unprepossessing shrine was unlocked and we stepped into the small stone building, entering a room in the center of which a raised dais bears a headless statue of Ptah. After taking in this desecrated sculpture, we gazed around at the reliefs on the walls that depict the great architect and healer Imhotep interacting with the deity Ptah, revealing this place to be a locality of initiation for healers.

Our guide's restless eyes darted toward a dark doorway to our right, and in a hoarse whisper, he told us that within this shrine is the only living statue of Sekhmet in Egypt—one that was placed in this crypt by the pharaoh Thutmoses the Third in roughly 1450 BCE. He then tipped the guards once again, and the gate across that door was opened, allowing us access to another small stone room.

As the group filed in a small hole in the ceiling let in a dim shaft of early light from the sky. We stood blinking as our eyes adjusted to the darkness, and then there in the shadows before us emerged a standing black stone image of Sekhmet, a slender female human form with a lion's head, on top of which was perched the sun disk, with the cobra uraeus in front. From her base to her apex, the goddess seemed to stand a good seven feet tall.

## SEKHMET

This was a dramatic experience, to say the least, and our guide closed the door after us, effectively shutting us into the shrine with Sekhmet. There was only just enough light to barely make out the outlines of the powerful figure before us. But as our eyes continued to adjust to the dim light and the sky outside brightened with the dawn, the goddess seemed to magically take on form and density, manifesting herself in the small room and intimidating us into silent reverence for a good five minutes or more.

I stood facing her, leaning against the back wall behind the group, taking it all in, and I watched as the group began to respond, their hands slowly coming up and their prayers softly being offered. I considered what our guide had said—that this was the only "living" statue of Sekhmet in Egypt. With that thought, I decided to try to access the shamanic state of consciousness—the same high-frequency brain-wave state described in the books of my Spiritwalker trilogy.

There was no problem. As the first ecstatic surge of energy gripped me in its invisible fist and my breath caught in my chest, I reached for those sensations. In response, the power swept into me like a wave engulfing a beach. I stiffened physically, my mind abruptly expanding . . . and I suddenly felt the goddess's awareness focused upon me.

There was no doubt. "She" was there.

I tried my best to remain still, controlling my tendency to shake by wedging myself against the back wall. The rest of the group was focused on the statue, and so we remained for another five minutes or more. When our guide finally opened the door, I remained propped against the back wall, while my fellow travelers slowly completed their rituals and quietly filed out the doorway.

Finally only I remained.

There I was, alone in an ancient stone room in Upper Egypt, standing in the presence of a goddess. I observed her feminine form closely . . . and it seemed that I could actually see her breathing. In those moments I suddenly remembered that I had my wife's little camera in my pocket, so I asked in a stifled whisper through clenched teeth if I could take her picture.

A brief snort of amusement jolted through my mind . . . and I felt her agreement. "Why not? Everyone else does and none of them ever asks permission."

My blood was hissing in my ears as I brought the little metal box to my face with extreme effort. No sooner had I snapped the shot than I realized that I had filled her sanctuary with a flash of shattering light. In the shocked darkness that followed, I wondered if this had been appropriate and, almost in response, two words appeared in my mind.

"Come closer."

Astonished, I remained rooted to my spot, my back braced against the stone wall. I glanced to my right and to my left. I was alone with this leonine goddess. Then again, almost impatiently, the words came . . .

"Come here . . ."

There was no denying this summons. Slowly and reverently I managed to jump-start my legs and feet and slowly shuffle forward until we were only inches apart. I stared up into her lion face and I could feel her cool breath upon my skin.

Then her words came again . . . "Kiss me!"

Somewhat shocked, I looked around me in the darkness, but I was alone with her. The group was outside the shrine. So I slipped off my shoes and stepped up onto the statue's base and slowly reached around and took her into my arms, suddenly aware that her breasts had become warm and soft against my chest and that I could feel her breathing.

The New Yorker born "I," who is very much a mainstream scientist, was stunned at this turn of events, and yet as my lips brushed across her's, I felt her face stretch thinly into a smile. And in that timeless moment the room suddenly brightened, filling with a blue neon light. It was as if an aperture behind her or around her had opened—a doorway into the sky. Thoughts moved through my mind—hers and mine . . . thoughts that conveyed the awareness that there is an inter-dimensional portal here in this shrine.

Without thinking, my hand came up and caressed her face and brow, scratching her as I know all cats like to be scratched. She felt organic, furry, with the bones of her skull and the cartilage of her ears very much alive, the vibrissae of her face stiff and rigid. In response, she bent and pushed her face against mine, butting me with her forehead in a distinctly feline greeting as the cobra on her brow watched me with a flat stare. Did her free hand grasping the ankh come around and clasp me to her chest? I don't know but it seemed so, or perhaps she generated a force that created this illusion.

In response, the feelings of power soared within me, virtually cutting off my breath. As I gasped for air, Sekhmet leaned down and breathed into my mouth, filling my lungs with her HA—her divine lion's breath of life. The doorway shimmered around and behind her and once more her words appeared in my mind.

"You will return to me in your dreaming . . . in your dreaming while asleep and in your dreaming while awake. And you may use this portal with my blessing, whenever you wish, now that you know that it is here. Perhaps you will call upon me from time to time . . . I can be of service to you. Until then, may you fare well . . ." And then almost as an afterthought, "It is nice to see you again."

I leaned my face against her breasts as a burst of sudden tears came, and then the softness of her breathing slowly stilled and once again she became a stone image. Simultaneously, the blue light ceased to exist and the crypt was once again in shadow.

I hastily disengaged and stepped back, wiping my face and her chest, concerned that our guide or one of the guards would come in and find me embracing the statue. Yet I was still alone . . . so I bowed with reverence and, digging in my pocket, I pulled out a small blue-glass crow bead. I breathed my gratitude and my respect into the hole in the bead with a whispered prayer to her and tucked it into a crack in the wall where no one would see it, my ritual now complete, my offering made.

As I emerged, blinking, into the light I saw that the group had drifted back to the sycamore and was taking pictures, and our guide was still joking with the guards. So I strolled slowly past the mute stone walls, alone with my thoughts, as I considered what had just taken place.

## RUMINATIONS

Now . . . I am much aware that the existence of spirits is problematic for us Westerners. We do not live in a society in which connection with spirits is part of our experienced reality on a day-to-day basis. There are, as well, the mainstream philosophical theorists of our time like Ken Wilber, Jurgen Habermas, and Jean Gebser who sidestep the whole issue of spirits.

Yet the fact that shamans claim that they are able to come into relationship with transpersonal forces, and accomplish various things through relationship with them, cannot be denied. There exists historical depth for this claim in the anthropological ethnography that stretches across several hundred years, like it or not . . . and then there are my own experiences described in my trilogy.

If I were to categorize Sekhmet in a mythic sense, "she" appears to have two polarities. In Egyptian mythology, Sekhmet represents the warrior as slayer in the negative polarity, the goddess of plagues and pestilence and all sorts of nasty stuff (directed at the enemies of Egypt in days gone by, of course). Yet, in the positive polarity, this leonine female is the warrior as healer—an archetypal force that expresses fierce compassion—a quality that comes through Sekhmet's willingness to stand with us while we embodied mortals are in the fires of transformation. She offers this so that we may become who and what our destiny holds out to us. And she has served me in this capacity many times during my shamanic healing rituals.

Now—aside from these mythic beliefs (which can be greatly supportive and sustaining in the short term), it is my understanding as one who walks the shaman's path that this archetypal force called Sekhmet does indeed exist in the subtle realm of things hidden. As such, "she" is one of those dense concentrations of energy plus awareness plus intelligence that possesses certain qualities and abilities that may be of use to us. Indeed, in reviewing her words to me in the shrine, this is what "the agreement" seems to be.

In fact, it may very well be that these deities of ancient Egypt (and elsewhere) embody and express the myriad aspects of nature as archetypal forces that have "overseen" the human experiment from the very beginnings of our long journey across eternity.

And in this sense, each of us has the potential to be partnered by many such benevolent forces that are hovering just offstage of the human drama, willing to constellate within us and through us in order to manifest effects that can be truly life transforming and very far-reaching.

We're not talking about religion here, in which our priesthoods and scriptures demand worship and deference to some monotheistic father figure in the sky. That's a belief system, and an archaic one at that. We're talking about authentic transpersonal experience of the subtle and causal worlds, in which we can come into relationship with forces that are real. But how those forces are experienced depends on how we, as individuals, are psychologically focused.

When we consider the societal games that we all seem to be playing with each other, it could be observed that many if not most of us are anchored in the negative polarity. We may proclaim that we are not—we may say that we are compassionate beings devoted to the greater good, that we pray to God in church or synagogue or mosque—and yet if we achieve success at the expense of others' failure, if we injure others with our words or deeds or thoughts, if we operate through competition, coercion, zeal, or deception, we are most definitely in the negative polarity.

If, on the other hand, we deal with our family members, friends, and coworkers through cooperation, persuasion, with compassion and authenticity, our anchor is in the positive polarity. This "law of polarity" is most important because the archetypal forces do not judge us. They simply exist in the spiritual realms and express themselves through us, amplifying who and what we already are. This reveals that the archetypal forces essentially expand our experience of whatever polarity we inhabit.

As I have said, over the years that have followed since that first contact, the transpersonal force called Sekhmet has come to me many times during the shamanic healing rituals that I facilitate in my training workshops. And when she arrives, she is always the black leonine woman who exudes qualities of fierce compassion and dark grace—the warrior as healer.

When I visit the Metropolitan Museum of Art in New York, I always walk through the Egyptian collections in that vast building. And there, in the huge room housing the temple of Dendur, brought stone by stone from Egypt, there sits a series of images of Sekhmet, all in black stone, facing the temple.* They were brought from the garden of Mut at Karnak.

And although they are not "alive" as was the image in the shrine

---

*The image I favor has now been moved into the main gallery with one of its compatriots, where they sit before tall walls covered with painted images from Egypt.

*Seated statue of Sekhmet at the Metropolitan Museum of Art*
*in New York (Photo by Hank Wesselman)*

of Ptah, I sit in contemplation of them for a while and then I make my prayer to her while holding a small blue-glass bead in my hand . . . and when the guards are looking elsewhere, I breathe my love for her into the hole in the bead and tuck it into a crack in the image that attracts me. It's one of my responsibilities . . . and it's part of what it means to walk the shaman's path.

HANK WESSELMAN, PH.D., is an anthropologist and author of nine books on shamanism including *The Re-Enchantment: A Shamanic Path to a Life of Wonder,* the award-winning *Awakening to the Spirit World* (with Sandra Ingerman), *The Bowl of Light: Ancestral Wisdom from a Hawaiian Shaman*, and the *Spiritwalker* trilogy. He lives with his family in Hawaii and has a website at **www.sharedwisdom.com.**

# The Origins of
# This Alchemical Process

I first heard the name of the goddess Sekhmet in about 1982. My teacher at the time, the late Nadia Eagles, showed me a small relic that she said came from the leonine goddess. She spoke of her in hushed, reverent tones and made it clear that this was a goddess of great power, one with whom she hoped to have a deep and lasting relationship. I learned from her that Sekhmet is a goddess in the Egyptian pantheon, the daughter of the sun god Ra. While Sekhmet is mostly known and feared as the goddess of war and destruction (see color plate 1), she is also the quintessential healing goddess of Egypt.

Sekhmet's name means "Power" or "Mighty One." The word for the power she generates is *sekhem,* which is the ancient name for what we now call the universal life force, and is much like the *kundalini**
(life-force energy) expressed by the cobra she wears on her diadem. Sekhmet appears most often in a woman's body with a lioness's head, usually crowned with the sun disk. In her role as a desert goddess, she is often seen running wild as the lioness, her very breath creating the *khamaseen,* the hot winds in spring, the scorching of the land before

---

*Definitions of terms such as this, which may be unfamiliar to the reader, can be found in the glossary at the back of the book, along with descriptions of the major goddesses and gods of Egypt, temple sites, and certain scientific terms.

*Statue of Sekhmet at the Metropolitan Museum in New York showing the cobra on her diadem (Photo by Hank Wesselman)*

the inundation, and the droughts and plagues that brought death and unspeakable misery to the people who lived in Egypt. The ancients both feared and revered her: she could cause plagues, yet if you were suffering from one, it was Sekhmet whom you beseeched to heal you.

Sekhmet is called by many names, perhaps, as Robert Masters suggests, as many as four thousand.* These include: the Daughter of Ra, the Eye of Ra, the Lady of Flame, the Feared One, the Great One of Magic, Great One of Healing, Protectress of the Divine Order, and many

---

*Robert E. L. Masters, *The Goddess Sekhmet: Psycho-Spiritual Exercises of the Fifth Way*, 53.

other epithets that describe her audacious and various functions. To me Sekhmet has become protector, guide, healer, and staunch ally. But it was not until some years after Nadia introduced her to me that I really began to understand why Sekhmet was such an important goddess to her, and for all of us.

I was teaching a workshop at a venue called the Long House somewhere not far from Seattle, back in the late 1980s. I knew nothing about the place before I got there; my colleague who was sponsoring my workshop simply rented space there. It turned out to be primarily a nudist colony that rented space for others to do workshops—clothing optional I presume . . . I was somewhat amused as well as surprised and was glad that the location of our seminar space provided us with sufficient privacy to avoid distraction.

It came to my attention that the Saturday evening entertainment for the Long House that weekend was to be a fire walk, and we were all invited to join. Fire walking was in vogue, and until then, I had successfully avoided participating in one. During our lunch break, I found myself walking with my husband, Mark Hallert, to where they were preparing for the fire walk. I had no idea of what to expect, but the length of the fire was about fifty feet, and I could not imagine the need for such a huge fire. The amount of wood sacrificed for the occasion could possibly be measured as the needs of several families for their woodstoves for a winter. My hackles were up at what my uneducated mind calculated to be a waste under any circumstances, and the sheer size and heat of the fire was daunting, to say the least.

When class resumed, I found myself expressing my opinions to my students in a way that caused me to pause. Other than the waste factor, I could recognize that something deeper was behind my eagerness to denigrate the idea of fire walking. It didn't take much self-examination to reveal the true source of my ire—fear. Once recognized, I had no choice but to challenge myself, and, to make sure I would follow through, I told my students of my intention.

By the time our class was over for the night and we made our way to where the fire walk was happening, things were not going well. Apparently the instructions, all of which we missed, were inadequate, and the leader was no longer present. Several people had been burned, including the leader, and there was no one who could give us guidance. People were milling around in the dark, the bright glow from the coals casting the only light, eerie and foreboding.

Having made a public commitment, I felt I had no choice but to walk across the coals. As I felt my panic grow, I turned to my staunch ally and personal visionary, my husband, Mark, and he suggested, "Ask for help." I knew the traditional fire walk was meant to be powerful and sacred, because I had talked to many people who had participated successfully in them; however, the essential ingredients of positive input and focused group mind were missing here. I was on my own, and no one in my group was willing to attempt the walk under the circumstances.

It was Sekhmet who showed up when I asked for help. No surprise there, as she is the feminine face of the sun, the potent expression of fire itself. She turned into a lioness and stood by my side so that I could put my hand on her back. Immediately I felt more secure, though still out of balance. I asked for another lioness, and one immediately appeared at my other side. I couldn't see them, but I felt their presence, and they gave me the confidence I needed to move forward.

I studied the coals and then picked a point some distance from where I was entering to where I would step out of the river of glowing coals. With a hand on the back of each etheric lioness, I confidently stepped onto the coals and walked my chosen distance.

The biggest surprise was the feeling of the red-hot coals under my feet. There was a soft coolness that defied the laws of physics, and the urge to play with fire grew in me as I completed my walk. Once I stepped off the coals, I reached in, picked up a burning coal, and tossed it farther into the path. Then another. I wished I knew how to juggle. At a certain point, I knew that I was done and should not tempt the fire any further. I thanked Sekhmet from my heart and felt the reflection of the glow of the burning coals radiating from me as I felt a new confidence grow within.

Although I never became passionate about fire walking, and had no desire to repeat the experience, I learned some great lessons that night at the nudist colony, and from that point forward my relationship with Sekhmet has deepened and grown to what it has become today. She is my mother, my teacher, my friend, and a powerful goddess whom I have been most honored and privileged to priestess for over the many years since.

## OUT OF THE BRIGHT NIGHT: SEKHMET'S ALCHEMY FOR OUR TIMES

January 23, 1997, was an auspicious full moon night in Bern, Switzerland, a night when people all over the world were taking part in a global meditation for peace. My dear friend and associate Dr. Christine Fehling and I were planning to join a group ceremony/meditation that night to commemorate the unique six-pointed star configuration that was said by astrologers to be amplifying the power of ritual and ceremony. We were also preparing for a class that we planned to teach together the following weekend.

I had been given a special "jewel pill" that came from a pharmacy in Dharamsala for just such an occasion. The jewel pill was almost an inch in diameter and made of ground-up minerals and herbs (I do not know the exact ingredients) tightly mashed together into a ball and wrapped in colored foil. It was kept protected from the sunlight and other radiations. I had been assured that the effects of this herbal medicine would be subtle and that I would be able to handle a social occasion and ceremony.

The precise directions for preparing the medicine had been given with the jewel pill, and great care was taken to prepare it properly: a process that I have since found readily available on the internet, and one that involved opening it in darkness, mashing it thoroughly, and preparing it for consumption in just the right way at just the right moment. Before consuming the resulting potion, I learned the Medicine Buddha mantra so that I could repeat it over and over again while I lay wrapped in blankets for quite some time before any effects could be noticed.*

*Tayata*
*Om Bekandze Bekandze*
*Maha Bekandze*
*Radza Samudgate Soha*

MAY THE MANY SENTIENT BEINGS
WHO ARE SICK,
QUICKLY BE FREED FROM SICKNESS.
AND MAY ALL THE SICKNESSES OF BEINGS
NEVER ARISE AGAIN.

Having spent the previous several decades as a psychedelic explorer, fully aware of the sacredness of consciousness-expanding sacraments and medicines, I expected that the effects of the jewel pill would be subtle, as indicated. Much to my surprise, my journey that evening could by no means be described as "subtle." Although many details have escaped me since the event, I recall being taken into trance by piano music that was being played by our hostess's husband at the dinner party we went to. That's when I began to notice that I wasn't "in Kansas anymore." I managed to hold it together until we got back to our flat.

---

*Since I learned the Medicine Buddha mantra verbally so many years ago, I recently looked to the internet to find out how to spell it. The transliteration and free translation reproduced in this text are from the following site: www.worldwidehealingcircle .net/medicine_buddha_mantra.htm. I found this site to be useful and think it would be helpful for anyone wishing to ask for or send healing to others. In addition to giving the long and short versions of the mantra, the site includes instructions for its use and the option to join a community that recites the mantra simultaneously for optimum effect. It also offers options for listening to the mantra, with clearly recorded correct pronunciation. The short version is the one I was taught. I recite it in groups of seven repetitions when I wish to invoke Medicine Buddha.

The next thing I remember (unfortunately I didn't take notes at the time) is talking to my husband by phone—he was in Oregon. Many of the details of the conversation have also evaporated; however, I do remember quite clearly that my fingers and toes began to tingle and go numb and how that numbness moved through my body in such a way that at some point I had to terminate the conversation by saying, "I have to hang up the phone now. I'm dying."

Dismemberment, death, illumination, and rebirth are at the heart of both the psychedelic and the shamanic journey experience and were not new to me. There was no fear. Rather, this was without compare the smoothest and gentlest shamanic death I had experienced in this life. I don't remember details of the renewal or rebirth, but I do remember that Christine and I had only one or two days to prepare for a class that we were presenting together on the weekend.

It was in the illumination stage of the experience that the teachings for the weekend came in. It was as though my radiance created a field in which Christine could perceive quite clearly the details of what we were to teach and how we would teach it. It took the form of an offering to Sekhmet, in an alchemical process to transform rage. We were shown that if every person who felt rage could somehow find the root of the rage in their fear, loneliness, or despair, then it would be possible to change it. If each person in our class could perceive clearly the source of their angst, and hold a clear, strong intention as they offered a symbol of their suffering to Sekhmet, she would devour the entire thoughtform and transform it in her belly.

When Sekhmet devoured the offerings she became an exquisite, decorated cauldron with lion's paws for legs and the sky for a lid. Together we spent a couple of days observing while each offering was digested and transformed as the alchemy unfolded. Part of the beauty and elegance of the process was that the person remained fully conscious in both the physical and spiritual worlds. As the mystery revealed itself, the change turned out to be not only undeniable but also forever engraved in the person's DNA and memory. No longer could they avoid the absolute knowledge of their personal choice and responsibility regarding the issues that instigated the work.

Thus began the work with Sekhmet—transformation in the belly of the goddess.

Over time, the alchemical process evolved. The concept of transforming rage is still a good one, but we each have to deal with a zillion issues, many of which have caused us to develop habit patterns over time that we can't seem to control, no matter how smart we are or how much we try to change our reactions to various situations. There is no one characteristic that we can change in ourselves that will magically turn us in to the potentially wise being who lives consistently in the natural state of joy that is our most basic right—to love and be loved and to cherish ourselves and all life.

When it came time to commit Sekhmet's alchemy to this book, it became apparent that she wanted readers to make the most of the potential of their full experience. Consequently the alchemical process we share here offers the most potent possibility of transformation, inclusive of all issues, judgments, characteristics, attributes, and disease—no matter how obstinate or deeply ingrained they may be—that keep you from reaching your highest level of potential as a fully realized human. It is a process that nurtures your capacity to be awake, fully present, and with full comprehension of the choices you make moment by moment and the consequences that potentially develop as a result of those choices.

The magic that comes from Sekhmet's alchemy is a blessed, precious mystery that, although it cannot be fully explained, can be experienced. May these pages inspire the gratitude, the presence, and the attention that give you an opportunity to participate in the miracle of transformation.

# Introduction

My first job as a writer was as a journalist for a small alternative newspaper in Sonoma County called *The Sonoma County Stump*. My first article was on the Hopi prophecy as told by Richard Kastl, an Osage Native American who was representing traditional Hopi elders from Hotevilla on the Hopi Reservation in Arizona. Kastl was spreading a message to get the warning out about the strip mining for coal and the pollution and depletion of the ancient groundwaters that were desecrating Hopi lands. This was in 1977. According to the prophecy he related, the decision would soon have to be made whether to bring the world back into balance with a fist or an open hand. At that time there was still choice.

Apparently, in our apathy and ignorance, we have crossed the line. It appears that the world is split, and many of us are being subjected to the fist and the madness that is the result of our refusal to take seriously our job as stewards of our precious planet.

In this book, we will be working with a very specific initiatory process—one that was given to us by Sekhmet in one of her primary roles as Guardian of Ma'at. Although Ma'at is the goddess of truth, order, harmony, and cosmic law (not people's laws), whenever the balance of cosmic law swings too far in one direction or another on this planet, it is Sekhmet, as fierce Protectress of the Divine Order, who is called to bring things back into balance.

Sekhmet teaches us to transform our rage and anger into the creative impulses that result in benefit for one's self and community. This requires presence of mind, skill, commitment, and the ability to stay awake and aware, fully conscious of the consequences of every stray thought as well as action. Today more than ever, we all must learn to transform our outrage and fury into creative solutions and actions that will help bring our planet back into balance and bring healing to ourselves and our precious home.

All people develop patterns during infancy and early childhood that, regardless of how conscious we are, influence our responses to the challenges we face throughout life. Because of these patterns, we often automatically react with helplessness, rage, or any of the possibilities between. We lose our center, hide, or act out in unconscious ways, creating chaos and causing harm to ourselves and those around us. We may yearn for the embrace of sweet Morpheus—intoxication or sleep during which these feelings seem to magically disappear—until the next time. Often we develop life patterns that result in the attraction of experiences that are harmful or limiting. If we can transform these deeply rooted negative patterns, the energy used to maintain them can be released and used for more productive, constructive applications. Then our responses to life will be different—richer and more conscious.

## THE TRANSFORMATIVE NATURE OF THIS BOOK

In a sense, this is a cookbook filled with recipes designed to bring about total transformation at the deepest levels of your being. It will guide you to make appropriate preparations, then meet and give your offering to the goddess. While it is being digested, absorbed, and assimilated by her, you will be initiated into the alchemy that will bring about your transformation. Throughout the book, you will be given initiations, rites of passage, and transmissions to renew, regenerate, and restructure the most important aspects of your being.

The alchemical process that you will engage in will bring you to the realization that you have the capacity to transform your most deeply ingrained negative habit patterns, including your inherent rage at people's inhumanity to one another and disrespect of the planet. You will experience directly the entire alchemical process while your offering is safely gestating in the belly of Sekhmet. The alchemical gold, the universal medicine that is the result of your commitment and attention to the work at hand, results in the opportunity to heal at many levels—physical, emotional, spiritual, and at the level of your soul. Sekhmet's teaching results in powerful internal transformation and shamanistic healing attunements and techniques through which you become a fully realized adult child of the goddess, self-confident, wholly in your power, and strong and clear in everything you do.

This transformative process transmutes the lead of your deeply ingrained reflexive responses into the gold of enlightened choice. Like alchemy, it is a process of cooking, similar to baking a loaf of bread. It requires you to search within yourself to find the character flaws and weaknesses that hold you back from becoming a fully realized human. You create your offering to the goddess through an intensive self-examination process in which you seek out and find your pain, your fear, your rage, your self-sabotage, and your perceived faults and disease. Your obsolete, ignored, and unconscious habitual patterns are the *prima materia,* the prime matter, to be transformed. You can invite these patterns to rise into consciousness, work them into a symbolic representation of the demons that plague you, and offer them to the goddess for transformation.

Sekhmet called this process into being because we are in urgent need of radical change, now. Although there are other traditions with appropriate corresponding archetypes, this alchemical formula requires a trusting relationship with Sekhmet. If you are new to this type of work, or to Sekhmet, you will develop the bond as you work through the preparations. What is extraordinary about this work is that you will experience directly the entire alchemical process of transformation, and your renewal and regeneration is dependent only on your ability to maintain attention, intention, and consciousness throughout the journeys through which you will be guided.

I cannot make these claims of transformation without explaining the principles behind the process on which they are based. Alchemical Healing is the comprehensive healing art form that is the foundation of all my work. The four principles were given to me by Thoth, the Egyptian lunar god of wisdom, who is my primary mentor and teacher and the architect behind most of my spiritual expressions. Alchemical Healing is based on four principles that are fundamental to any act of creation or intentional manipulation of reality. These four principles of Alchemical Healing, simply put, are

1. the skill and life experience you bring to the table;
2. your relationships with Spirit, and your discernment regarding how to develop and utilize those relationships;
3. the recognition, honoring, and inclusion of that which is beyond the comprehension of our limited mind and the wiring of our brain—the invitation of the participation of the mystery; and
4. gratitude for all participants in the co-creation of the healing/ alchemy/transformation in which you are engaged.

Most of the book requires engagement in the alchemical process through the form of guided visualizations, which can be approached in a number of ways to assure the deepest experience. Although some of you will be able to take the journeys as you read them, many prefer to hear them read by someone else or to record them so they can hear them in their own voice. Having the journeys recorded offers the advantage of being able to use the pause button to make sure you have enough time for the full experience of each instruction. Another powerful way to go through this alchemy is with a friend, taking turns reading to one another, or even in a small circle, structured in such a way that everyone gets a chance to play both parts. The more you can share your observations and experiences, the more deeply you will realize the profundity of your personal transformation and the lessons learned.

Another aspect of engagement in the alchemical process is that of keeping a journal. Journaling is helpful in many ways, so between initiations it is important to journal your experience, the sooner the better. Sometimes there will be space during the journey when you will want to pause and write down something significant or jot down some notes that will help remind you of what is important so that you can fill in the details later. It will get easier to go in and out of the visionary state during the journeys as you become more comfortable with the work. These visionary experiences are somewhat like dreams and will fade quickly if you don't have a way to remember them. While you are having the experience, regardless of how vivid it seems, you are using a different part of your brain, and, even though it may seem quite dramatic in the moment, it often doesn't stick. Try to capture as many details as possible, even if you don't understand what they mean when it is happening. There will come a time when it will be important to return to what you have written. Even the small details that may seem insignificant now will help clarify the revelations and lessons as the process continues.

I've noticed in the classes that sharing is very helpful for those who are experiencing this work, especially for the first time. Throughout the book you will "hear the voices" of prior participants. In some cases, they are journal entries written in the midst of the process, conducted either as a teleclass or a retreat. In others, they are letters or essays written short or long periods afterward. They appear under the heading "Shared Voices."

The work of this book is a co-creative activity, a gift of knowledge and sensitivity that most of us have lost over time, and we have to earn it back. This requires you to submit yourself to the magical processes of the goddess. It's an extraordinary set of arcane practices that, if done with full awareness, will reward you with happiness and health. It is not a job. It's about opening yourself to magic and surrendering yourself to the ancient, magical powers—the basic natural laws of the universe—and letting them work within and through you. Although it requires your full attention, life continues, and you quickly learn to live in multiple dimensions simultaneously.

All ancient shamanic work carries the same obligation, to honor the power and spirit of the magic and not take it lightly. Know that you are safe; yet treat the magic with deep respect. The process you are about to enter is a ritual and therefore requires you to look at your intentions and what is drawing you to it. Sekhmet will always be guiding you through the alchemy, and you will have ample opportunities to pause and assimilate the magic.

You can take as long as you need to prepare and are advised to wait until you feel ready, safe, and secure in the knowledge that Sekhmet is your true mother in this alchemy before you give her the offering you have prepared. In the end, you are responsible for your own experience, and, as in any true initiation, there is a level of unknown—the mystery that is both the unknowable and the source of the magic.

It is ultimately your decision whether to participate. It is important to note that once you commit to the process, you are encouraged to follow through and complete the entire ceremony. However, if it becomes more than you choose to undertake, you have only to be straightforward in your communications with Sekhmet, and you and she can work out a graceful exit or postponement until such time as you are more prepared for the required trust and surrender.

## RELATIONSHIPS OF TRUST AND POWER

These gods and goddesses, the Egyptian neteru, are our ancestors. However, most of us have simply forgotten who they are and how to work with them. Fortunately, they live within our DNA, and as we align our awareness with that knowledge, it becomes more and more obvious that they represent all the various parts of who we are. Once you fully understand that, you develop the trust required to give yourself fully to the experience of the relationships that are available to you.

When we were given consciousness, we were also given free will. For reasons that I cannot understand or explain, we have chosen to use the gift of our free will to gain power *over* the forces of nature rather than use it to co-create *with* them. The gods of Egypt are representations of nature. The word *neteru,* as the pantheon is called in ancient Egyptian, became the word *netcher* for the Coptic Christians and eventually morphed into *nature* in the English language. In an uncorrupted, harmonious world we would all be enlightened beings working together with each other and the neteru to create beauty and joy using the power of love and the skill we develop through our curiosity and attention.

We each offer two eyes and two hands as well as our minds to the collective of seven billion plus people, but many of the billions of collaborative minds are driven from a place of greed, power seeking, lust, or survival by any means, adding to the chaos that is currently tearing us apart and creating fear, misery, and despair. Yet there is another way.

These times require more from every one of us who is awakening in order to deal with the trauma that plagues our planet every day. There is no single, primary problem, although they are all connected. It's not just the pollution. It's not just the arrogance, fear, rage, and all the conflicts. In the chaos that permeates and surrounds our world during these transformational times, the entire planet is traumatized to some extent. That requires those of us who are waking up and learning these new skills to show up and use every ability we have to respond (response-ability) to whatever is needed, whether it's whatever is in front of us in the moment or on the other side of the world.

When many people first begin doing transformational and healing work, they may feel a sense of shyness, a sense of not being enough, or not having or knowing enough. We don't have time for that anymore. If we believe something needs doing and feel, from our own experience or inner knowing, that we can possibly do it, we should go ahead, especially if we are willing to work with appropriate spiritual guidance. Likewise, if we are encouraged to take action by someone we trust, or we see somebody accomplish something seemingly miraculous, which inspires us to try, we can often accomplish our goal, again especially if we have direct access to someone with skill in the spirit world. It may not look exactly like what another person does, but we can all use our own gifts and skills in our unique way, based on our own clear intention and desire to help. And, of course, it's never just us—our relationships with life's processes and the neteru, and/or other trustworthy spirit guides, are vital.

We have seen Sekhmet come from relative obscurity three or four decades ago to become one of the most important and beloved goddesses for those whom she has called. If you are reading this, chances are that you have been called. Many of us are being called and trained to awaken her power within ourselves, so that each of us becomes a powerful guardian of Ma'at.

Sekhmet has come into our lives, incarnated in each of us, to remind us that it is our duty to transform the chaos into harmony, the misery into joy, and the hate and discrimination into compassion and healing.

PART I

*Who, What, and How—*
*Beginning the*
*Alchemical Journey*

# 1

# Sekhmet Face-to-Face

As part of the blend of Hawaiian Huna, Western magical tradition, and ancient Egyptian mysteries teachings that I was studying with Nadia Eagles in the early 1980s, we were to choose a word of power that would be used like a trigger to set the universal life-force energies into motion. I was a total novice at the time, so I asked her what she meant by "word of power." She explained that it was a word that had intrinsic qualities or characteristics that I wished to add to the energies I was generating in my healing work.

She suggested using the name of the goddess Ma'at, telling me that she was the goddess of truth, justice, balance, and order. My first thought was that, although I could appreciate to a certain extent what she stood for, I didn't like the sound of her name, but I quickly realized the sheer stupidity, if not downright impudence, of that thought.

I chose Ma'at, and invoked her almost daily, sometimes several times a day, in my healing work. However, it took me many years before I understood the concept of Ma'at and all that she represents. Ma'at is the weaving, the pivotal feather at the center of the vibrant web of all inter-relationships. As the dynamic equilibrium of love's field of connections and true will, she provides the transdimensional access to and from all. We were brought forth by Ma'at. We were born to serve Ma'at so that harmony and order can be maintained. At the end of our lives, like pharaoh Seti I at Abydos in the illustration on the facing page, we are meant to return all of Ma'at back to Ma'at, having changed not a thing.

*Fig. 1.1. Offering of Ma'at at the Temple of Osiris in Abydos
(Photo by K. Indigo Rønlov)*

Because I called on her so often, I eventually learned that serving and enlivening Ma'at was very much a mainstay of my sacred purpose in this life. What I didn't know until many years later, while writing and teaching with Normandi Ellis, is that all ancient Egyptian children grew up knowing that they were put on this Earth to serve Ma'at. As my relationship with Sekhmet grew, I came to understand that her role as Guardian of Ma'at lent courage, passion, and the necessary power required to live up to the gifts that came from my naive yet constant invocation of Ma'at and the lessons that came with it.

## THREE GODDESSES IN ONE

As I began to learn more about the Egyptian pantheon, particularly when I met and communed with them directly during my travels in Egypt, I began to realize how important Sekhmet is in the cosmic scheme of things.

According to many historical anthropological texts, Sekhmet is inextricably linked with Hathor, the ancient mother goddess of the night sky, the golden cow whose nourishing milk is that of the Milky Way. They are like flip sides of the same coin. Sekhmet represents the mighty power of kundalini energy, or sekhem, and is the main goddess of the Egyptian pantheon to use that power for healing. Hathor, whose name means "House of Horus," is the magical medicine woman, goddess of love, joy, intoxication, sensuality, celebration, and sexuality. Although they share many of the same qualities, Hathor is generally considered more passive, like the water buffalo whose head or horns she sometimes wears, and Sekhmet is definitely seen as more fiery, passionate, and violent.

All humans, especially women, easily slip from manifesting Sekhmet to Hathor and back in accordance with both natural and human-created cycles, moods, and external and internal forces. In ancient Egyptian mythology, many of the myths that are attributed to Sekhmet are just as often ascribed to Hathor, and usually include aspects of both.

*Fig. 1.2. Lioness goddess at Hathor's temple at Dendera*
*(Photo by K. Indigo Rønlov)*

Sekhmet and Hathor were part of an ancient trilogy completed by Bast, also known as Bastet, initially a local goddess of the Lower Egypt town of Bubastes. She is the domesticated cat goddess who kept the grain silos free from vermin and came into great popularity during the Second Dynasty. She is a goddess of fertility, sensual pleasure, strong drink, protection, self-love, and nurturing. In her role as a fertility goddess, she once showed me through vision that she is the one who connects mothers with the children that will be born to them.

In *Feasts of Light,* Normandi Ellis tells us that Sekhmet is the Crone, Bast the Mother, and Hathor the Maiden.* That said, it should be noted that Hathor, along with Thoth, also known as Tahuti or Djehuti, are by some considered the oldest of the Egyptian pantheon. It is my personal theory that Thoth passed into this universe during the big bang—if such an event is indeed true—fully conscious and with

---

*Normandi Ellis, *Feasts of Light,* 10.

© Nicki Scully

*Fig. 1.3. Hathor at Hatshepsut's temple (Photo by Nicki Scully)*

full knowledge of all that came before. Hathor might also have come through that black hole with consciousness intact. Sekhmet, as the feminine face of the sun, could be perceived as more local—or perhaps the sun in this instance pertains to all stars. If that is the case, her sekhem, the power from which she derives her name, is universal.

Occasionally Thoth appears spontaneously throughout this work. Pay attention to how he shows up, and honor it, for he can bring levity into the most serious of situations. There are always reasons for his presence, even if it seems incongruous. He enjoys guiding and teaching through riddles, so don't be surprised if he shows up as Groucho Marx with a cigar in hand. I have seen him sitting at his desk with a cigar and martini, cutting his ibis talons with a cigar clipper. When he shows up in full regalia, know that you are entering a sacred opportunity that requires extra attention and a more respectful demeanor. Every opportunity to learn from Thoth is a reason for gratitude. Like all gods, totems, other allies, and even children, Thoth would prefer that you meet him at his level, eye-to-eye and heart-to-heart.

For the purposes of this book, we will focus primarily on the Sekhmet element of the trilogy of Sekhmet, Hathor, and Bast. Although her functions as healer and guardian of Ma'at are at the core of this book, many of her epithets describe her fierceness and reflect the dread and fear that was felt for her throughout the ages. Although she was most certainly a goddess of war and her wrath is legendary, she was also the healing goddess of Egypt. Full comprehension of her powers was kept secret, the knowledge being directly related to the initiatory level of her priests and priestesses. It is important to remember that Sekhmet's expressions of power were, regardless of how they appear to our smaller view of reality, always in service to justice, balance, cosmic law, loyalty, and protection.

Sekhmet's force is expressive of the sun. Just as heat melts away stagnation and poisons within the body, so it is that Sekhmet is the healing intelligence of nature. Her presence chases away those who would do harm to her pride, the kingdom, or empire. Force is not always violence,

*Fig. 1.4. Thoth (Photo by K. Indigo Rønlov)*

especially if there is no abuse or malice. Healthy force of life shakes up stagnation and sets the vigorous dynamic of Ma'at into the often severe justice of any self-organizing and self-healing living system. Sekhmet works for justice—without judgment.

Although there is controversy regarding who is the oldest of the goddesses, when seen as the crone in the triad of Sekhmet, Hathor, and Bast, Sekhmet bestows her wisdom for the benefit of the younger, less experienced, and more impetuous generation of women, although we never outgrow the need for her wisdom and can awaken to that need at any time.

## SEKHMET'S MYTH

Sekhmet's most common myth speaks of a time long, long ago when Ra—the sun god who was said to have created the Earth, the Sky, and all that dwelt herein, including humans—was seen to be growing old. Although he had ruled over our precious planet for millennia, humans began to perceive him as aging and losing his power and ceased to pay their respects, not only to Ra but to each other and the planet as well. No longer did they express their gratitude for the blessings and miracles of life, and they openly disrespected the sun god, having forgotten the source of life itself.

As Ra felt mocked and disregarded, he called on his daughter Sekhmet to incarnate on Earth to deal with the upstart humans. When she saw how disrespectful people were to one another and to Ma'at as well as to Ra, she went into a rage and began a slaughter that evolved into carnage with no end in sight. Her bloodlust knew no bounds, and it appeared as though no human would escape her wrath. She started her rampage in Nubia and continued northward throughout Upper Egypt and into the Delta in Lower Egypt. She became so intoxicated by the taste of human blood that she made no distinction between good and evil.

Ra loved the children of the Earth; they were his creation. So he called upon all the great Egyptian deities for help, but no one could temper the rage of this out-of-control goddess. Finally, Thoth, the god of wisdom, came up with a plan. He told Ra to have the women of Heliopolis brew seven thousand vats of barley beer spiked with powerful herbs, such as poppies brought from Elephantine Island in the south, mandrake root (a plant in the *Solanaceae* family), and other magical, mind-altering substances, with pomegranate juice to dye it the color of blood. When Sekhmet lay down to take a nap, the priests and priestesses crept as close as they dared and poured the beer around her in puddles that she would not miss, hoping she would mistake the brew for human blood.

Sure enough, when she awoke, Sekhmet discovered the beer and gleefully lapped up the bloodlike brew, continuing until she became intoxicated. Most versions of the myth say she became drunk; however, I believe that rather than being subdued into a drunken stupor, Sekhmet's mind was expanded and her heart opened. When she was able to see with the new eyes of compassion what she had done, her rage was transformed into love.

As the story continues, Sekhmet, having been pacified and now of a more docile nature—some say as the water buffalo, the Egyptian cow, while others say it was as Bast, the tamer version of the cat—traveled south to Nubia and disappeared. Ra was quite upset at the loss of his daughter and finally sent Thoth and his entourage to coax her back to Egypt. Thoth promised her that she would never be forgotten, that there would be a great feast awaiting her return and a celebration every year in her honor. Always one to love a good party, Hathor/Bast/Sekhmet returned to Egypt, and the celebration continued every year, probably practiced in some form to this day.

It should be noted that beer was very different in Egyptian antiquity from what it is today, especially in Egypt, where it was often cleaner than the available water from the Nile. It was also nourishing. In *Feasts of Light,* Normandi Ellis says:

The sacred drunkenness of the ancient Egyptians provided an entrance into the altered state of the shaman where one might experience high forms of ecstatic union and feelings of love. It offered humanity a means of approaching the Divine and of experiencing an intoxication of the Goddess and God. For the most part, drink and song served a religious purpose, as they do in a number of modern religious practices. Drink allowed the devotee an opportunity to participate in the mystery of life, to understand the nature of offering and sacrifice, and to focus on the abundant love readily offered to humankind from the hand of the Divine.*

A celebration known as the Inebriety of Hathor commemorated the yearly inundation that brought soothing comfort to the parched earth and her people following the scorching summer heat. Similar celebrations were also held at the end of battles as a way of transforming the bloodlust energy of war so that the warrior could resume his life as a farmer or artisan in the peaceful, laid-back state that was more common in the ancient country of Egypt.† It is thought by some that sacred, mind-altering substances were used specifically at those times to aid in the transformation that needed to occur, and the celebration brought joy and refreshment to the people.

## AT HOME WITH SEKHMET

Sekhmet's primary home was in Memphis, the great capital city of Lower Egypt in the north, near Cairo. Memphis was in its glory during the Old Kingdom, although it continued functioning throughout Egypt's history until the time of the Greeks and the strengthening of Alexandria. It was situated on the border between Lower and Upper Egypt. Ptah and Sekhmet's huge and magnificent temple there was first

---

*Normandi Ellis, *Feasts of Light,* 8.
†Ibid., 8–10.

destroyed in 1650 BCE by the Hyksos, Asiatic invaders from the East. Almost nothing is left today.

However, Sekhmet was well represented in Upper Egypt at Karnak, the largest existing temple in Egypt and built in honor of the triad of Thebes (Luxor), the capital of Upper Egypt, which consisted of Amon, Mut (pronounced *Moot*), and their son, Khonsu. Several hundred seated Sekhmet statues, many of which are still in situ today, were sculpted for the temple of Mut and for his own mortuary temple on the West Bank by Pharaoh Amenhotep III, father of the controversial pharaoh Akhnaten. Although the temple of Mut is closed to the public, I have had the privilege of seeing the many remaining statues. Apparently, Amenhotep III was ill and had the Sekhmet statues sculpted for rituals designed to cure him. My Egyptian Egyptologist friend Emil Shaker also tells me that they were carved to propitiate the goddess because, as a guardian of warriors, she was considered unbeatable. At the time of this writing, more than twenty of her statues were recently unearthed across the river in excavations beneath the remains of Amenhotep III's West Bank funerary temple. And they are still excavating.

Thutmoses II, whose name means "born of Thoth," was also responsible for many of Sekhmet's statues, possibly including the one found in the chapel at Karnak honoring Ptah and Sekhmet. Karnak was the seat of power in Upper Egypt, next to the city of Luxor, the ancient capital of Upper Egypt known as Thebes. The current temple was constructed on top of a previous one built with wooden pillars. As was most often done throughout ancient Egypt, materials from the previous temples were used to create the next incarnation, and there were certain stones known as seed stones that were most important in laying out the temple.*

After I led a number of tours to Egypt, it became apparent when most people stood before the magnificent statue of Sekhmet in her

---

*For more information on seed stones, see Normandi Ellis and Nicki Scully, *The Union of Isis and Thoth*, 33–35.

chapel at Karnak that all previous assumptions regarding the reason they thought they were called to explore the area were literally blown away! Her stone presence—imbued with intention, energy, and *ka** by the adepts who initially carved and consecrated her—came alive and, in some totally unexpected and magical way, touched each of them. For many, their lives as well as their ways of perception, and for some even their belief systems, were challenged or changed forever. When a person discovers that they are a child of this goddess, regardless of the style of their human parenting, they feel motherly love, protection, and support. Eventually, if they persist in developing the relationship, they also discover their reason for being, on a new, often cosmic, level.

The first time I entered Sekhmet's chapel at Karnak was no exception, and nothing in my past or my training prepared me for what happened when I met her face-to-face for the first time. Although I'd stood before her at museums in New York, London, and Cairo, and also at the Tut exhibitions, and although every statue is imbued with ka, there is something to be said about a statue that has lived in the same place for nearly 3,500 years. Yes, she has been broken and repaired, there have been attempts to steal her, and her chapel has been reconstructed around her, yet her magic remains very much alive.

Sekhmet's room in the chapel is quite small, surrounded with plain stone blocks. The only light aside from the doorway comes through a small opening in the stone ceiling. When I first visited this sanctuary, the sun had not reached its full height. As I turned to see her, the light that reached her reflected a softness on her magnificent, tall, black granite body. There was no great drama—no lightning bolts or bellowing voices in my head—simply the feeling of return and of pure love. As I walked toward her, transfixed by her majesty, a glittering tear appeared in her right stone eye. She is alive! Her magic was alive and well. Although to some it might seem subtle, to me, a (reformed, non-observant yet watchful) Jewish-raised, upper-middle-class skeptic, it was

---

*Ka is the etheric double and connection to ancestral spiritual lineage.

*Fig. 1.5. Statue of Sekhmet in her chapel at Karnak*
*(Photo by K. Indigo Rønlov)*

as real as real could be. All vestiges of doubt and the obstacles of my upbringing were blown away in a flash of comprehension—this statue exuded love, the love of a mother gazing upon her firstborn, one of her pride. I was especially deeply appreciative that I could feel her recognition and joy—she was glad to see me, and I felt it flow directly into my heart where it lives, and shall continue to live for as long as I have breath in my body. The goddess is alive, and I had been touched.

## SHARED VOICES

*I very much appreciate the opportunity to add my thoughts to those who have participated in the life-changing alchemical process known as "Sekhmet: Transformation in the Belly of the Goddess."*

*For me, the timing could not have been better. After many years of research, my own journey began to focus on both lions and ancient Egypt. A unique combination to be sure. And in Sekhmet I was blessed to find them together, united as one being.*

*And in the class you offered, which I promptly signed up for, I was introduced to a teacher who had the experience and the integrity to walk me down this path in a way that I could trust and allow myself to fully embrace. And the gifts I received have been both immediate and long-term. The class itself gave me further insights and information on the shamanic tradition. But rather than being a short-lived "weekend seminar," I feel that Sekhmet continues to walk with me as I move forward and discover myself. As such, and I feel Sekhmet would agree, "We've only just begun."*

*So it is that I heartily recommend this work to anyone who wishes to take a walk on the wild side, one that ultimately leads to greater understandings that cannot be accomplished by any other means.*

STEPHEN DUKES

*Sekhmet has become my mentor and spirit guide. This beautiful goddess has helped me to relate to the shaman who is conscious within me. I am Sekhmet. Through her transformative fire energy, she has helped me to overcome my fears and doubts. Sekhmet devoured my inner child issues in the belly of the goddess.*

*On a daily basis I call upon her archetype for strength and courage, and healing, as she is a compassionate healer. I also call upon the goddess Sekhmet to restore balance in my life.*

*I have also used her archetype and energy to do Mother Earth healings or ceremonies. Her presence has been very powerful in those ceremonies.*

*The goddess Sekhmet has forever changed my life.*

SUSAN NANCY BOUTHOT

# 2

# Preparing for the Work

As you gear up for and pass through these tumultuous and often difficult times that are happening in your life and throughout the world, there are things you can do, individually and communally, to steel yourself for the changes happening to and around you. What you learn here will help as you find your way to the potential golden age or whatever opportunity succeeds these transformations and mutations. Confusion generally precedes clarity, so don't be put off if it takes you some time to get into the rhythm of the work.

We hope to accomplish a number of things through this work, and many opportunities will arise to assist us to clear away confusion and clouded vision. Fostering, feeding, and growing our courage and healing while satiating the hunger of the goddess Sekhmet is a good start. What is happening in the world is a reflection of that which lives in our own hearts. Everything, as horrendous as it looks out in the world, is something contained within ourselves, for we are ultimately all connected, all one organism. There is no way that we can fully hide from the horror that is happening on the planet, regardless of where we put our attention. At some point, we have to step up to the plate and own that we are part of the collective consciousness that is creating the insanity. In this work we look for those things inside of us that we can transform, and, in so doing, we are doing our part to heal the world.

In learning how to develop and join with communal consciousness—

when we come together and facilitate change on an exponential basis by gathering with other like-minded people of heart—we feel the power as it grows in the collective consciousness of all humans. When we honor and invite Sekhmet to assist us, we get to be part of an alchemical process in which she receives, digests, and ultimately transforms a satisfying meal. It is up to each of us to give her the raw material—the food—that is the prime material with which she works. When we first started doing this work we only worked with one problematic characteristic at a time. It soon became apparent that the larger the meal, the happier Sekhmet became and the more she is able to transform for those willing to hold the required focus.

## THE MAGICAL POWER OF KNOTS

Over the years, as the Sekhmet work evolved, I tried a number of different methods to help us find the roots of our issues. We started out molding wax—just a small piece of the kind of wax that becomes malleable when you form it as you work it with your fingers. Molding the wax worked well because we could put a lot of energy and creativity into the process, either purposely designing and creating objects or symbols, or simply noticing what shapes emerged as we worked the wax. The wax was also effective because it burned up entirely when we offered it to the fire in the final ceremony of completion. However, it was difficult to find the kind of wax that was pliable enough to work and would allow us to continue returning to it without hardening until it became too difficult to mold.* We tried other methods too, including working with paper and drawing our way back into a deeper understanding of the source of our challenging qualities, but most of these methods did not carry us deep enough into an understanding of

---

*Many Waldorf schools have small sheets of wax that—when warmed sufficiently in the hands—can be shaped and reshaped into unique forms, each pressure of a thumb informing the wax with one's intention. If you feel drawn to use wax you can give it a try, but it is not easy to get, and it grows more difficult to mold the more you work with it.

ourselves at the necessary level for the full transformation to occur.

Of all the methods we tried, organic twine offered the most positive results. For about a year preceding this writing, I worked with jute or hemp twine to prepare my offering for Sekhmet, and it worked perfectly. Kite string also works well if it is thick enough, as long as it is made from hemp, sisal, jute, cotton, or any natural fiber that will not create toxicity when it is burned. I particularly like the texture of the jute or hemp twine, because it's thicker and makes more interesting shapes as you continue adding knots. Although you are free to find the way that works best for you, this what I recommend. The other benefit of using twine is that if you run out before your offering is complete, you can simply add more.

I suggest starting in this way: Consider a recent moment when you experienced dealing with an ugly habit pattern, such as undue judgment or jealousy. Or you can focus on any recent uncomfortable situation that created stress and caused you to react rather than respond. Tie a knot in the twine to mark that moment, and then turn your attention to a previous, similar situation, the response to which also created unnecessary stress. As you work your way backward in time, you will find patterns developing; you will begin to see how your choices caused problems. With each new recognition, tie another knot about a half inch from the previous one.

As you continue to focus on your thoughts and your actions, your ball of knotted twine will grow, and you will be led deeper and deeper into your unique thought processes. Soon you will become aware of the results of the choices you made and how your life and the lives of those around you were affected.

To link with the core source points in your life, particularly those that are precognitive, requires communication with your subconscious mind. You can't think your way back there, yet you can follow a thread by remembering the last time you experienced what a certain situation felt like and let that carry you to the time before, and so on. In your explorations you may discover a pattern, and as you seek to understand

and find insight about a particular characteristic in that pattern you will remember another layer, and then another and another. Layer after layer you will discover a different trait or quality as each new nuance reveals itself. Each new discovery will lead you deeper and deeper into the recognition of all the attributes that need to be transformed.

Each knot that you add to your twine as you think of a pattern that you can recognize helps you as you work your way back to its source. Most important is the intensity of your concentration and the willingness to stay focused and work your way back through time and depth. There are some things you'll remember and some things you won't. What you are doing is imbuing the twine with the experience, the knowledge, and the deeply held belief or thoughtform within yourself, regardless of whether you remember details.

The work that you have to do to complete your offering between now and when you enter Sekhmet's temple is to continue to identify what you want to transform, tie it into your twine, and then work your way back and see where that leads you. It may ultimately take you beyond cognition, so there may not be articulation, yet those pieces are significant parts of this transformation. You will need to take some time to continue this as a form of meditation, and hold your focus while you explore yourself deeply until you know that you have created sufficient knots and are ready to give your offering to Sekhmet.

In my most recent personal journey with this alchemical process, one of my knotted paths took me back to a shameful experience where I acted out of a hunger in myself that superseded what I knew was right. The release of that experience of greed had a huge effect when it was transformed through this work. Another had to do with loss—the first time I really, fully experienced loss in my life. We all have various emotional triggers that we can begin to identify while knotting the twine. Any one of them could lead you back to the originating thoughtforms for your addictive patterns, be they drugs, alcohol, food, or needs you think you have, hungers you think you are dependent upon. It could take you through rage to more deeply hidden fears behind the anger. It could take you through any one of the whole potential gamut of emotions and possibilities that exists within all of us.

Be sure to add a prayer and gratitude to many of the knots for the understanding you receive as you delve deeper and deeper into your actions, thoughts, and motivations. You can add knots of gratitude at any time as you go through the experiences that follow. As you proceed with this part of the preparations, you are likely to discover new allies that naturally appear and show you how they have been assisting you.

When you find yourself entering difficult terrain in your youth or your marriage, in your parenting or your work relationships, traumatic events in your life, or whatever you happen to be working on, notice when you recognize the need for forgiveness, especially for yourself. Forgiveness is an essential ingredient that will pave the way to return to the time before the giving of the hurt. It also opens the way for more energy to replace the blockage that was created by the initial judgment. It should be noted that to share such epiphanies directly with someone from your past may come with a certain amount of risk, particularly if they have not grown as you have or if they are hanging on to hurt caused when you reacted blindly and without compassion. Using a spiritual forgiveness ritual may be sufficient to transform the situation.

If you need help with the forgiveness work, see the chapter on forgiveness in *Alchemical Healing*,* or look up *ho'oponopono,* the Polynesian forgiveness ritual shown in its many forms on the internet and numerous books on the topic.

When I was in Egypt preparing for the alchemy in this book, I carried my twine with me so that I would have it available when the inspiration arose. When my dear friend and favorite Egyptologist, Emil Shaker, realized what I was doing during our tour, he was blown away. He told me that many women, especially from rural villages in Upper

---

*Nicki Scully, *Alchemical Healing,* 62–71.

Egypt, particularly around Luxor,* use the practice of knotting dolls out of twine, using crochet needles, when they feel bad about someone or want to change or transform something specific. He told me that currently this practice is being used primarily to resolve situations involving revenge. The women use this magical way to confront their anger, sadness, and rage, or anything that they consider the "evil eyes," by putting their feelings into dolls and pinning specific body parts when necessary. They then burn the dolls.

Upon further research, Emil discovered that they not only use dolls, but also knot their concerns into twine, in exactly the way I have been doing and teaching. Once they tie each knot with the intention to transform whatever insult, injury, disease, or problem they are dealing with, they put the string of knots into a bowl and burn it. Emil's excitement at the magic of this synchronicity was more than palpable, as you can imagine. He assured me that this craft, still practiced in rural villages in the south of Egypt today, is inherited from ancient Egyptian, continuously living folklore.

## BUILDING AN ALTAR

While you are creating your offering, which could take several days or even longer, it is helpful to have an altar where you keep your twine when you are not working with it. An altar is also useful as a home for Sekhmet and whatever other spirit beings with whom you find yourself working. While you are doing your work, finding the particular attributes and traits that require modification, it can also be helpful to have a comfortable place that is used specifically to help maintain your focus and attention.

The altar can be as small and simple or as elaborate as suits you. If available, choose a quiet place where you can be alone from time to time.

---

*The Nile is one of the rare major rivers that flows from south to north. Lower Egypt is, therefore, in the north and includes the Nile Delta, which stretches from the Mediterranean Sea south, including Cairo, Memphis, and the pyramids, while Luxor (Thebes to the ancients) is in the heart of Upper Egypt, in the Nile Valley, and whose southern border is the first cataract south of Aswan.

You can use a small table, or even a part of a table that can be defined by a cloth, upon which can be placed a candle, an image or statue of Sekhmet, incense or sage, a lighter or matches, and space for your growing ball of knotted twine. The addition of a crystal or any object that has symbolic meaning regarding this ceremony is also appropriate.

I find that whenever and wherever I choose to do the work, it's clearer and more potent, and seems to flow through my fingers more easily, if I take the time to invoke Sekhmet, to light the candle, and to smudge (purify with smoke from sacred herbs, resins [incense], or certain fragrant wood) before I begin. Ancient Egyptians used highly valued imported resins such as frankincense and myrrh, as well as fragrant pressed oils of roses and other, often exotic, flowers. At the same time, it's best not to get hung up in details. Often I prepare in my mind, purify myself with my breath, or call on the spirit of sage or juniper and invoke Sekhmet wherever I am, or whenever I feel the need or have a thought of something that needs to be added.

Regardless of where you are or what you are doing, look for any chance to add knots to your ball of twine. These knots will reflect all of the qualities and characteristics that you wish to transform in your body, your emotions, your mind, and your spiritual relationship with life, ranging from reactionary and judgmental responses to any weakness, disease, or other undesirable attribute. Be flexible—while traveling on the subway to work is an equally fine time and place to focus your energy on this project, especially when you realize that you are only a breath away from your altar. Sometimes the magic comes to life in the most surprising of places.

## HOW THE ALCHEMY WORKS

Most of the time our responses to events or situations in our lives are based on reactions that were programmed into our psyche from conception to about age six.* As the grooves in our subconscious mind deepen

---

*Bruce Lipton, *The Biology of Belief,* 172.

and create patterns, we tend to react automatically to many situations in our lives. As we become older, it is harder to change the habit patterns that we developed and that direct the majority of our actions and reactions.

Our subconscious mind does not distinguish between visions, dreams, imagination, and real-time, three-dimensionality. Consequently, when doing active meditation practices, such as guided shamanic journeys or visualizations, it is important to engage as many of the inner senses as possible. Then you will have a better chance of experiencing the potential changes this kind of shamanic work offers. It's quite similar to hypnotherapy, although you don't need to be in a trance to have the experience.

What you perceive, whatever you see, feel, smell, hear, or imagine in your inner landscape will translate to your subconscious mind as reality, and the physical body will respond accordingly. For example, if you have a tumor, or a kidney stone, or cyst, and you have an inner experience of a serpent, a cobra perhaps, entering your body and eating the unwanted mass, either in small bites or one gulp, your body will react as though it actually happened, and the tumor or cyst will disintegrate. When the spirit is removed from an organism, it dies. Although this alchemy can work spontaneously, the more a person's inner senses are engaged—the more they "see," "hear," and especially "feel" or simply "know" that the cobra is eating their tumor—the more quickly and easily the transformation will occur. Imagination works as well, as imagination is the lightning rod of the shaman. I-Maji-Nation: Each of us is the magician that creates our own reality.* One's sensitivity in the inner realms is an important asset and is developed or amplified by practicing visualization meditations.

Because science cannot measure these types of effects, the proof is in the experience, and the result. Because each person experiences such journeys in their own way, and in accordance with their unique

---

*This concept was first spoken to me by Christine Payne Towler some thirty years ago.

sensitivity, it is difficult to measure these activities in a way that reaches the bar of science. In my decades as a practicing healer, however, I have had countless experiences of "miraculous" healings, many of which were instantaneous. More times than I can count, symptoms that were recorded in a hospital or clinic have simply disappeared. (These include a broken foot, cancer, and just about everything in between.) Many allopathic doctors have difficulty accepting the evidence before them and write it off, claiming that the first X-rays or tests were mistakes or mislabeled. To me and the people who receive these miracles, such results are more like validations or proofs. And yet there are inconsistencies that, although a good practitioner can usually figure out why and overcome the problem with appropriate language, cannot be explained. For example, according to a person's core beliefs, they may not respond well to a cobra or a spider, both of which have a whole host of healing skills. (Imagine a spider, or multitudes of spiders, stitching together torn tissue, or weaving a supportive, medicinal web as a splint.) Finding and utilizing the gifts of nature in all her forms is another key to this method of transformation.

Once your offering has been accepted by Sekhmet, you will learn to be conscious in more than one dimension simultaneously. For some of you that will come easily. For others, it will take some time and practice. The most important thing is that you allow yourself to be present for the alchemical process, using all your senses, even though you will be living your ordinary life at the same time. If you have the luxury of sequestering yourself throughout the time that you are working with this book, of course that would be ideal, but it is not necessary. By living your life as usual while the alchemy is happening, you will learn to hold your focus in spiritual dimensions at the same time as you are fully functioning in the "real" world, taking care of business as usual.

As you continue knotting your ball of twine, you are working toward that place in the core of your being where the primal characteristics or habit patterns that are set in your subconscious programming have been engraved. When you bring those specific patterns into your higher consciousness as you focus on the knotting process, they will be more easily available to Sekhmet. As soon as she receives the twine and the discordant patterns are in place to be transformed, tremendous amounts of energy are released that can be used to help you rebuild yourself and move forward with much more ease and clarity.

Doing the work with your heart open is the most important factor. I recommend practicing the Heart Breath, given below and on the following pages, as often as possible throughout the entire time that you're involved in reading this book to achieve an optimum outcome.

## STARTING WITH THE HEART

To be most effective in any intentional act of healing, co-creation, or transformation, much of my work starts from and is threaded through the heart center. True wisdom is perceived from the heart. Every process, every meditation, every act of healing and conscious creation that you will encounter in this book starts with you becoming centered and focused, developing and directing your intention from the heart.

The Heart Breath process, through which we can quickly and easily bring ourselves into alignment with the higher purpose of the work, was initially published in *Alchemical Healing* and has been included in every one of my books since.* Its practice has been employed by thousands of practitioners around the world. The Heart Breath is fast and effective, and its value expands with use. We will begin with a powerful induction that prepares you for whatever work is at hand in this book or in your life. Later in this book we will also add the Belly Breath, inclusion of which gives additional power to your individual will and intention.

*See Nicki Scully, *Alchemical Healing,* 275–78.

##  HEART BREATH INVOCATION

*[Relax and take a couple of deep, grounding breaths. Look within to find the eternal flame that dwells in the sanctuary of your heart center. As you bring it into focus, accessing whatever inner senses are available to you— sight, hearing, feeling, knowing, or imagination—feed your heart flame with love.]*

As you continue to pour love upon your flame, notice how it responds. Notice how your ability to love grows. Love is the fuel. As you continue to pour love upon your flame, it may brighten, intensify, or in some way grow and spread warmth and light throughout your being.

While you continue pouring love upon your flame, begin to breathe as though you are drawing the power, vitality, and intelligence from the heart of the Earth up through all the strata of the Earth, drawing from all the elements, minerals, and plants. Pull the energy that comes with your in-breath upward, into your body. . . . Inhale the power and vitality of the Earth, drawing it with your inhalation up through your body to your heart center. . . . Hold your breath for a moment while the power and intelligence of the Earth mingles with the love that you are continuing to pour on your heart flame. . . . As you exhale, your nourished breath radiates out from your heart center, igniting every cell of your body with vitality, intelligence, life-force energy, and love. . . . *[Pause.]*

After several strong earth breaths, continue pouring love on your heart flame while you inhale from the heart of the Earth. . . . Now, simultaneously extend your consciousness upward toward the heart of the universe. While you are inhaling the power of Earth, you can also inhale from the Sky, drawing down the power, vitality, and intelligence from the star nations and all the intelligence of the universe that surrounds and permeates all of creation. . . . As the power of above joins the power of the Earth in your heart center, see-feel-know-imagine the further nourishment of your heart flame. . . . Hold your breath for a moment as these energies combine with the love you are continuing to pour on your heart flame. . . . With each exhalation, experience the growing life-force energy, intelligence, love, and radiance that extend throughout your body and beyond. . . . [*Pause.*]

Once you feel yourself in alignment with the consciousness and powers of Earth and Sky, you will be prepared to enter into the journeys and rites of this Sekhmet work and each meditation and initiation.

The Heart Breath practice helps to establish a direct connection with the intelligent sources of our universe and can be used at any time to bring you back to center if you've strayed. It also helps you to maintain your center as you function throughout your day. It can serve as a beacon with which to call forth appropriate guidance to help you meet your needs at any time. Consistent practice of this process, either as part of a daily meditation or by simply choosing to take a moment to focus, will result in a sustainable awareness that is sane, balanced, and rewarding.

Although the practice itself will become smoother, easier, and will eventually integrate so that it is only a matter of your attention to bring yourself into centered and balanced equilibrium, you need to remain vigilant so that it does not become a rote formula. The Heart Breath requires revitalization and a conscious awareness of the sources of energy required to keep this practice alive. Done by rote, it is in danger of becoming devoid of the spirit and intelligence it is meant to invoke, not unlike many religions that have resorted to dogma and lost the vitality of their initially inspired spontaneous magic.

The Heart Breath is a starting point that also holds the position of a fulcrum, the nexus point between the grounded, dense, solid, and often volatile energy of earth (matter) and the magnificent, radiant, and complex intelligence of the stars and the universe that enfolds and surrounds us (spirit). It is a road map to your place of power as a lightning rod, capable of transforming the energy and intelligence of Source into a coherent matrix of information and power.

The Heart Breath serves as a basis for all of your journey work and hopefully will develop into a natural breathing pattern that helps to keep you grounded and centered. When we introduce the Belly Breath there will be a shift in source and direction that will help you ground your alchemical work from the spiritual into the physical.

## SHARED VOICES

*When I took Transformation in the Belly of the Goddess in June 2009, I sensed that my experience was different from what had been expected. I was never in Sekhmet's body. In my notes I wrote, "Sekhmet, you feel like my mentor. I am not inside you; we are cuddling." I experienced myself as one of her cubs, wrapped in her lion arms. "Instead of being in her, it was more like we have merged." There was a feeling of being in a vast, heart-shaped space. There was no sense of fierceness. I still have a vivid memory of Sekhmet in a journey that you offered, showing me how to hunt a desolate, devastated landscape, stalking the beauty that sustains me.*

*Sometime between this class and my trip to Egypt in 2011 with you and Normandi, I became so used to feeling that Sekhmet was always available to me that I hardly thought of her. She had become a part of me. And rereading my notes from our class I see how that is true. Those things that you asked us to think about—our fears, what holds us back from embracing our power, those things that I frankly did not even know how to name—are no longer with me. Now, in 2015, I found these notes describing the intention of a journey you offered us. "My intentional creation/co-creation of myself: take time to focus on the attributes that I wish to foster and imbue. We are doing this work in alignment with cosmic forces, a co-creative process. Think of Sekhmet as my mother/mentor to achieve my very highest potential. Take time and space to receive the love she is lavishing upon me. Pay attention, observe the process. Participate! If we take hold of Power from the perspective of the Heart, then we will not abuse it, misuse it." I felt no great change in my approach to life, in my living of my life, but the power of what you offered me clearly supported what was always my intent. It is as if what you offered helped me to become more available to the partnerships that I had already been offered, that were already at play in my life. And the truth of the power of your offering is made manifest in the living of my life to this day.*

MADELYN PITTS

*I cannot describe the joy and gratitude I am feeling from this journey via the telecast of "Transformation in the Belly of the Goddess." I feel truly blessed to have been a part of this.*

*I am not good on computer and could not get on Skype or see any of the photos. It did not matter for I AM TRANSFORMED! I know that it was working with Sekhmet and Thoth, who kept showing up all the time, and the magical alchemy.*

*I was ready for this releasing, healing, and transformation. I had been working on releasing old patterns and belief systems that did not serve me. I've been living the Four Agreements by Don Miguel Ruiz, which has been wonderful. I even attended a seminar last weekend to hear Tara Brach, which was fabulous. But nothing I have done or tried has ever lifted me or changed me to how good I feel now as did working with you and alchemy.*

*I really took to tying knots, releasing, showing gratitude, and feeding Sekhmet. I was doing it all the time and everywhere. I adapted to switching back and forth very easily almost right away. I'm actually relaxing in Sekhmet's belly under the sycamore tree as I am writing to you.*

*During our journeys I was often a step ahead of you with Sekhmet. For example, I was feeling fire coming into my body and igniting my heart flame when shortly after you said, "You'll know when it is time to call in fire." Also, even before the journey to receive our skeletal system, I could feel my muscles, tissues, and ligaments forming.*

*Nicki, thanks to you and the program and ancient deities, I can actually say that I love myself unconditionally. It has taken me seventy years to feel this. My gratitude and appreciation to all of you.*

*I was working on mindfulness, knowing my boundaries, being grounded, knowing who I am, loving myself. I can truthfully say that I am now totally all of those things since Thursday's session of transformation.*

TRISH BLOCK

# 3

## Paying Respects to the Mysteries

The next addition to our offering to Sekhmet came when Indigo Rønlov and I were preparing to take a group we were leading in Egypt in 2014 for their opening ceremony, which we like to do between the paws of the Sphinx, the guardian of the mysteries.

Although we were staying in our hotel at the foot of the pyramid at the time, the night before our sunrise ceremony we found ourselves having a meeting with Ptah, Sekhmet, Anubis, Ma'at, and others from the Egyptian pantheon in Ptah's chapel at Karnak. They suggested that we add a new piece to our usual Sphinx ritual, one that would become part of our offering to Sekhmet. It was then that we realized that the alchemy of that particular Egyptian mysteries pilgrimage was to experience as much of the work of transformation in the belly of the goddess as we could fit into our schedule and that this was our dress rehearsal for the book.

The Sphinx is a huge statue carved from the bedrock of stone on a direct alignment between due east and the second pyramid in the Great Pyramid complex on the Giza Plateau. It is traditionally said to have been created by the pharaoh Khafre, the son of Khufu, also known as Cheops, about 2500 BCE. The controversy surrounding its origin spans thousands of years. Equally controversial is whether the animal was meant to be a lion or Anubis, the jackal god who, among other funerary tasks, was found to be the guardian of the treasures in King Tut's tomb. There are compelling arguments for both options based on a number of interesting points of view. I choose to leave it to you to decide from your own experience. What's truly important to this work is that you make a connection and develop a relationship with the Sphinx that will help to ground you throughout this process and any other work you do regarding the great mysteries hidden beneath the sand and locked in the stones of Egypt.

I am including a variation of this journey now for several reasons: It is advisable to pay your respects to the Sphinx because he/she is the guardian of the mysteries, and it is important that you acknowledge that and ask for guidance and protection as the alchemical process carries you through the mysteries and sacred places and monuments of Egypt. The Sphinx is also an Earth altar that gives us a direct connection to our source in the stars. As the keeper of the Akashic Record (the subtle field that contains all past, present, and potential future events) for our planet, as well as for each of us, he/she holds information and perhaps some specific instructions that you may need further along in the process. This is also your opportunity to honor and invoke your own spirit guides as well as to ask for protection and guidance from the Egyptian pantheon. Offering prayers from your heart for this land, its family of neteru, its people, and, perhaps most especially, its waters and the turbulent politics that surround the region.

## ☀ SPHINX JOURNEY

*[Prepare for this journey as you would any ceremony or initiation. Smudge yourself with sage or other incense, light a candle and get comfortable in a peaceful, quiet place. . . .]*

Breathe the Heart Breath, intentionally drawing in the vitality and power of the Earth and the intelligence and energies from the Sky as well as its celestial bodies and the field of consciousness in which all are

*Fig. 3.1. The Great Sphinx (Photo by Debbie Clarkin)*

suspended. . . . Be sure to continuously offer your love into the mix, paus-ing at the apex of your breath to allow the power and intelligence of Earth and Sky to mix with your love. . . . As you continue breathing the Heart Breath, your radiance grows and glows. . . . [*Pause while you continue to breathe the Heart Breath until you come into resonance with yourself at the nexus point between spirit and matter.*]

As you become more fully present, you will be able to see and feel yourself drawn to the ancient Sphinx, which has been standing for ages at the entrance to the Giza necropolis. Soon you become aware of yourself standing between the paws of the Sphinx. It's the quiet time between dark and dawn, and you can begin to hear the sounds of the city waking up behind you. Look up at the head of the magnificent being, the Earth altar where you are standing. You can see the eyes of the Sphinx staring ahead toward a point at some distance over Cairo.

Gather your intention to request permission to enter these myster-ies, the ancient Egyptian mysteries that include the powerful transformation to which you are committing by doing the work of this book. With humility and respect, offer your next deep Heart Breath directly into the heart of the Sphinx, including your love, your commitment, and your request for safe passage through the coming rites. . . . [*Pause.*]

Immediately, as the first ray of the rising sun touches your back, the heart of the magnificent Sphinx opens and you are drawn forward, closer, until you are pulled into and become part of the great stone statue, leaving the sunlight behind. . . . The molecules within the stone expand along with yours, giving the sense of being in a great and spacious room. Even though it's very dark inside the stone, as you become accustomed to the darkness you become aware that there are many beings coming into form all around you. It is the light of their essence that fills the heart of the Sphinx and allows you to see and recognize some of the members of the Egyptian pantheon that have gathered to greet you. Certain of them may be more prominent for you, and you may or may not know their names. . . . [*Pause.*]

Greet those whom you know, and receive welcome from some that you are meeting for the first time. One of the neteru steps forward and hands you an etheric bundle wrapped in red cotton cloth. Be sure to thank the deity that gifted you with it. . . . Certain of the other deities offer you specific messages, tools, or information to help you on your journey. . . . [*Pause.*] Once you have greeted and communicated with those who wish to connect with you at this time, the neteru dissolve back into the walls. It will begin to feel as though the stone is closing in around you as you are squeezed back out of the Sphinx and find yourself standing once again between the paws. . . .

As you gaze up to the eyes of the Sphinx, receive any final message he/she has for you at this time, remembering that the Sphinx not only maintains direct access to the intelligence of the stars but also holds the blueprint, the Akashic Record, for this planet and its inhabitants. Offer your gratitude to the Sphinx, and tie some knots of gratitude to add to your offering for Sekhmet. . . . Ground and center yourself.

◆ ◆ ◆

Be sure to write as many details as you can remember of your meditation with the Sphinx in your journal. Try to recall the names of those who connected with you. If you don't know their names, often what they are wearing, especially on their heads, and what they carry in their hands can be clues. Also, many appear as humans with animal heads, or occasionally the other way around. You might wish to do some research to get the names and functions of those you didn't recognize.

## A BUNDLE OF TRUTH

After you come out of this journey and record your experience in your journal, it is a good time to open the etheric bundle you were given. Although this bundle is composed of spirit rather than physical matter, it and its contents are quite real in the spirit realm. When we work in this way we cross back and forth between realms, worlds, and dimensions, and our recognition of these spirit objects gives them validity and power in our three-dimensional reality. The more you practice focusing in these visualizations, the more you will awaken your inner senses and the clearer and more potent the images (or whatever senses you already have and the new ones that you are developing) will become.

The bundle you were given in the Sphinx contains symbols of all the significant things that you have neglected or discarded in your life and for which you may still carry regret. As you study its contents one item at a time these memories will awaken; you have the luxury of time to fully understand the importance of these events or patterns and the influence they still hold over you. As the memories come to you, be sure to tie a knot for each and let each take you deeper into those experiences you might have forgotten. Whether or not you consciously remember the details, these situations or patterns have been adding to the burdens that you have been carrying and will open up more space for positive energies once they are transformed. For now, simply make note of those choices and any detritus that may remain as a result. Continue to mine for the delicacies that will surely spice up Sekhmet's meal.

As you seek to expose the truth of yourself, it's good to remember to be grateful for the truth and carry it with honor and dignity. Record your experience. However, after you tie whatever knots may develop as a result, you will want to wrap up the bundle again and bring it with you as part of your offering to Sekhmet. You may choose to place something on your altar as a symbol for the etheric bundle and a reminder of the truths that it holds.

## SHARED VOICES

*As I journey to Egypt and look up into the eyes of the Sphinx, he carefully wraps his paws around me in greeting. Old friends reunited once again.*

*He invites me to enter into his heart center. I feel as though I am moving quickly through the center of an hourglass. I feel a tremendous amount of density as I am squeezed through from the outside, through the stone into the chamber of his heart. Once inside, the stone opens into a vast room where all my neteru friends are awaiting my arrival.*

*I step into the center of the room, and the goddesses and gods circle tightly around me. Ma'at steps forward and hands me a bundle in red cloth. It was strangely light and heavy at the same time. Each of the neteru then reach out with their hands to touch my shoulders, and as they do so, we become a connected web with me in the middle. I feel all the power, vitality, love, and wisdom of these ancient and ever-present allies pulsing around and through me.*

*As I am given the bundle, I am told to remember to be strong and that strength sometimes comes in softness. I am also told to remember to be true and that even when I doubt myself I will always know what to do. They tell me that everything I need is in this moment, and this moment is eternal. They remind me that neteru are everywhere and universal, and all I have to do is ask and they will assist.*

*Once I am complete and it is time to leave the Sphinx, I am squeezed through the constriction of the looking glass yet again as I return out of the stone. Under the blue morning sky, I notice that I am now wearing a thin gold band—a very simple crown—around my head, and I am holding the red bundle in the crook of my left arm.*

*Next I become aware that Ma'at has come through with me and is standing to my left. Together we face the dream stele between the paws of the Sphinx. The Sphinx relays to me that I am a daughter of the stars. He says, "Remember your work, show up fully, and all will be as it is meant to be." His enormous paws again reach out to gently hug me and Ma'at.*

*I give gratitude to the neteru for bearing witness and informing my experience within the Sphinx, to Ma'at for teaching me Truth and bringing me this bundle, and to the Sphinx for being an ever-steady guardian. As I come out of the journey, I feel both a bit of trepidation and a welling of curiosity to open this bundle to see what aspects of my life and self I had discarded and previously thought were useless. I am excited to refashion these aspects into whomever I am currently becoming.*

*With full engagement in the alchemical process of recycling or reclaiming them, we can become fully actualized beings, living in* hotep *(an ancient Egyptian word meaning "peace," "blessings," and "offerings").*

INDIGO RØNLOV

# 4

# Dealing with Fear

Fear is one of our greatest teachers. From the time you had your first childhood lesson of keeping your hands off the hot pot or cookstove to your current ability to recognize danger and get out of the way, fear has earned our respect and has tremendous influence and sway in our behavior. The ability to discern the difference between fear and paranoia is basic to the mature enjoyment of life and the management of stress.

There are things that get in the way of the kind of progress we wish to achieve with regard to fear, which is often behind many of the most deep-seated issues that interfere with our ability to locate the main blockages to our personal energy and power. Fear has many causes, including all manner of traumatic experiences ranging in time from conception throughout our lives, and sometimes even including past-life trauma. The older and more extensive the trauma, the more deeply it is ingrained in our soul's memory. It can still affect our ability to achieve consistent clarity in our lives, even if we don't have conscious memory of the event or events that caused it. Those fears, at the time they were set in place, were likely important survival mechanisms.

Fear's wide range of causes includes not only our direct experience of frightening events but also the phobias that are handed to us from our parents, such as fear of spiders and other judgment-based decrees.

Many of our cultures are fear based and create and feed unreasonable fears like homophobia, xenophobia, and other fears embedded in propaganda, while war and conflict generate PTSD with all its complexities and anxieties. Poverty, disease, pain, and death forge an endless array of other problems over which we have little or no control. Even scary stories in our youth can implant fears that can last a lifetime.

Whether your fears are rational and realistic or totally unfounded, they have a huge impact on your life; the transformation that occurs based on how you face those fears can make a great difference in the quality of your life. The importance of dealing with fear cannot be overstated. The powers that control the world have chosen to use fear to manipulate, dominate, and oppress huge segments of the populations of our country and many other countries around the world. We are going to have to stand up and face this. Bringing your fears as close as you can to consciousness is an important part of the alchemy so that they will stand out to Sekhmet as particularly delicious tidbits. The more you can offer up your detrimental patterns to Sekhmet, the more satisfying will be the offering and the results more clear and potent.

Have you ever studied how traditional Native Americans hunted for their food? There is great respect for the animal. Before a shot is fired, a bow drawn, or a trap set, a prayer of gratitude is made for the creature, honoring its family and acknowledging the sustenance that is the gift of the hunt. Every part of the animal is utilized, and nothing is wasted. As you enter into this covenant with Sekhmet, there is a level of trust in the container itself, a knowing that Sekhmet will be able to transform that which you are offering her and utilize every morsel in a good way. Therefore, your desire to give her an exceptional, nourishing meal is paramount. The entire process, when treated with a high level of respect and gratitude, will help assure that we can truly stop the insanity that has become so pervasive in our world.

Fear is particularly important, because courage, an important quality dispensed by Sekhmet, is gained through meeting your fears directly. During this journey we will work on making your fears more conscious as you cleanse and prepare yourself so that you can give your offering as fearlessly as possible to the goddess when the time is right.

To accomplish this you will need to find a way into a direct relationship with your subconscious mind. You cannot think yourself there; your subconscious is too deep. Although you can't get there directly, you can knot it into the twine, starting with the last time you felt fear and working backward until you know you are ready to move into a different arena.

## TRANSFORMING FEAR WITH SEKHMET

Fear can be helpful in keeping us alive. Yet we also have irrational fears that do not serve us, and some can be very debilitating. It's important to be able to distinguish irrational fear from true threats to our or another's safety.

The survival mechanisms that we employed when we were young, even precognitive, set patterns in our subconscious mind. If we do not recognize, outgrow, or otherwise change these patterns as we gain in our understanding and discrimination, they remain our first and most available means of dealing with fearful situations. These fears can run the show and cause us to react in ways that are not productive and often magnify the danger. Throughout our lives, we learn ways to recognize threats and things that could cause pain, and we intuitively get out of the way. Each type of fear requires its appropriate response.

The following journey is an alchemical process that will help transform the layers of fear and open the way for the other levels of transformation. As you journey you will be looking for those responses that do not serve you anymore, the ones that are so ingrained that you act from your subconscious patterning rather than from mature, reasonable consciousness and skill. Each time you locate a reactive pattern that no longer serves you it will take you deeper into recognizing and bringing these patterns to the surface, where they can be added

*Fig. 4.1. Sekhmet*
*(Illustration from* Power Animal Meditations *by Angela Werneke)*

to the twine. Be sure to have your twine close by so that you can add knots as needed.

Fear puts us into fight-or-flight mode, affecting our adrenals and making it difficult to form a conscious response. The aim of the transformation is to be able to take action with responsibility rather than reactivity. Sekhmet is here to help you recognize and find those fears, identify them, and work with them in a way that allows you to bring them forward and tie them into your twine. You may wish to do this fear journey in a place where you are alone or with a trusted group so that you will not be inhibited when it is time to roar as a lioness.

## ☀ FEAR JOURNEY WITH SEKHMET

[*Allow yourself to be very comfortable as you close your eyes and ground and center yourself. Take a moment to find your heart flame and feed it with love.*]

As you pour love upon your heart flame, inhale the powers of Earth and Sky. Reach with your breath into the heart of the Earth and then draw up Earth's vitality, power, strength, healing energies, and vital life force. Gather the elements, minerals, plants, and their intelligence into your body, drawing them all the way up to your heart center, where they enter your heart fire and mingle with the intelligence, power, and love that you have drawn down from the Sky. . . . [*Pause.*]

Continue to pour love on your heart flame throughout. As you inhale, experience the breath through your entire body, and let a new level of alertness and clarity enter every cell and molecule of your being. As you exhale and the radiance of your heart flame grows, look outside the circle of light that surrounds you like a halo. Look into that place of darkness that inevitably surrounds us all. As you put your attention beyond the comforting glow of light into the darkness, you will see the eyes of Sekhmet gleaming in the darkness. On your next exhale, send your heart breath to Sekhmet as you ask her to join you and help you deal with the fears that inhabit your being. . . . *[Pause.]* As you connect with Sekhmet, she stands before you in her goddess form, a woman's body with a lioness's head surmounted with a uraeus crown holding the sun disk.*

If this is the first time you are meeting Sekhmet, allow yourself to connect with her eye-to-eye and heart-to-heart. She may place a hand or paw upon your chest. . . . Allow yourself to feel her sekhem, her power, moving into your heart and through your circulatory system into every cell and molecule of your body, waking up the ancient memory that resides in your DNA, reminding every part of you that this goddess truly lives within you. . . . *[Pause.]* Notice how you experience being filled with her courage and power. . . . *[Pause.]*

Sekhmet has come to help you work through your fears. As you continue to feel her power coursing through your being, she morphs into her beautiful lioness form, nudging you to become a lioness with her. . . . She is going to take you on a journey into the savanna. Feel as you begin to transfigure into a lioness. You can feel as your breath, your body, and your muscles change. . . . As your whiskers grow, you begin to sense how they communicate information to you. . . . Stretch into the fullness of your lioness being, and follow Sekhmet, experiencing the grace and strength with which the two of you are running across the savanna. Although you are following Sekhmet, you know that she knows exactly where she is going. Notice your senses as they become more acute with each stride of your graceful lioness body. . . . *[Pause.]*

In the distance you begin to perceive the first fear that is coming to meet you. Sekhmet shows you how to stop and crouch in the grass to watch. . . . Once you are still and hidden, observe this fear closely. Listen very carefully. Sniff the air. You can smell it. You may even

---

*The uraeus is a stylized image of an upright cobra that was worn by deities and high initiates of ancient Egypt. It is emblematic of the serpent power (also known as kundalini energy) that was accessible to them. It's also a symbol of an awakened being.

be able to taste in on your tongue. Is this a fear that is serving your higher self? Is it keeping you safe? Notice where you feel it in your body and how your body reacts to it. Can you feel it? [*Pause.*]

If this fear is something that still serves you, then honor it. If it has served you in the past to keep you safe, honor it and thank it. If it is a fear that you wish to transform, Sekhmet may nudge you to stand and look directly at this fear. . . . You hear a low grumbling, rumbling sound, possibly before you realize that it is coming from you. Let the sound build as you face this fear. . . . Let loose with a great roar! Notice how the fear reacts. . . . Do not be shy. Sekhmet is right there with you! The roar seems to have a life of its own. As it diminishes, take a moment to tie this fear into your twine. . . . [*Pause.*] It is not necessary to know the story behind the fear, yet isolating it in this way helps you to let go of it. . . . [*Pause.*]

Continue hunting more of these fears, following the same process. As you seek out each fear, remember to honor and give gratitude, then roar and let go of that which no longer serves you. Sometimes you will know the source of the fear, the specific situation that caused it, and sometimes it will be obscure. In either case, tie a knot in your twine and continue on your hunt with Sekhmet. . . . [*Long pause.*]

When there are no more fears showing up, you and Sekhmet walk side by side enjoying the sun in the aftermath of the hunt. . . . She has shown you how to hunt and how to face your fears. She is always available to you in the future, if you need to come back to this place again. . . . [*Pause.*]

Take one last stretch in your lioness form, relishing the power and strength that is the natural state of a healthy lioness. . . . Now feel yourself come back into your human form as Sekhmet returns to her goddess form, while you slowly walk back to your place in present time and space. . . . Walk with Sekhmet now and ask if she has any further instructions for you in preparation for what is to come. . . . [*Pause.*]

Be sure to express your gratitude to Sekhmet for this teaching.

You may find a need to repeat the hunt as memories surface or new events occur. . . . Thank yourself for having the courage to face your fears, and offer prayers for others whom you know and the world in general to be able to live free of fear. . . . When you feel complete, take a deep earth breath pulling up the earth energy to help to ground you in your physical body. Wiggle your toes and fingers, and slowly open your eyes.

Write every detail that you can think of in your journal as soon as possible, and add any knots to the twine that you may have missed. It's okay to make more than one knot for a particular fear or other pattern that may return again, including knots for gratitude for lessons learned, and any prayers that develop as a result of this journey. Regardless of whether you are working with fear or any other issues that come up as you are preparing your twine, it is important to know that you do not need to remember the story behind every knot. When you leave your memory and move beyond, Sekhmet will know what to do with the knot, regardless of how putrid it might seem to you. Knots for gratitude and prayers are especially appreciated.

Take as long as you need to continue to delve more deeply into your psyche to find those characteristics that require transformation. Look for any weaknesses, places of illness, discomfort, and trauma that remain from old injuries as well as emotional baggage that causes reactions that you have yet to fully control. Continue to tie knots for any remaining instabilities that surface, for both acute and chronic pain, and for damage to any of your body's network of systems. Tie knots until you run out of reasons and then tie more knots for gratitude and prayers.

### SHARED VOICES

*That was a journey! Wonderful, deep, scary, and joyful all at the same time. During the Transformation in the Belly of the Goddess webinars last October (2015) I received many messages, and some of them are still unfolding. One of the most insightful and direct effects, however, concerns a profound liberation from a fear that was so well hidden that I did not even know it existed in me.*

*Throughout the journeys, Sekhmet took us on a quest to hunt down, recognize, and heal the obstructions in our lives. During the period that ensued—between the webinars and the last ritual, which I performed more than two and a half months later—my reality shifted, bringing into focus how much of my life was directed from the fear of "not being loved," fear of "not being loveable." Some of the people whom I considered as close friends suddenly changed their behavior and have shown their dark side in most disturbing and unloving ways. Other people, whom I did not see as intimate or even familiar, changed their ways and have expressed their love and support in a surprising chain of events. Now I know it was not they who changed but rather my perception and energies, newly guided by Sekhmet's fierce compassion.*

*And she was with me all the time! Her presence is what allowed me to dive deeply and have a hard look at what was revealed. Every time I would confront a situation or a person whose existence in my reality was a consequence of the fear, I would call upon Sekhmet, and we would observe both through her and my eyes and act through our combined energies. Needless to say, that brought a number of closures but also opened a way for understanding and forgiveness. There were also numerous occurrences where I was given the occasion to see, feel, and receive love, in—until then—unsuspected ways; and this novel perception is still unfolding.*

*This journey and work we did together also liberated a huge amount of energy that was buried with the fear, serving the purpose of containing it. These energies, which were safely tucking the fear away from my consciousness, became available and were suddenly seeking expression! Unused for their previous purpose, they were at first coming up raw and wild, transforming me at times into a volcano. My intentions were and are harmless, so I did not hurt anyone, but I know I was rather intense at times. Now I am learning to use this volcano and direct its energy so that it acts in both powerful and loving ways. I am learning fierce compassion. ☺*

*I am immensely grateful for all of it. To you, to Sekhmet, to Ptah, and to Nefertum.*

*I now know I am Love and am on a quest to discover ways to integrate this truth into my operating system, my personality. My intention and my endeavor is to integrate this knowledge into both my "daily life" and into my spiritual practice as a meditation guide. Through both, I am in constant contact and relationship with many people of various constitutions, so occasions to exercise are many. I am now on a journey to discover how to keep Love in my consciousness and how to best express it—this is what best describes the outcome of the journey with Sekhmet.*

*I thank you, I thank the neteru for the presence and the guidance on this journey of profound transformation.*

DANIJELA NESTOROVIC

*Little Rewards. When fears are identified, tasted, faced, and then put away, the feeling of accomplishment is almost palpable. As the process is repeated and the size and depth of my personal monsters are faced, even if it's just identifying them for the first time in years, years of hiding from them, the little rewards become bigger rewards and have a lasting impact on my life. It was almost as if I was trapped in a loop and I could see no way out—every year on the anniversary of a horrible and scary situation I could feel the moment approach. When the day arrived I would be haunted, and I would move on knowing that the next year, on March 25, this process would repeat. This work with Sekhmet fills me with hope, with the promise that it will be different next year, and that every March 25 after will be different.*

MARK HALLERT

# PART II

❧❧

*The Offering*

# 5

# Taking Your Offering
# to Sekhmet

You will know when you have completed your preparations and are ready to take your offering to Sekhmet. Choose a time when you are sure that you won't be interrupted and a place, perhaps at your altar, where you are comfortable and can return again and again if possible to continue the work. Enter this phase of the process with reverence, full presence, and an open heart.

To give our offering to Sekhmet, we must journey to her chapel in Karnak, which we will do in two phases, first as a journey to Karnak, and then, in the next chapter, as a journey to Sekhmet's chapel. From this point forward, you will want to give extra attention to where you are while taking the journey, and in the breaks between try to stay with the work with as few distractions as possible. Please note that I have included supporting images of both parts of this journey in the color insert so that you will not be distracted during the actual journey, which is a rite of passage that requires your total presence. Please study color plates 2 through 9 carefully before beginning the Journey to Karnak (the first phase of the journey) to help yourself visualize the actual surroundings on the way to the chapel.

It is almost time to make your offering to Sekhmet. However, you will still have ample opportunity to complete your work with the twine as we get closer to your face-to-face meeting with her in her temple.

##  JOURNEY TO KARNAK*

*[Begin by grounding and centering yourself. Breathe the Heart Breath to clear your mind and help you to focus. Offer your breath in gratitude to Earth, Sky, and all the beings that you may have already invoked and will invoke at this time to witness and support you throughout this initiation and all future initiations and journeys throughout this alchemical process.]*

As you continue breathing the Heart Breath, feel the space filling with your supporters and guides. . . . As your light brightens and radiates out from your heart, remember that many others have gone before you on this journey. On your next exhale, link your heart flame with all the heart flames of those who have come before you. The radiance brightens and extends farther and farther out, creating a light that works like a beacon that attracts ancestors, deities, ascended masters, plant medicines, animal totems, galactic councils from throughout our universe, and other spirit guides who recognize the light and come to assist. You can feel it as your heart opens wider and when your heart flame merges with the heart flames of all those in attendance. . . . [*Pause.*]

As you inhale your next Heart Breath, focus your attention on your intention to offer the gift you have been creating to Sekhmet so that she can help you transform all the issues that you have knotted into your twine regarding the health of your physical, emotional, spiritual, and mental bodies. As you exhale, direct your intention to Sekhmet from your heart. . . .

---

*An original version of much of this journey was published in *Heart of the Sun: An Anthology in Exaltation of Sekhmet,* by Candace C. Kant and Anne Key (Bloomington, Ind.: Universe, 2011).

In the center of the light that is radiating from you, there is a tiny dot that grows with each breath. It soon takes the form of a right Egyptian eye, the eye of Horus, or Ra, the all-seeing eye of the sun. As it grows, it draws you toward it. . . .

When you approach and pass through the pupil of the eye, you will find yourself on a boat docked at the edge of the east bank of the Nile River in Egypt. You are helped off the boat and directed to walk up the wide stone roadway, through a massive open square that leads to a great temple pylon that is the entrance to the magnificent temple of Karnak. If you look west to the opposite bank you will see the tiered funerary temple of the female pharaoh Hatshepsut looking as though it is grow- ing out of the cliffs that reach from the sugarcane fields below to the top of a pyramid-shaped mountaintop, the other side of which is the Valley of the Kings.

Walk toward the pylon that is the entrance to Karnak. Soon you will find yourself passing between rows of ram-headed sphinxes. If you look straight ahead toward the temple, you become aware that each ram is looking directly at you, and you can feel its gaze pen- etrating your being as it knows you completely. When you arrive at the giant front gate, a priest or priestess opens the way for you and guides you into the temple and toward the chapel of Sekhmet, Ptah, and Nefertum. . . .

When you first enter Karnak temple, you find yourself in a large courtyard. If you have walked back in time, there are people doing vari- ous tasks, and, depending upon whether there is a festival, there could be a lot going on. In current time, it could be filled with tourists from all over the world. . . .

On the other side of the square you enter the hypostyle hall, which is filled with carefully placed columns as large as the girth of giant redwood trees that are carved, painted, and covered with hiero- glyphs. Sunlight shines through the missing places in the roof, and you might be drawn to a specific hieroglyph that has special meaning for you on one of the pillars. Take a moment to see if you can grasp its meaning, and then enter the details into your journal. . . . [*Pause.*]

About half way through this great hall of columns, you will turn left and proceed to a small opening in the north wall, which at one time marked the outer edge of the temple. As soon as you exit the main temple, what you see depends upon whether your observations are occurring in the present or in ancient times, perhaps thousands of years ago. Now it is dry and sandy with a few palm trees and a number of cut stone blocks waiting to find their place in the still incomplete puzzle that is Karnak. If you find yourself in ancient times, there is likely to be a beautiful garden filled with exotic plants and trees with distinctive fragrances. There are unusual, colorful birds and exquisite fountains all laid out in perfect symmetry and beauty. . . . [*Pause.*]

Follow a path that goes off to the left and then swings around to the right toward the northern outer wall where you will find the temple of Sekhmet, Ptah, and Nefertum, a modest chapel complex compared to the grandeur of Karnak, and yet a place of immeasurable power. Where the path ends there is a lush, green sycamore tree on your left.* This tree is several hundred years old and bears the scars of hundreds of cuts made by people seeking the milky substance beneath the cambium layer of the bark.†

This is a good place to rest in the shade of the sycamore and reconnect to the ball of twine that you have been creating. Take a few moments to breathe the Heart Breath and notice how layered the work with the twine has become. . . [*Pause.*] Thank the guide who brought you here, and ground and center yourself. . . . As you return to your ordinary reality, try to keep as much of your spirit self sitting in the

---

*Emil Shaker tells me that some years ago he and our land agent, Mohamed Nazmy, discovered that this tree was dying for lack of attention and water. They paid the local guards to care for the tree and water it. I personally observed this sycamore tree, sacred to the goddesses Sekhmet and Hathor, come back to life over the past decade. It is now a lush source of shade in an otherwise desolate landscape.

†This medicine is known to have many purposes, most commonly for its use on eczema and other skin disorders. The juice of the sycamore fig that grows in abundance on this tree is also used for medicinal purposes.

shade of the sycamore tree in front of the entrance to the chapel of Sekhmet, Ptah, and Nefertum as you write about your experience in your journal. . . . [*Long pause.*]

## WORKING THE TWINE
## AND THE SUBCONSCIOUS

As you continue to work the twine to complete your offering, notice that you are maintaining awareness in two dimensions simultaneously—you are at your altar, or wherever you have chosen to make your final preparations for your offering, and at the same time you are at the sycamore tree in front of the temple. You are learning to move easily between the realms and dimensions and are able to bilocate, to be in two dimensions simultaneously. It gets easier as you practice.

Continue breathing your Heart Breath as you add more knots to your twine. When you either feel complete or need to take a break, take a moment to ground and center yourself, and know that you will return to the sycamore tree when it is time to resume your journey.

If you find that you are having trouble moving back and forth between the tree and wherever you are reading this book, reengage the Heart Breath. It will help to bring you into the resonance of the temple that you are in along with the one that you are preparing to enter. Keep adding knots to your ball of twine until you feel complete for the moment and are ready to make your offering to Sekhmet.

Continue working with your twine for another few moments as you bring your intentions into focus. Keep working with the twine, coming in and out of the space according to how this work is being woven into your life. You may be complete by now or it could be several days or longer before you have reached the depth for which you are striving. You will know when you are finished with this part of the preparations. You will be able to add more knots after your offering has been given to Sekhmet throughout the alchemical process if new things come up or you wish to add more ties for prayers or gratitude.

## SHARED VOICES

*I took a class you led years ago at the Goddess Temple of Orange County. . . . During the class you led a guided meditation in which you described walking through Karnak to Sekhmet's temple. Your words, your energy, your connection to Sekhmet was palpable. I could see exactly what you described almost before your words were spoken. And for the first time, I had a profound felt experience of the goddess. I felt the strength and power of her unyielding form and beauty, and, just as equally, I felt her envelop me with her soft, motherly love and support. Words cannot describe it, as you know. Tears and amazement flowed from me that day. I went on to take your class via phone and again felt her work deeply within me. Over the years, I have continued to honor and be led by her.*

*For the past five years, she has watched over the Center for Living Peace in Irvine, which I created, in part, inspired by my work with Sekhmet. I am deeply grateful for the work you do and so grateful to you for introducing us!*

KELLY HALLMAN

*Sekhmet has influenced my life greatly and still does to this day. I took with me to Egypt a "Shakespeare stone," which I placed on every altar we made. When I was with Sekhmet at her temple I confessed my secret passion to become a Shakespearean actress. I felt embarrassed to admit it, even to her, and my main path since then has been to shed the embarrassment and fearful emotions that have thrown up obstacles to my heart's desire. The biggest hurdle has been loving myself in the present, just as I am. Every encounter with Sekhmet has shown me that nothing will happen if I do not love myself. Over the years I cheerfully plunged along the path of shamanic initiation, confronting old wounds to heal them. It was as if I were on a freight train of healing: nothing was going to stop me. But nothing has made me more fearful than the idea of loving myself unconditionally. And that is what Sekhmet has hammered in to my heart both in meditation with her and through others who have channeled her message.*

*An example: Last summer I took a series of Shakespeare training classes. One of the instructors, Michael, a professor of theater from LA and a working actor and director, told us at one point to get ready for a certain exercise with the texts we had brought and referring to our group of "fine actors." I snickered at his use of the phrase. He turned and looked me directly in the eye, "Why are you laughing?" It was as if Sekhmet were turning her fiery gaze into my soul to expose the lack of confidence I had in myself. I had been standing at a door looking in to the acting world, and Michael pushed me across the threshold.*

*I've been taking classes since then and will be doing a general Shakespeare audition in Portland next month. I'm even scheduling a photography shoot for a needed headshot to include with my résumé. All of these acts are steps I would've been afraid to take without Sekhmet's influence.*

KATHERYN SHAMRELL

# 6
# Feeding Sekhmet

Sekhmet is the consort of Ptah, the creator god who is the patron of all craftsmen and builders. Together they ruled Lower Egypt from their city and temple at Memphis. Their necropolis at Saqqâra holds many of the tombs of the Old Kingdom, including the first pyramid, the Step Pyramid, which is said to be one of, if not the, oldest buildings of its size.

Now, at Karnak, we will be entering the chapel of Ptah, Sekhmet, and their son, Nefertum. Inside the chapel, on the far side of the small courtyard, is a large stone altar that was originally used as an offering table (see color plate 10). Because this temple celebrates Sekhmet's healing attributes, the blood that was collected from another slab of stone where circumcisions occurred was given as an offering to Sekhmet. Births also happened here, as well as healing activities.

Behind the main altar there is a large wooden door (obviously newer), behind which are three rooms: the middle room contains a headless statue of Ptah, the room on the left is empty but is dedicated to Nefertum, and the one on the right contains a bigger-than-life-size statue of Sekhmet carved from black granite. Although it is usually described as having been originally sculpted approximately 1400 BCE, Emil tells me that the exact time is uncertain, and it could be much older. What's known is that it was later found broken into many pieces and put back together so well that her ka is still vital and alive from the power of the initial intention invested in her when she was first sculpted and consecrated. That vitality continues to be sustained by the thousands of pilgrims who visit and honor her to this day.

For the past several years there has been a French archaeology crew working to find out what is underneath the temple. I just learned that they did find some objects under and behind this chapel. As mentioned, many temples are built on top of one another, using original stones and artifacts as seed stones. When we were slipping in to be initiated by Sekhmet during those years, we could see the great care the French crew was taking as they dug around and under Sekhmet and in reconstructing the temple so that you can hardly tell it had been taken apart. Much of Egypt has been examined in this way.

## PTAH AND THE IMPLEMENTS OF POWER

Ptah is closely related to Osiris. Ptah owns the entire domain between Sky and Earth, between the spiritual and material worlds. If you were looking at Ptah in his full glory as an upright man, his legs would be wrapped in mummy cloth like Osiris. This describes a being whose feet are firmly embedded in the inner world, or underworld, while his blue domed head reaches all the way to the stars, fully connected to the intelligence available above. He also wears a beard like the one that pharaohs wore. Ptah maintains dominion over all the planes and dimensions between and including the stars and the underworld. As the great creator god of manifestation, he was worshipped by craftsmen, builders, and artisans throughout the ancient civilization of Egypt. Masons and Egyptologists the world over associate him with the square and the compass, the most fundamental tools of architecture, as written in some of the most ancient Egyptian texts.

The *djed* is the part of Ptah's staff that symbolizes the steps of manifestation from both the earthly plane to the spiritual plane and from the spiritual plane into earthly manifestation. The djed is like a pillar with four rungs crossing it. It functions like a ladder of consciousness between the worlds. It also symbolizes the backbone of Osiris. The living, upright djed represents the living, upright being and assures his stability, strength, and power. The raising of the djed symbolized the resurrection of Osiris; it was an ancient Egyptian ceremonial practice for bringing one back to life—giving or renewing life (see color plate 11).

Ptah carries other important implements of power, including a *was* staff (or scepter) and the *ankh* (see color plates 12 and 13). The ankh is the hieroglyph that conveys life itself and is sometimes referred to as the "key of life." It is similar to the astrological symbol of the planet Venus; both the ankh and the astrological symbol precede the Christian cross. You will see an ankh held in the right hand of Sekhmet's statue in her sanctuary. It is often depicted on the walls of the temples with a god holding it up to the nose of a pharaoh who is breathing in the essence of life from the round loop at the top of the ankh.

The was scepter signifies dominion over the forces of nature; it was usually held only by gods, and some pharaohs and priests, as a statement of their power and self-control. The top is surmounted by the head of an unknown animal that looks similar to Set, the sibling of Osiris, Isis, Nephthys, and the elder Horus—the children of Nut. Although nobody knows for sure what the animal is, it seems to be a combination of a donkey and/or an aardvark or jackal, with several other possibilities noted according to the source.* At the bottom of the was staff is a curved bar

---

*I should note here that Set represents "the Saturnian influence of limitation, the constriction of ego, and the boundaries of form" (Nicki Scully and Normandi Ellis, *The Union of Isis and Thoth,* 57). Although he was initially a respected god of the desert, storms, and chaos, he is most remembered for murdering his brother Osiris, twice, and for his lengthy battle with the son of Osiris and Isis, Horus, who was conceived after his father's death and raised to avenge the murder. Set ultimately lost the battle with his nephew, and Horus is the reigning head of the pantheon to this day. Every pharaoh is called Horus, yet Set remains a vital member of the pantheon and works with Horus to help support those who have crossed over. The fascinating legend, the myth of Osiris and Isis, is one of the most important stories in Egyptian mythology, and the best version I've seen is threaded throughout Normandi Ellis's *Feasts of Light.*

similar to a tuning fork. This rounded bar connects the frequencies of that which is above to that which is below and gives them grounded stability.

Ptah is considered by some to be the god who continues to hold the dream of the fully realized, potential human. Hopefully, we who are the result of what some call an experiment that was implemented millions of years ago when consciousness and self-awareness was first infused onto this planet, can still bring Ptah's dream into being.* He has been holding that dream, that vision of the possibility of how things could be if we allowed ourselves to become fully realized humans. If we can clear our filters sufficiently to be able to listen to, learn from, and be guided by the trustworthy pantheon of Egypt (among many other avatars), we can, using our collective heart/mind intelligence, still find our way back to that vision.

## SERVICE AND READINESS

Included in the timeless vision is the imperative for free will. The gods can cheer us on, watch in amazement at the choices we make, make suggestions, and offer guidance. Ultimately, what we do is up to us. An individual can be swayed by the negative currents created when many speak in the voice of fear and hate, and at the same time that individual can stand strong while being in awe and in gratitude for this great gift of life and the cosmos.

What happens to us, including all of the interconnected forms of life on this planet, is ultimately up to us. None of us can do it alone, and we who are gaining in awareness have to work many times harder, not just to survive as individuals and families but also to counteract the

---

*See the *Anubis Oracle* (Nicki Scully and Linda Star Wolf) for the story we were given on how humans were seeded with consciousness and how Ptah continues to hold the original dream. According to Egyptologist Emil Shaker, mixing the gods is somewhat like mixing colors; when you mix Ptah and Sekhmet together you access the healing aspect of Sekhmet and the essence of life in their son, Nefertum. According to Emil, Ptah would be passive without the ignition that happens when he is stimulated by his consort, Sekhmet.

*Fig. 6.1. Ma'at*
*(Image adapted by Lauren Raine)*

negativity that is plaguing our world through the desires, needs, and wayward thoughts of others. Together, however, those of us who are ready and willing to show up, to awaken, and to use the tools that we are given can find the solutions to our challenges and co-create a world of peace, beauty, and joy.

Before you enter the chapel, you need to remember your underlying service to Ma'at and carry that thought in your heart as you enter the temple. Truth reigns supreme, and it's important to honor and bear in mind that if you aspire to be a guardian of Ma'at and the truth, justice, and balance she represents, it is essential that you be fully present and engaged in the preparation of your offering.

When it is time, you will walk silently through the colonnade and into the chapel courtyard. This courtyard is fairly small. When you enter it, you are facing a large, heavy wooden door, which is usually kept closed. The door opens into the middle room, which is dedicated to Ptah. There is a headless seated statue of Ptah in the center toward the back of the room (see color plate 14). Paintings and carvings throughout Egypt show that if his head were still on his body, he would be wearing a blue skullcap, which has always indicated to me that his head reaches up into the starry sky, fully connected to the intelligence above. His feet are bound like those of Osiris, with whom he is closely associated. This would indicate that he has dominion in the under or inner worlds as well, including all spaces in between.

In the temple, the room on the left is dedicated to the son of Ptah and Sekhmet. Nefertum, known as the Lotus Born, is considered the essence, or fragrance, of life. Nefertum's room at this time is empty of any furnishings. The wall decorations are quite faded, so when it's time to pay your respects to Nefertum, simply appreciate the stillness and enjoy a short journey if he chooses to take you on one. You may wish to take a few moments to consider the potential of the son that Ptah and Sekhmet conceived together.

Please study color plate 15 before beginning the following journey.

## ❀ JOURNEY TO SEKHMET'S CHAPEL

[*Ground and center yourself and breathe the Heart Breath, invoking your deepest desire for the transformation that you seek and all those whom you wish to have witness your process. Be sure to express your gratitude for all that you have learned about yourself so far. Take a moment to honor Hathor and the unconditional love and joy she represents. Allow yourself to feel that love and know that regardless of what you think you are facing, Hathor's love permeates Sekhmet and remains a constant throughout the alchemy. Try to remember to continue to breathe the Heart Breath throughout this rite of passage.*]

Are you ready? Is there anything you have forgotten? Remember the bundle that you were given inside the Sphinx. . . . Now take a moment to recall those situations along with your own discoveries that you have knotted into your twine. . . . [*Pause.*]

Now that it's time to meet Sekhmet in her chapel, gather your ball of twine and hold it close to your heart along with the bundle. Accept the hand of the priest or priestess who comes for you. Together you walk past the guardians and through the colonnade to the inner courtyard. There you stand before the altar and reconsider your intention for being here. . . . [*Pause.*]

The priestess, seeming to have read your mind, lets you know that all is in order and that you are expected. The guardian of the chapel opens the big wooden door for you. You find yourself in the entranceway in the dim light of Ptah's chapel. Walk up to and stand directly before the headless statue of Ptah and pay your respects to this great creator god. Though the physical stone of his head is gone, his essence remains—the aliveness and energy of this statue has the power to touch you deeply, to your very core.

In whatever way you perceive him, Ptah will also show his pleasure at your presence. He greets you, and you can tell that he sees all of you— he knows you better than you know yourself. After you have exchanged greetings, he has a message for you . . . [*Pause.*] Now Ptah reaches into a small tool chest and brings out a miniature of the staff that he's holding: the djed with the was scepter on top. As he holds it, it magically grows into a full-size staff, and he taps the ground with it. When the rounded tuning fork at the bottom hits the ground, ripples of energy radiate from the point of connection, and you can feel yourself instantly come in to alignment at the center of the horizon between Earth and Sky and between this physical world and the spirit world. . . . [*Pause.*]

He then shows you a small ankh, perhaps three or four inches in height. What is unusual about this ankh is that the circle at the top of the would-be cross encloses a magnifying glass. After he holds it up and shows it to you, Ptah offers it as his gift to you. This lens is something that you can use to increase your focus on whatever you choose to look at through it. It will also magnify whatever you wish to manifest. You may be able to see what you are missing in the process in which we are engaged, or be given a different perspective of the changes that are happening while you are going through the ceremonies.

Take a moment with Ptah while he shares with you other possibilities for this tool and perhaps some further specific message he has for you at this time. . . . [*Pause.*] When your time with Ptah completes, be sure to offer your gratitude to this great being. Now turn and enter the chamber to the left, which is the empty room that is dedicated to Nefertum.

It's a rectangular, walled room, empty except for the fragrance of the blue lotus blossom, the plant emblem of Upper Egypt. As you deeply breathe in the lotus fragrance, pay close attention to Nefertum as he appears as a young lad of around fourteen to sixteen floating on a lotus pad. He wears his hair in a side lock that identifies the Egyptian youth as a young initiate. He has a beautiful brown body, and he is blowing bubbles—beautiful, iridescent orbs. As you connect with Nefertum, there's a sense of the essence of joy and beauty, regardless of whether you can see him. Wherever the bubbles land they become like crystal balls, yet they are very light and appear more like large soap bubbles. They seem to contain and emit pure joy. As Nefertum happily blows these bubbles, he picks out one and gives it to you as a gift. As you accept it, feel the joy it radiates. It's always good to have a little joy of life hanging around. You can place it in your space as you wish. . . . [*Pause.*]

Take some time to simply be there and breathe in the fragrance of the lovely lotus blossom, allowing its intrinsic power to move throughout your body, bringing clarity and focus. Listen closely to receive any further message from Nefertum. . . . [*Pause.*] When you feel complete, thank him and bid him farewell. . . . As you leave his sanctuary, you will walk past Ptah and pause when you come to the iron gate at the entrance to Sekhmet's sanctuary. . . . [*Pause.*]

Take a moment to reiterate to yourself your reasons for being here— your personal desire to better yourself and transform those things that have plagued you, many of them for your entire life. You can feel them encoded within the ball of knotted twine that you are holding. It is imperative, as you meet Sekhmet for this purpose, to remember the deeper intention for being in this life, as a servant of Ma'at and the truth and balance she represents. As her primary guardian, Sekhmet will see and know your commitment to the truth.

Know that at this point, it no longer matters if you forgot anything, as you will have created enough prime material for Sekhmet to digest and transform beyond the individual experiences that represent your journey so far in this life and the patterns that have been created to make up your character as well as your physical and spiritual bodies.

Hold your twine and your bundle close to your heart as you recite the following invocation to Sekhmet by Lorye Keats Hopper.

[*Breathe the Heart Breath to Sekhmet before and during your recitation of this invocation.*]

### Hymn to Honor Sekhmet

*Lion-Hearted Lady of the Solar Ray,*
*dwelling within the realm of Light . . .*
*we ask to blend with your powers*
*of Courage, Strength and Honor,*
*so we may reclaim the Beauty back*
*to our earthly Life.*
*Oh Great Goddess, devourer of time,*
*destroyer of illusion!*
*Help us clear the destructive and*
*heavy stagnant patterns,*
*within our body and mind.*
*Bring Life, Vitality, and Willfulness*
*to our Soul Destiny,*
*and Joyful Healing to our Hearts.*
*Great Sekhmet . . . we greet your Glory,*
*this day in Gratefulness.*

*Fig. 6.2. Head of Sekhmet's statue*
*(Photo by K. Indigo Rønlov)*

Open the gate and enter the stone room. It too is unadorned except for her huge presence, which you feel even before you turn to the left and see her standing tall in her graceful, granite body, her stone eyes bright, perhaps glittering as you feel her pulling you toward her. Remember to breathe. Her presence can be overwhelming the first time you come face-to-face with her in her sanctuary.

Walk right up to her, offer a deep Heart Breath, and hold out your offering of twine and the bundle you received in the Sphinx that contains the symbols of all that you have found inside yourself that is in need of transformation. Sekhmet scrutinizes you and looks directly into your heart. She sees the truth of what lies within the knotted twine, the prime material for your transformation.

As you stand, riveted to the stone ground in front of her, there is no time for words of greeting. She lets out a huge, rumbling roar, then . . . devours you . . . *all* of you. She may take you in one single gulp, or she may take her time, savoring every morsel of the delicious meal that you have brought to her. . . . [*Pause.*]

While you might find yourself faltering at the idea of giving up some of what you are, your organs are being scrubbed clean by Sekhmet with her lioness tongue. . . . She loves these parts and takes great care, carefully deploying her claws when necessary to open a place so that she can suck out the best parts. . . . Right now you are hyperaware and you sense the change as she shifts from her goddess statue form to that of a lioness. . . . [*Pause.*] You can feel the absorption begin to take place in yourself and are aware of how it is working for Sekhmet as well. Feel the fluidity as well as the acidity of the various enzymes as they begin their digestive work. . . . [*Pause.*]

Notice how you feel, using all your senses as Sekhmet's digestive fluids move through all the parts of your body, piece by piece. Allow your awareness to capture each part of the devouring as it is happening and as each organ or bone or knot from your twine unravels and is consciously absorbed and disintegrated as you slide down her esophagus and into her stomach. . . . [*Pause*]

There is no hurry. You will be safely held in this vessel, the belly of this goddess, for quite some time. Sekhmet licks her lips as she leaves the chapel in her lioness body and makes her way out through the colonnade to the entrance, where she finds a comfortable place under the sycamore tree to lie down and contemplate her meal.

As you begin to feel the space where you are inside her belly, let all your senses be open to the experience. . . . [*Pause.*]

Ground and center while continuing to maintain awareness of what is happening to you inside the belly of the goddess. . . . Enter the process into your journal as soon as you can do so without disturbing your ability to hold your focus on all the things that are going on. . . . [*Long pause.*]

Take as long as you need to become accustomed to being inside the goddess. Sekhmet is still relishing her meal, and there is more for you to do to complete this part of the process.

## AFTER DINNER

This next part of the journey should be read quite slowly as you undergo the completion of your devouring by the goddess, experiencing it bit by bit, bite by bite, much as Sekhmet is experiencing the wonderful meal you have brought her.

### MERGING WITH SEKHMET

[*Breathe the Heart Breath to stabilize yourself in your unusual surroundings. You are inside of Sekhmet, who is now lounging in the shade of the sycamore tree. After you heard the roar and were swallowed by her, it will take some time before all of you arrives in her stomach. Every reader has a different experience. . . .*]

From your new vantage point, having discovered yourself inside Sekhmet, in whatever way that perception happens for you, you come to awareness of a strange landscape as you move, all at once or bit by bit, down her throat and into the various organs that are involved in the digestive process and the alchemy of calcination, dissolution, and separation that happens on the way down to and inside of her belly. . . . [*Pause.*]

Notice that once you are inside of her and her juices start flowing to dissolve the hard parts of you and begin the process of digestion, she is also inside you. You are no longer two beings. Now that you and everything that has accumulated to create you has been consumed, you have become Sekhmet, devourer of you and all that you are. As parts of you dissolve, the landscape changes. . . . There is the sense of an inner world, with a barren landscape. Here Sekhmet moves about, looking for and finding bits and pieces of things. . . . Every time she finds something she is looking for, she grabs it with her teeth and pulls it out of wherever she found it. Parts of you are being devoured that you have to consciously give up—things that are not nourishing for either of you.

Allow yourself plenty of time to observe this process. Neither you nor Sekhmet are in a hurry. . . . Many parts of you are healthy and good, nourishing and strengthening for aspects of both of you. You may or may not recognize some of them as they are separated out and converted to appropriate energy, some going into Sekhmet's body, and some reserved for yours. . . . [*Long pause.*]

You can perceive how the waste products are separated out and eventually move through the outer Sekhmet to be released as scat. The scat that originates with you is now a welcome and nutritious contribution to the desert ecosystem.

## THE ALCHEMY OF DIGESTION

During the many breaks in this ongoing meditative process, you will ground and center and return to your life, but you will remain in the belly of Sekhmet from now until you have been thoroughly digested and transformed. The first thing you do every time is journal, because recording the details of your experience will be of great value as you move forward as well as when you need to look back.

During this time, you will also have a number of opportunities to witness the transformation of all that you have brought forward for her and for yourself. The main object of this next phase is to develop your observational skills—to be engaged in this digestive alchemy—because this is where the breaking down of the old patterns happens. In addition, some of these patterns will not disappear that easily, as much as we'd like to think, "Chomp chomp burp, they're gone." Rather, you're going to watch them throughout the process, as you've got all this gristle in you, and all of it is going to have to work its way through. And, of course, some of the patterns will want to return.

Lions, although they have a short digestive tract, can wait a while between meals. It can be awhile between hunts. There is a part of Sekhmet—the part that takes the lioness form to hunt down her meal—that just wants to lie down underneath the sycamore tree at the front of the sanctuary and enjoy savoring her meal as it is digested. As you become more accustomed to being in her belly, let your awareness also be very clear as to where you are and what is happening in the world around you as well as in her belly.

Outside of Sekhmet's belly, place your ball of twine on your altar so that you are reminded of the issues you are transforming. Occasionally, if you feel the need, add more knots and look within to see where they or any other particular issues are still clinging to the soup that's being created in her belly. This process continues at many levels. It even begins anew if something awakens within you, something of great importance that you have been keeping hidden and secret, even from yourself. Her strong digestive acids break down the shield that you created that may have been the perfect protective defense for a younger you, but it is dissolving now.

Although the main body of the work is the transformation of the undesirable characteristics that you uncover within yourself, that is only one piece of the process. As you go through various initiations while being digested and gestating in Sekhmet's belly, you can take as long as you need for the alchemy to cohere the new possibility that is developing within you. Other teachings, empowerments, and rites of passage will help to shape the new being that you are becoming.

### SHARED VOICES

*In the belly, facing Sekhmet, I felt inner contortion and trembling, actually, because of the profundity of what was taking place—any facade, any outer layer just crumbled.*

*As soon as I was devoured in the belly I felt myself almost drunk, all my senses in a totally altered state like I was fluid and in fluid. My head rolled around, my whole body was in that space. The best feeling about it was the absolute surrender. The feeling of "this is all that I am, naked, and I can let go and surrender." I loved that feeling.*

*I spent a long time in the belly. Sekhmet sucked out and showed me that I had the belief that solitary is safety—she devoured it. When we went to the riverbank Sekhmet was licking my face with her tongue; she was so loving. As she went in on what there was to devour, I stood there in front of her and simultaneously in her belly I went straight into the deepest, deepest grief—this deep sorrow. It was my mum's absolute heartbreak about the dissolution of her relationship with my dad. The sorrow felt crippling, so deep, so profound; true grief. It's where I've sat for so much of my life; it's where I came into. And then I was in the guilt, the guilt that I was at the center of their demise, and that had linked into so many situations I have found myself in my life. It was actually quite stunning to see the pattern and how it's played out, and I was so grateful to just hand it over to Sekhmet, to not have to dissect it and work with it but just to observe, let go, and just release it to Sekhmet.*

*After that I instinctively lay down in my actual physical body; I lay down in the fetal position and felt really nurtured and taken care of by Sekhmet. I was so grateful to just lie there, feeling cleansed, cleared, and to just bathe in the love.*

ELOISE JOSEPH

*It took me quite a while to find the journal that I wrote all my Sekhmet thoughts in. Deciphering them and remembering all this was also a bit of a challenge, but then you mentioned in class that we are always remembering and forgetting and not stepping into our power. What I know for sure is that I did release a lot of my fears and issues in the class and feel like I have grown stronger. I still have fears whenever something new comes up, but I seem to be able to just do whatever I fear anyway. I have more confidence that I will figure out how to deal with the challenges.*

*While in the belly of Sekhmet, I found it very useful to have a physical string to tie knots into, and the more I acknowledged my fears and concerns, the more I was able to pinpoint my patterns and core issues. This Sekhmet class came after losing my mother and boyfriend, who both passed away. I faced my loneliness, sadness, abandonment, and insecurities about my own abilities to support myself and the lack of respect I felt from my mother and a couple of my friends. I kept tying knots and tying knots for each of my issues while in the belly of Sekhmet until I realized that this process could go on forever and it was time to stop. Being in Sekmet's belly allowed me to feel her fire, which gave me strength, and also her mothering energies that made me feel protected. It felt like being contained in a warm and loving vessel that contained all the necessary ingredients for my transformation: love, warmth, fire, strength, blood, and trust. Sekhmet is a goddess who commands respect, and that was one of the issues I was also dealing with. I don't think I learned these lessons from my own mother, but I did from Sekhmet.*

*I went for a soul retrieval soon after your class and saw Sekhmet during the session. I saw myself inside her statue, and when the stone cracked off of me I was an Egyptian priestess with an Egyptian-style red-net dress on. This was kind of like being rebirthed all over again. . . .*

*Throughout my life, I have always identified the most with Isis, because for many years my life followed her story . . . the infighting, dismemberment of my boyfriend, gaining wisdom. Recently, I have begun to identify myself as a sea priestess . . . and am doing what I can to help conserve our oceans. However, writing this, I am once again remembering the warmth, love, strength, and fire of Sekhmet, which is a good balance to the water energies. She seems like a very useful ally in this battle to protect our oceans and forests from the greed and unconsciousness that is destroying this beautiful planet. . . .*

*The process of revisiting my notes on your Sekhmet class has made me feel like I am in her belly again, and it feels GOOD to have this lioness around when life throws those curveballs. I am looking at challenges in a whole new way and feel somehow supported, when before I felt like I was doing it all alone. My adrenals just got pumped up a notch . . . and I am just taking care of business, and I don't have to drink blood unless it is absolutely necessary.*

JAN PRESTON DUNN

# 7

# Fierce Compassion

Although Sekhmet is delighted with her meal, there are still some chewy parts and gristle that she wants to deal with in a way that shows her fierceness and gentleness at the same time. This will vary from reader to reader according to your preparation and the things that you want or that still need to be brought into consciousness to be transformed.

Every action that you have discharged, or that has happened to you, creates the various emotions that express your personal lessons. Once you've learned the lessons, you can move on. Sometimes you must be fierce in your process to be compassionate and find your way to love and healing. At the same time, you must be gentle with yourself and not judge yourself for holding on to things, for we are still as children, learning and growing. Likewise, we must be gentle with others. Besides, you have already submitted all these things to Sekhmet, and they are now hers to deal with as she pleases. It is only for you to be present and learn discernment from her choices, allowing her to digest as she will.

To fully step in to your power you must embrace your divinity. Leave behind the accumulated trash that you hold on to unnecessarily—those qualities do not serve your highest purpose and only bog you down with burdens that you do not need to carry, thus wasting energy that could be much better utilized.

To use a personal example, I have carried a tremendous amount of guilt regarding my perceived lack of parenting skills and decisions I made that have had consequences that I have borne with little grace and lots of guilt and judgment. Despite all my healing and priestessing skills, until I was truly ready to give up my arrogant judgments and my dysfunctional guilt, my prevailing attitudes held me from attaining my full potential and, more particularly, the best possible relationships with my daughters. I am not saying that I have as yet achieved enlightenment—I am very much a work in progress, and still have much to do and learn, yet with the understanding I have achieved from doing this work I am much more conscious and present, thereby catching myself more often when I begin to backslide.

In actuality, regardless of how poorly any of us may have behaved in our youth, guilt is never an appropriate or useful burden to carry. It also builds a barrier to love that makes it difficult for everyone in our complex family relationships—and that creates consequences. I am seventy-three as I write this and can truly say that this work with Sekhmet over the past several years finally loosened the knot of guilt and let the love flow in, and I have finally let go of my greatest burden. The effect for those concerned has been remarkable, not so much because they have changed—although life itself brings a certain maturity to those who care enough to work on themselves—rather it is my perception that has changed and, consequently, my reactions and my recognition of the amazing capacity for love and the joy that brings.

## ☀ FIERCE COMPASSION JOURNEY

[*You have never fully left, so it is easy to get back into the meditative mind-space. Simply breathe a few Heart Breaths and acknowledge those that are closest to you at the moment, in this case Sekhmet and any prominent spiritual witnesses and supporters. . . .*]

Remember, you are living in at least two dimensions. Ever since you were consumed, you've shared consciousness with Sekhmet. You are a combination—you are a witness and a participant. When Sekhmet roars you can feel the mighty roar emerge from your chest. All the while you stand in awe as her hot breath moves around and through you. . . . [*Pause.*]

Sekhmet rises, still in her lioness form. She stretches and yawns and begins her trek from the temple of Karnak down to the Nile River's edge. You may find yourself adjusting to being inside her moving body while still aware of where you are sitting or lying quietly in this physical plane as the work continues. You will also be aware of the sand and stone under your/her paws as you pick your way to the river. . . . [*Pause.*]

As Sekhmet walks along a peaceful, lush part of the riverbank, you can hear her making a low rumbling sound, between a purr and a growl. . . . She stops and grooms herself, licking her paws and running them through her fur. . . . She feels your presence inside of her, and somehow you find yourself once again outside of her body. . . . She greets you with a low rumbling growl, then stands and approaches you, sniffing as though she is reading your scent and taste by licking the air as she slowly circles you. . . . She checks you out thoroughly, looking you up and down as she stands in front of you. . . . [*Pause.*]

Sekhmet changes into her goddess form. . . . She tells you that it is time to learn about fierce compassion—to be able to recognize what needs to be let go of or removed so that true healing can take place. . . . Suddenly lots of things begin happening simultaneously. All of the knots you've labored and prayed over come to life and hit you all at once. . . . The work has been opening you, preparing you for this moment. . . . There are many images coming almost simultaneously, like a kaleidoscope that includes flashes of situations that have happened in the past and bring together all the emotions you felt at each moment. It feels as though your life is exploding before you. The emotions you may hold on to that are still affecting you in some way include guilt, jealousy, joy, envy, desire, desperation, terror, insanity— the gamut of feelings around events, injuries, abuse, various traumas, relationships, and so on—these are unique to your life. . . . [*Pause.*]

Sekhmet retains her goddess form, both lioness and woman, as she goes about dealing with what she has been observing in her meal. Although it's already in her stomach, it's also part of the you that stands outside of her body. . . . Without further ado, she begins to claw at and dig out all the extraneous stuff with her claws and her teeth as if it were a diseased or damaged branch on a tree that she can just rip off so that it does not continue to damage the tree. . . . [*Pause.*] You can feel it being pulled out as she tears it out of your energy field. . . . Her growls grow louder as she finds especially contentious bits and pieces. All that does not serve must be removed, and it is your job to relax and release. . . . [*Pause.*]

After working on you for some time, Sekhmet becomes very gentle, like a mother cat stroking her kitten or a lioness her cub. You are likely to feel as though you've been through a purification, a washing away of the detritus of past events and energies that no longer serve a positive function. It's very peaceful and calming after the fierce, violent energy of the ripping away. . . . [*Pause.*]

You return with the goddess to the sycamore tree by the entrance to her chapel at Karnak. She reaches up with her claws and carefully scratches the bark just deep enough that it bleeds a viscous white liquid, which she feeds to you along with a sycamore fig. The fig is somewhat sweet (although very different from the figs that we are used to, and much more like medicine), and you can feel the thick milk move through your body, refreshing, energizing, and healing all the torn places of separation from that which was removed. It mends and seals those wounds as it flows through your partially digested body. . . . [*Pause.*]

Sekhmet pours what smells like lotus oil over your head. . . . It has a very silky feeling as it permeates and coats your body parts while it mixes with the digestive acids, fig juice, and enzymes. . . . Now you are ready to enter the temple once again. Together you walk through the colonnade into the courtyard of her chapel. It is as it was in ancient times, painted and decorated with beautiful carvings. You find yourself holding blue lotus flowers in your hand. This is your offering to the goddess in gratitude for the healing and the initiation that you have just received from her. When you make the offering to her, she invites you to step in to your power and to become or walk the path of your life's purpose. . . . [*Pause.*]

She touches your third eye and your heart, and you instantly notice that you feel as though you are peacefully floating in the belly of the goddess. . . . There is a feeling of total peace, supported and connected, as though your heart is expanding and filling with love. This is the blessing of compassion—to be loved, to be accepted, and to be your true self. . . [*Pause.*]

It is time to return to your place of digestion and comfort under the sycamore tree, and you take this lesson with you. The knowledge has always been there; you just have to remember. As Sekhmet settles down for a rest, you notice that your perception of things has changed. It is as though you see from your heart rather than from your ordinary subconscious patterning or your usual mind-set. . . . Ground and center yourself. . . . Use the earth part of the Heart Breath to ground yourself further before you open your eyes in your three-dimensional world. . . . [*Pause.*]

Write down your experience in your journal. In addition, it is also important to maintain constant vigilance, noticing all the changes that are occurring, regardless of what is happening around you in your life. Take some time to rest and integrate before you continue with the next part of the dissolution.

### SHARED VOICES

*Where to begin . . . In Alchemical Healing and my life the three main allies who support and guide me are Thoth, Anubis, and the glorious Sekhmet. A trinity of magnificence. My first real experience merging with Sekhmet was not intentional . . . it was during a healing class. Sekhmet showed up (for another student), but she just couldn't let go and allow her in. I agreed to let her work through me, and wham, she jumped in and went straight to work. It was quite ferocious, with much sounding . . . growling . . . a little overwhelming I have to say. Since then I have learned to truly merge . . . to work with Sekhmet instead of allowing her to take over. It was what both the other student and I needed at the time, though, for sure. . . . She needed that force to break through the strong barriers she had put up to contain what was ready to be healed, and I needed to feel that strength and potency followed by gentle compassionate support. Such an incredible balance of intense force and power. . . .*

*And so my relationship since then with Sekhmet has refined and strengthened. I usually experience her in her lioness form, and I know that when she shows up that there is deep or even dangerous work to be done. She can stand guard like no other; breathe fire to transform virulent energy; devour dark and dangerous beings; remove deep pain, trauma, and emotion; and heal the heart with deep love and compassion. Her presence warrants a confident authority, and I know that together we have the ability to handle absolutely anything that crosses our path. . . .*

*Each time I embody her I experience the ability to stand in my power and feel her deep strength and compassion more fully and intensely, into my very core and knowing. She has shown me that when the big work comes it doesn't have to be fierce . . . it can become gentle in the presence and strength of Sekhmet. She has shown me my own strength and brought a steadiness and poise into my life that I was lacking.*

*More often now she is standing before me in her human form, which feels significant in how our relationship has evolved and refined . . . in how I have grown . . . in how I am able to receive her. I recognize now that she has been instrumental in the healing and recovery of the wisdom of the sacred feminine within me. Sekhmet has gifted me the courage to step in to my own fullness and let my unique light be seen. With Sekhmet, I arrive fully present, in gratitude . . . daring to put love into action.*

NICOLE BALOGH

# 8

# Lost Hopes and Forgotten Dreams

You may feel that the majority of the digestive process has been accomplished, but this lioness goddess is going to take as long as she pleases, knowing that it's best for you to have enough time to fully devote yourself to the experience of the calcination and dissolution steps in the alchemy. A lot of this work is designed to give you a new start, or at least an upgrade, and there will be more on that part later.

As you prepare for the next journey during the disintegration process, be aware of the split between the realms that you are experiencing simultaneously. There is the you that is in your body wherever you are meditating, and there is the you that is dissolving in the belly of the goddess while she is lounging under the sycamore tree, perhaps enjoying a few burps while the part of her that's digesting and enjoying her great meal just wants to bask in the filtered sunlight coming through the branches. While you're held in that sacred space, another part of Sekhmet will guide you to yet another dimension. Follow this new track as Sekhmet, in her lioness form, takes you out to a desertlike place that is so barren that it makes most deserts look vibrant and alive. This is truly another dimension of things, so it's as though you are living in three places simultaneously.*

---

*A version of this journey has been published in *Daughter of the Sun: A Devotional Anthology in Honor of Sekhmet*, edited by Tina Georgitsis, in which my chapter was coauthored with Debbie Clarkin.

85

## ☀ JOURNEY TO THE LAND OF FALSE HOPES AND BROKEN DREAMS

[*Breathe a few Heart Breaths to ground yourself in preparation for yet another journey into the unknown, while at the same time you are present to your known reality.*]

Sekhmet has left the tree, with you inside of her, to stalk out certain life-forms in this vast, barren desert place. This harsh environment looks as though it's been burned, as though a fire had raged through the region; or maybe it was hit by lightning. Like the *wadis* in Egypt, it appears to be a dry riverbed that runs through the center of this desert. Perhaps there was a civilization here at one time, yet that civilization is long gone. As you explore this desolate terrain you will encounter remnants of old bridges that have been burned to skeletal remains and a few hand-hewn stones here and there, but not much else. . . . [*Pause.*]

Sekhmet is scavenging for bits and pieces of things, using her nose and her whiskers to locate them. When she finds something, she snuffles it up into her mouth. . . . Some of the pieces aren't even big enough to eat, but she's looking very intently and drawing them up into her as she moves through this lost and neglected terrain. . . . There is very little life here. It feels similar to exploring the aftermath of some great conflagration, and she just keeps working her way through the vast emptiness until she reaches a mound in the center where she lies down. . . . Although you are in her belly, you are also able to witness her as she lies there with her great big belly, which has just gorged on the wonderful meal you gave her. . . . [*Pause.*]

Soon ghostlike wraiths begin approaching her. . . . Imagine what you think a ghost might look like in a movie—a wraith is an apparition and is generally transparent. There's not much to these wraithlike beings, but they're starting to come around her and look at her and into her. . . . They can see right into her belly, and they're looking inside to see who you are. . . . [*Pause.*]

Some of these wraiths, the ones that belong to you, are your broken and abandoned dreams. And when they recognize you and you recognize them, they realize they can be reunited with you. You are the person for whom they were looking. They joyously leap in to the belly of the goddess. . . . As that happens, you sense that these wraiths help complete a missing part of yourself. Perhaps it was a road not taken; perhaps it was something that you didn't even know you missed. Some of these things are great desires that you wanted but never received, or things that you wanted to manifest but never followed through to make happen. . . .

You discover that you can actually recognize what some of the wraiths represent as they come into you—"Oh yes, that was that particular dream. That was that road not taken, that possibility or hope that never manifested." Depending upon how much you had invested in these dreams and desires, part of you stayed with them when you abandoned or left them, or when they didn't work out. And so you are being reunited. . . . Notice the effect that this reunification has on you. . . . Perhaps there is a sense of fulfillment in you that makes you whole again in some way. . . . [*Pause.*]

Not all of these wraiths belong to you; when those that don't look to see what Sekhmet has in her belly, they realize that you're not who they are hoping to find. They may appear sad as they turn away, for there is incredible desolation in the dimension they inhabit. . . .

Eventually it becomes quiet and still; although some have come in and some have left, there are no more wraiths to be found. Sekhmet, still in her lioness form, rises, stretches the length of her body like big cats do, and then slowly returns, walking back the same way she came, sniffing the ground for any bits and pieces that might have been missed. . . . You might choose to give her belly a scratch or tickle from the inside in gratitude for the time and effort she took to bring you to this desolate place and help call back your neglected hopes and dreams. . . . [*Pause.*]

As Sekhmet reaches the edge of the dimension of this plane, you find yourself in a position where you can see her looking into your eyes, or whatever part of you is observing. You may not even have eyes at this point, but she's able to create that eye-contact experience. As you feel the interaction, notice if there is a message in her gaze. . . . [*Pause.*] Now you depart the land of lost hopes and dreams, crossing back through the veil between dimensions, back to where Sekhmet is lying under the sycamore tree in front of her temple at Karnak. . . . [*Pause.*]

Once again Sekhmet stretches and yawns and then pulls herself up and returns to the sanctuary. Here you find yourself in both worlds once again; you're in her belly in her sanctuary, and you're wherever you are focusing on the journey. This is an additional layer of what's happening for you while you're being digested and while those parts of you that you wish to be changed are being transformed. You are also in a place where you have the opportunity to reintegrate not just the lost hopes and dreams, but the energy that dissipated when those dreams were lost. . . . [*Pause.*]

Notice how you move back and forth between dimensions. . . . Allow the part that is observing the three-dimensional plane to strengthen as you continue to focus back and forth, again and again, until you suddenly realize that you can be in two or more places simultaneously. . . . When you attain that ability, you will have accomplished one of your immediate goals. . . . [*Pause.*]

Be sure to give heartfelt gratitude to Sekhmet. Allow yourself time to become complete with this experience. . . . Thank Sekhmet and then ground and center, and be sure to record your experience in your journal. . . . [*Long pause.*]

## ❀ A FRESH START

[*Part of this alchemy is about is giving yourself a fresh start. You will be aided in that by the following practice. In your journal, write the story of your journey into the land of lost hopes and dreams, along with exploring the possibilities introduced by the questions that follow.*]

Perhaps you recognized a particular lost hope or dream that would have resulted in a different life for you if you had taken that road, or won that prize, or persevered to make a particular dream come true. What would your life have been like? Would you still choose the same road? What would you have gained if you had chosen differently? What would you have lost? What would you still want to retrieve? If you still had the full amount of energy to put in to any one of those things, which would you choose? How would your life be different if you could add "Ph.D." to your name, or "philanthropist" when introducing yourself? What would you do, and how would you do it?

If you prefer, you can express the answers to these questions with pictures or some form of art. It is a part of the work you can do while you are disintegrating to help trigger a deeper understanding of yourself and the choices you made that brought you to be the person you have become. You can also find a physical way to focus on which of those dreams you would invest in if you had the energy. Is there anything still useful to you at this time in your life from those old hopes and dreams?

This is also another opportunity to use the magnifying ankh lens that Ptah gave you to help discriminate and discern what is important. During this part of the process, you may come to a place where you see an array of choices. The tool that Ptah gave you will give you a discriminatory eye so that you can sift through the possibilities and discover anything of value that's there for you. It's as though you are mining for gold from these broken hopes and dreams, shining a light in the shadows, honoring what is important, and then your writing or art project is a way for you to create something to symbolize the experience and the new understanding.

In the event that grief (or sadness or anger) comes during this part of the process, remember that Sekhmet has already consumed the grief, and you do not have to hold it anymore. At the same time, grief (and other feelings) are respectable emotions that deserve to be honored.

Spend some time being quiet and observing the process before you take another journey. Write and work with your twine a little more if you feel the need. Be with the altar that you created for this alchemy. Use as much of your time as possible to stay aware of yourself in the belly of the goddess. Be with that process. You are going through a shamanic death. It will eventually be succeeded by a shamanic birth. There is a renewal involved, but first you have to give yourself to complete disintegration to fully renew and reintegrate at the next level of your potential.

You can revisit the land of broken hopes and dreams at some time later in the process. Sekhmet will let you know if and when it would be useful.

### SHARED VOICES

*After the journey of broken dreams I processed intensely, so I asked Sekhmet to help me. I went and asked Sekhmet to clear the loss and grief, I told her about the babies and the abortion vibration. She in her lioness form went into a high-speed hunt, chasing down an antelope. She pounced and caught it and bought it back to me. I asked her why she gave me this, and she said, "I am bringing back to you the vulnerable scared parts of yourself. Reclaim them and make them strong." She told me the work is already happening with the loss and grief. She just said, "Honor them," and then showed me the image I had painted. I asked her who the babies were, and she said they are me. I am what went before.*

ELOISE JOSEPH

### In Love

*In love, I stared at the blank page before me, tears streaming down my face. Walking with Sekhmet, I know I have walked with her for so long now, in the blank, barren, deserted, empty land; we lay together at the water's edge. In the land of lost hopes and dreams my sorrows lie. In the land of lost hopes and dreams my lost love lies. I allow Sekhmet to lap at* the wounds in my heart, sucking gently on the forgotten moments in the bank of my memories, the highs and lows, the gifts and the promises. The way I loved him was not of this world, and he and I will never exist here. He was my muse and my catalyst; I saw his face every time I came to write, the words were my haven and my peace, the words were my gift and my dreams, the words, they were my heart and the dreams were my soul. I was a wordsmith, I would weave and etch patterns, scribing the beat of my heart onto the page in long-forgotten hieroglyphic texts, sonnets of tomorrow's dawn, I would vision through the word, the word was where I witnessed God flow through me.

The night he entered my soul I dreamt him for years to come, his gift was my promises, his gift was my pain in the form of the soiled wound that lay beneath my chest in the perpetual broken heart. He was my brush stroke in the art of perfection as he introduced me to my core; he tore the layers of my well-constructed armor and whispered promises of love, love, love; where ever you go I go, he whispered; in his poetry he reminded me, you and I we are one, the oneness the heights of forever; the gift of grace and divinity incarnate quickly became the sodden pillow I wept into from morning till dusk; when the night time came I would pine for him, in emergency positioning I sought solace in the dreams we had whispered into manifestation. Here was my initiation into the power of the magic, the catalyst for my bliss. His words, round and round and round my head, the nonstop, the mythical land of forever loving no one here and barren solace in nothing and nowhere land of lost hopes and dreams, and here I stand as Sekhmet growls, "Rise," she orders, he is not the answer, he will not fill those holes, he will not be the one, he will only be my muse and as I travel deeper into the pain I must remember it is safe to open and it is safe to reclaim the gifts, I must stop longing for his presence, I must forgive him and myself. I must not equate this with opening; I must re-file this in my brain. This land, this barren land of forgotten promises is not my home.

I have come home, the home is in my heart, I must not travel this land, I must stand in the flow of reclamation. As they tore me apart *piece by piece so they taught me my strength and courage. As they tried to rape my essence so they taught me the power of my ancestors, as they held me down they taught me the gift of freedom, as they showed me the fear in their eyes they taught me the power of my grace and divinity. I will not fall down this time; it's morning dawning and the gifts, the hollow etches of the gifts I lay to rest in this barren land are once again mine to birth anew. These gifts I will allow to wrap around my tongue, these gifts I will allow to etch themselves as I scribe in love for love in the black indelible ink of forever. My mind I will allow to wander over the fruitful pastures of the promised land, and as I remember his promises I will remember the love that we shared as my heart sets him free in love.*

LIZZIE MCCALLUM

PART III

# Dissolution, Emptiness, and Regeneration

# 9

# A Sunset Walk

When you are ready to move forward with the work at hand, prepare yourself to continue with the next journey. From here forward, we will be engaging in one guided journey after another as the process of digestion is completed and you develop the blueprint for your regenerated body, mind, soul, and spirit. In preparation for each journey, it is important to ground, center, and practice the Heart Breath. Now that you are more practiced, you can more easily change back and forth between states of conscious observation, between the instructions, meditations, and reflections. As with all things, it gets easier with practice.

The rest of this chapter can be experienced through reading or in conscious meditation. You may already be able to move your attention quickly between left and right hemispheres of the brain and still maintain depth of focus. Try doing both simultaneously.

## ☀ JOURNEY TO LUXOR TEMPLE IN THE BELLY OF THE GODDESS

[*Back under the sycamore tree, Sekhmet is again feeling the urge to go for a walk. As you breathe the Heart Breath you will be able to recognize yourself in at least two dimensions: the you that is taking the journey and the you that has been digesting and disintegrating for some time in the belly of the goddess. . . .*]

As Sekhmet in her lioness form rises and begins to saunter down the path toward and through the temple of Karnak, you can feel yourself sloshing around inside her. You are rocking with the rhythm of her gait, which is unhurried as she moves with a sense of direction and purpose. . . .

Sekhmet's first stop is at the temple of Khonsu, the moon god who is the son of Amun and Mut (a nurturing mother goddess as well as, in her vulture form, the alchemist and protector of Upper Egypt). Khonsu is known as the Wanderer and is the protector of travelers. He is closely related to Thoth, and is often depicted as an ibis or a baboon. Like the moon, Khonsu has many faces, each reflecting one of his phases, for he is also the lord of time and the one who counts the days of each person's life.

Khonsu's temple is a good place to stop and rest and to contemplate the cycles of the moon. You are aware of how the moon circles around the Earth as it waxes and wanes through all its cycles, into and out of view—yet you always know it is there. Allow your thoughts to focus on questions that seek to understand how your own cycles, such as consumption, digestion, excretion, composting, sowing, planting, growing, and harvesting, are integral cycles in your own life. You will discover more understanding about each new level of teaching that is introduced, for each is a part of this intimately interconnected web of existence.

During this part of the gestation you also become aware of the Earth as it circles around the sun. Our solar system is a small part of a huge universe, and you are incontrovertibly linked with all the cycles and grand gestures of time and space. Allow yourself to feel and express your gratitude in whatever way comes to you at this time.

Sekhmet leaves Khonsu's temple and exits the main Karnak complex through the southern gate, which leads to an avenue just over a mile long and lined with human-headed sphinxes. In ancient times the line of sphinxes went uninterrupted along the edge of the Nile all the way to the temple of Luxor, also known as the Temple of Man. Most of these sphinxes have been unearthed in the past few years, and the

*Fig. 9.1. Nicki with Khonsu as a baboon in Karnak
(Photo by Tarek Lotfy)*

3/4/2019

reconstruction of this avenue is just now being completed. The Nile River has moved quite a bit to the west since this avenue and the temple at Karnak were built.

As you and Sekhmet continue walking and sloshing it becomes dusk, and by the time you arrive at the temple of Luxor, the lights have been lit on the front of this magnificent Temple of Man (see color plate 16).*

As you approach Luxor Temple, you are conscious of the power of dusk, the magical time between day and night. From within the belly of the goddess, you are aware of the darkening as night takes over and the stars glitter above, filling Sekhmet with their nourishment. You can feel her paws pad gently yet powerfully along the worn, ancient stone, still warm from the heat of the day. . . .

As darkness falls, Sekhmet sniffs the night air, and you feel it circulate throughout your now fully liquid being. As you experience this sacred temple through Sekhmet's eyes, you come to recognize that her breath and all of her senses are felt by you as she moves through this temple. It is through the depth of your connection with Sekhmet at this time that your senses begin to awaken further.

At the same time, you are keenly aware that you and all the juicy morsels from your bundle and twine are nourishing every cell and molecule of the goddess. You can also tell how she discerns what goes where—which parts of you will go back into yourself, which will build her body and her strength, and which will be separated out to be excreted.

As Sekhmet moves through the temple, she comes to a large courtyard surrounded by numerous pillars, many of which have doves nesting in their capitals. It is here that she stops to lie down on a rounded boulder that gently rises up through the paving stones near the entrance to the courtyard. Take a few moments to focus on the beating of her heart. In the quiet stillness you can feel not only the rhythm of her heart but also how each beat moves the stew that is gestating in her belly. The flame in her heart creates bright kaleidoscopic patterns that glow in the darkness. As you breathe the Heart Breath, the patterns brighten and you resonate with the thrumming of the heart of the goddess. Simply rest and pay attention. . . . And, of course, write in your journal. . . .

---

*Luxor Temple has been called the Temple of Man since R. A. Schwaller de Lubicz described it as such in his seminal work, *The Temple of Man: Sacred Architecture and the Perfect Man.*

*Fig. 9.2. The entrance to Luxor Temple at night*
*(Photo by Hank Wesselman)*

*Fig. 9.3. The inner courtyard of Luxor Temple*
*(Photo by Jacob Cohl)*

## SHARED VOICES

*So many thoughts of Sekhmet flooded my memory as I sat down with this journey. Even my cat named Sekhmet knew it was important and joined me while I meditated.*

*My walks with Sekhmet go back to even before I knew consciously who she was. As a kid I was the one who had cats follow me home, loved to go to the zoo and sit before the lions in awe, and as a Southern Baptist minister's daughter was fascinated with the story of Daniel being thrown into the lions' den and coming out unharmed. That seemed so special to me. She has always walked with me even if I wasn't aware it was she.*

*Although I had always been fascinated with Egypt, it wasn't until I was in my fifties that Egypt became part of me. In 1999, I had been looking for a place to celebrate the millennium. I "happened" onto Marianne Williamson's website and saw that she had visited Egypt. I clicked on the link to the tour operator and there, jumping out at me, was a trip to Egypt for the millennium! I booked it a year and a half out. It was a fabulous trip, but not until I entered Ptah's chapel at Karnak and stood before the living Sekhmet statue did I realize I had found my heart. I now understood that it was Sekhmet whom I had been walking with all my life. After that I met Nicki at a Sekhmet: Transformation in the Belly of the Goddess workshop in Tucson in 2001 or 2002. Again, my heart leapt at the sight of the Sekhmet statue we used in the workshop. I also was part of the first telephone conference for this workshop and, of course, several times since then have visited Sekhmet at Karnak, also with Nicki.*

*As I meditated I heard Sekhmet call me to join her on her walk. We didn't speak much. It wasn't necessary as we have always understood each other. I could hear her soft paws move through the sand and felt some of the sand on my face even inside her. Her rhythmic gait as I rolled back and forth inside her reminded me of sailing the Nile on a* dahabeya, *gently swaying as the boat cut through the water. As we approached the temple of Khonsu, I was so caught up in the moment that I bumped against her belly inside as she stopped to honor him. I thought I heard a tiny laugh, but one done with love. Although I knew I was inside her belly, part of me felt I was also outside, moving along beside her. We live in two worlds at once, so that didn't seem strange to me.*

*As we entered Luxor Temple, I felt her gait slow down just a little. I felt myself wanting to go farther, faster. When she sat down, I told her I needed to soar a little. She said that was okay but to remember we're all attached through the silver cord. I leapt out of her belly and soared upward, my silver cord expanding upward with me. I could see the setting sun, the rising moon as it began to cross the water, wanting to go higher. I felt a tug on the silver cord and knew it was time to come back. As I again nestled in her belly, I could hear her heart and feel its flame. Although I knew I had more gestating to do I knew that she and I would continue our walks. She is always present with me. That comforts me.*

*Thank you, Sekhmet. Thank you, Nicki.*

PATRICIA HAYNES

# 10

# In the Soup
# with Wadjet

Wadjet, the cobra goddess, is known as the Great Awakener. As one
of the pair of ancient sister goddesses known as the "two ladies," she
was initially the guardian and protector of Lower Egypt. When the two
lands merged, both she and Nekhbet, the vulture goddess who was the
guardian and protector of Upper Egypt, were joined together, as were
the crowns upon which they sat. It is this cobra goddess who spits fire
at the enemies of pharaoh from her perch on the double crown. Yet
Wadjet hails back to the Paleolithic era when she was the local goddess
of Buto, an important city of Lower Egypt during predynastic times. It
was her temple, Per-Wadjet, from which the great Egyptian oracle tradition originated, which may have later spread to Greece and beyond.
Wadjet and Nekhbet are seen as winged beings, alternating on the lin-
tels and ceilings of the passageways in many of the dynastic temples in
Egypt, overlooking and protecting the pharaohs and the priesthood
below (see color plate 17).

Wadjet represents the kundalini energy that is associated with
Sekhmet, who wears the uraeus crown upon which Wadjet is the central figure.

*Fig. 10.1. Cobra goddess Wadjet wearing the crown of Lower Egypt
(Illustration by Erin Alaina Schroth)*

##  ALPHABET SOUP—REWRITING YOUR GENETIC BLUEPRINT

[*You awaken and discover that Sekhmet (including the fluid you that is in her belly) has returned to the sycamore, under which she is resting peacefully in her lioness form.*]

You become aware that Sekhmet in her statuesque goddess form also stands beside you, outside of her. . . . The powerful cobra goddess, Wadjet, draws your attention to where she sits on the dais of Sekhmet's sun disk. She now enters Sekhmet's lioness body through the top of her head. . . . As you look up at this cobra, she opens her mouth so that you see her fangs. . . .

One drop of venom falls from one of her fangs into the soup that you are inside of Sekhmet. Golden and fiery looking, this drop of liquefied fire reduces you to your essence; it is a tiny speck of light that is the essential spark that ignites the awakening process. . . . As it mixes with the solution, it catches the light of the energy of creation and the kundalini fire that animates the life force. . . . [*Pause.*]

The soup starts to spin around and around, faster and faster as though in a centrifuge, and as it spins around everything starts to separate out and filter all that is not useful to the new body that is about to be created. . . .

The spinning also helps to unwind the DNA in what, when looked at from a certain perspective, has become an alphabet soup. This allows each DNA strand to stretch out and receive its new instructions from a different dimension. . . . Thus, DNA repair and the infusion of new DNA language occur during the spinning, as Sekhmet releases her power into your newly forming being. . . . You can feel it rise up from the earth through all the body's tissues and psycho-neuroendocrine-immune (PNI) networks, even before they come into physicality. . . . As the heat of the kundalini rises, you feel your consciousness expand. . . . The heat causes the molecules to separate, creating space for spirit to enter and carry with it the new level of intelligence that you are prepared to receive. . . .

You become aware of snakelike coils within each cell as they start to separate. When you are fully relaxed and the energy is flowing through your entire essence, the coils also relax. . . . In that relaxed state, they extend out beyond where the cell walls would be. . . . That's where the magic happens. However, it is part of the mystery and therefore unseen by you. It comes in the form of your unique blueprint, your DNA language, and what letters are highlighted. . . . This is somewhat different for each individual, depending upon who you are and where you are in the larger cycles of your life. The old and worn simply fall away and are incorporated into Sekhmet to be used where they can do the most good. Relax. . . . [*Pause.*]

As the coils re-form within the confines in your cells, you will become aware of a new level of foresight. . . . There is an energetic arc that moves out through time and awakens new organs of sensitivity that initiate your direct access to Source. This includes oracular knowledge of everything, everywhere, and everywhen. . . . [*Pause.*]

While this is happening, put out a prayer that this new blueprint will include some smart genes, genes that will help your intelligence to mutate so that the solutions to your personal and our planetary challenges will find fertile ground in which to grow in our collective consciousness. . . . [*Pause.*]

Soon everything starts to calm down, and the centrifuge begins to slow. . . . Everything settles in layers, so physical matter, the earth element, is at the bottom and looks like clay. Above that, the water is cleansing the emotional dimension of your being, which is very fluid and transparent. Lighter than water, air is less dense and feels like thought. It's mental. The golden drop of cobra venom has spread out and is floating above the other three layers—fire expressing the animation of your spirit. You are looking down at the four different elemental layers in which you are floating for a few moments while it's all settling into place. . . . [*Pause.*]

Be sure to write all the details of your experience in your journal before progressing in your reading.

### SHARED VOICES

#### Sacred Mission

*I have a sacred mission here on planet Earth. For years I lay sodden with wet tears in the no-man's-land of lost hopes and dreams. I begged to leave, the desire to return home so strong I lay paralyzed with the grief of being trapped inside my body. Today I open. The dreams reclaimed beat inside the heart of the remembered truth, the opening, the dawn and the light of the divine truth. Ripped inside at the core it was hard to remember the truth of who I am. For this I am thankful, for the humility I am grateful, for as Sekhmet whispers we can only know the truth through the delicate art of surrender. As we surrender we know divine grace; as we dissolve old patterning and re-pattern, our DNA spirals into the perfection that the divine coding of eternity creates. I lose the embodied trauma of ancestral grief as she laps at my open wounds. Sekhmet the goddess of the deepest compassionate grace feasts on the fear, the inadequacy, the broken promises, and the soiled infested cells in the core of my bones.*

*I have a sacred mission; I must leave behind all that does not belong to me, all that does not serve me, all that has hindered me and become all that I am. I am freedom, I am the dove, I am the sacred crested Ibis as he embodies me and teaches me grace through every cell, atom, and molecule of my being. Ripped apart at the seams I am rebuilt in the flow of the Divine. As the fire burns and transmutes the old, I serve grace. I have a sacred mission, a divine mission, and I will share this with the world. The fear shivers up my spine and releases through my crown. Sekhmet growls at the fear, the fear is the death of the truth, the fear is the dark moon where the light fails to shine, this moon is my gift; Khonsu holds the Divine in the form of timing, the timing of the ultimate alignment, the timing of the Divine. All that I am will be all that I strive to be. There is only perfection in the light and the shadow. I open deeper and wider. Sekhmet shows me the grace and beauty as I journey through that shadow, drawing and inhaling the light deeper into my being.*

*My mission is to serve Ma'at. My mission is to speak the truth into being. My mission is to share myself as grace flows through my thoughts, mind, and action. My mission is to call others to action, my mission is to awaken and connect those who slumber to their own truth, so that they may be invited to play their role. My mission is to allow the Divine to work through me to enable me to transform the encapsulating pain of yesteryear and share this with others so that they may shine the truth, the one truth, the only truth—the pure and unremitting light of divine grace and the ultimate perfection of unconditional love.*

LIZZIE McCALLUM

# 11

# The Oasis

Time can be manipulated. The flood of knowledge that we have been immersed in throughout our lives has been doled out at a pace that we can be comfortable with for the most part; it is our choice where our own comfort zone lies. The range of potential wakefulness is directly proportional to how each of us experiences time—numbness to life can allow decades to pass as we sleepwalk through time. Conversely, constant awareness and engagement with each moment and what it reveals generate a life crowded with epiphanies and adventures as your personal book of knowledge expands at an explosive rate.

Each of us has our own ongoing record, kept in a "book" that is part of the etheric library known as the Akashic Records. The next journey provides you with the option for access to the Akashic Records, where archives that include documentation of all knowledge and events that have ever happened reside and where changes can be made in present time that will affect everything that will happen in the future.

There is a choice to be made, a choice of involvement. There are some who will decide not to enter the Hall of Records, choosing to accept blind trust or destiny rather than full awareness and the choices that come with that level of wakefulness. There is no wrong choice, only the one that is right for you at this time. You will go through certain events in your life no matter which choice you make. Those are the things that you freely chose to experience before you came in to this life. With the capability to perceive the various potential realities, going forward you can see that, no matter which choice you make at this crossroad, the domino effects that will happen are apparent, and with that foresight, you will have the responsibility to do what is best, not just for you but for all others involved in your life who are affected by your choice. You are then responsible for your decisions and how you use the knowledge and power you gain in this journey. As you go forward, it is with your intentions and actions, and with your ability to perceive the connections and relationships with those around you and the Earth at all levels, that you co-create what happens around you . . . It's like being in Eden and taking a bite of the fruit from the tree of knowledge.

Those who choose to accept access to the Hall of Records, also known as the Akashic Records, will find comfort within the great halls of knowledge and will feel compelled to return often.

Please note that if you choose to let the chips fall where they will, and decide not to enter the Hall of Records, you can still read the following journey in its entirety without participating. You will have your own experience with Anubis, and the opportunity to pass through the eye will still be there if you decide to go there in the future. Its value is timeless and available whenever, if ever, you choose to make the commitment.

This journey includes working with Anubis, Thoth, and Seshet. Anubis, the jackal-headed god of the underworld, is known as the Opener of the Way (see color plate 18). He is the eldest son of Osiris, and although his mother was Nephthys, twin sister of Isis and wife of Set (another fascinating aspect of the myth of Isis and Osiris to be explored in *Feasts of Light* by Normandi Ellis), he was abandoned in the desert at birth by his mother and rescued and raised by Isis. When Osiris was subsequently murdered by Set, it was Anbuis who helped Isis and Nephthys find and put together thirteen of the fourteen pieces of Osiris's body that were scattered throughout Egypt after

Set threw them into the Nile. Wherever they found a piece, they buried that part and erected a temple. In the end, it was Anubis who performed the embalming and funerary rites for his "re-membered" father, for which he became known as the god of embalming. He is also the underworld figure who guides the dead on their journey back to the light. Anubis is a dependable guardian, guide, teacher, and shaman.*

Remember that whenever Thoth shows up you are entering a sacred opportunity for learning. Thoth is the scribe of the gods, acclaimed as the god of wisdom, teacher of teachers, and also Lord of the Moon. He has many roles, including magician, healer, architect, and scienctist, and he brings the unmanifest into manifestation though articulation with sound and symbols; he is associated with the system of writing, the storing of knowledge, and the maturation of knowledge into wisdom. It was Thoth who taught Isis the words of magic that allowed her to bring her dead husband sufficiently back to life to conceive their son, Horus. This virgin birth preceded that of Jesus in the later Christian iteration of the myth of Isis and Osiris.†

Seshet is the keeper of the libraries, including the Akashic Records. She is intimately connected with Thoth and can be described as the clear field upon which thoughts (as in Thoth) are impressed. She is seen more than once at the Temple of Osiris at Abydos, sitting behind Thoth with her hands generating energy to support him as he scribes. And she too is a scribe as well as a goddess of writing, astronomy, astrology, and mathematics. One of Seshet's most important roles is that of "stretching the cord" in the rituals she taught for the laying of the foundations of temples. It was she who instructed Normandi and me on how to build and consecrate the etheric temple at our lyceum as described in *The Union of Isis and Thoth*.

---

*See my books *Shamanic Mysteries of Egypt* and *The Anbuis Oracle* with Linda Star Wolf and Kris Waldherr, both of which reveal much of Anubis's story.

†See the various chapters on the Isis and Osiris mysteries in Normandi Ellis, *Feasts of Light*.

*Fig. 11.1. Seshet generating energy to Thoth at Abydos (Photo by K. Indigo Rønlov)*

Seshet is easily recognized by the seven-pointed star or flower petals surmounted by the upside-down horns of Hathor that you can see atop the pillar on her head. Some have suggested that the seven points refer to the seven sisters (perhaps the seven Hathors) of the Pleiades. The number seven represented perfection to ancient Egyptians and was considered a sacred number in women's magic.*

## ☀ JOURNEY TO THE OASIS TO CLARIFY YOUR DIRECTION

*[Prepare for the journey using your Heart Breath. . . .]*

Walk out into the desert. You are both in Sekhmet's belly and you are walking beside her. She stops to allow you to observe what is

---

*See Normandi Ellis, *Feasts of Light*, 79, and elsewhere throughout.

going on around you. There is an oasis in the near distance. Large rock formations enhance the scenery behind you and to the right, where the sun is shining. Anubis is on your left, where it is dark and you are surrounded by the night sky. You can see that your goal is to get to the oasis, yet first you must follow Anubis into the darkness. There is a surrendering that has to happen along the way. . . . The surrendering of your expectations and control over what is happening brings you to a place of trust—the final letting go—to trust Sekhmet, Anubis, the process, and whatever higher intelligence you rely upon. . . . [*Pause.*]

The sensation of floating in Sekhmet's belly blurs with the feeling of sand under your feet. There is a light in the darkness, and you are drawn, as though you are drifting toward it. . . . The light reveals itself to be an eye. As you near it, the choice of the depth of your involvement is just about, but not quite, within the grasp of your consciousness. . . . If you choose to pass through the eye, you are agreeing to take on the responsibility that comes with access to the Akashic Records and to consciously take a role in co-creating your life and making choices from that place of knowledge and wisdom, and it is not to be taken lightly. You should choose to enter the eye only if you are willing to go forward with the additional knowledge and foresight that can be obtained in the records—and the accountability that comes with the weight of that advantage. Once again, you are reminded of your commitment to serve Ma'at and to use any knowledge gained for truth, justice, and equilibrium. Choosing to enter the eye also requires an equally deep level of commitment to yourself and to the work that you are doing. You will know in your heart. . . . [*Pause.*]

If you choose not to enter the eye, you will have your own experience as Anubis guides you through the darkness to where Sekhmet is waiting at the oasis. . . . [*Pause.*]

If you pass through the eye you will find yourself in a large and crowded library space. . . . It's so vast that much of the walls and ceilings are beyond your sight. What light there is shows rows of shelves with books and scrolls, and one brightly lit desk. The surface of this desk is dynamic: some of you see reams of paper flowing as each moment passes. For others, it might be a digital experience, or you might see scrolls unfurling. However Thoth reveals information to you is the correct way for you. Focus. . . . Words may flicker into being and then disappear. Information comes in ingenious ways. In whatever form it is presented to you, you are able to grasp meaning from what you are experiencing. Find your own way, or ways—whatever works best for you. . . . [*Pause.*]

Thoth or Seshet is there with you—their presence fluctuates from one to the other and back again. . . . Keep staring at the desktop, watching the records forming as time passes. . . . [*Pause.*]

Reach out your hand; Thoth or Seshet will place a trimmed and inked quill pen in it. . . . You are being given an opportunity to rewrite where you go from here. Now is the moment to make a change, one that will ripple through time. . . . [*Pause.*]

As you record your intention, you can see how everything is interconnected. Instead of dealing with specific events or situations as they come up, you can see the influences that shape the bigger picture, including how you influence others and how they influence you. . . . [*Pause.*]

There will be one parting message for you from Thoth and Seshet before you pass through the other side and find yourself once again standing with Anubis. . . . [*Pause.*]

Anubis leads you out of the darkness, and you are now walking toward the oasis where Sekhmet is waiting for you. . . . Thank Anubis for showing you the way through and being your guide and protector on this journey. . . .

You are now back inside Sekhmet, and she asks you what you chose and what you learned. She tells you that whatever choice you made was right for you, because it was your choice. Sekhmet is drinking water from the oasis. As she drinks, the water washes over you and through you. . . . The water helps to refresh you. It also further separates out what needs to be for Sekhmet, what is for you, and what needs to be eliminated. It's the final cleansing before you begin your reconstruction and renewal.

Sekhmet is taking a bath and playing in the water. You can feel her joy. It's almost overwhelming as she splashes the water with one paw and then uses the other paw to bat at the droplets of water that are suspended in the air. She continues playing in the water with childlike delight, filled with innocence and joy. . . . [*Pause.*]

Worn out from playing, yet retaining her sense of joy, Sekhmet stands up, shakes herself off, and is now standing quite dignified and ladylike. Together you walk back toward the sycamore tree.

Be sure to thank Thoth, Seshet, Anubis, and Sekhmet, and record your experience with as much detail as possible as soon as you can, preferably while you are still in the field of the Akashic Records. Notice how much easier it is to be in both worlds simultaneously. . . . [*Pause.*]

## CREATING WITH JOY

Please note that joy is the most important part of the above journey, regardless of your choice. You need joy to co-create a new self. Creating from a place of fear, guilt, or the unfeeling place of neutrality will only create more of the same, or worse. The purpose of this alchemy is to co-create a new, better version of yourself and to learn how to co-create for the betterment of our planet and for life itself.

If you chose to pass through the eye, your experience—of learning how to read the Akashic Records in the process of being created and making a simple change that will resound through the ages—may have taken you to the edge of your capabilities. The more you do this the easier it will become. Your confidence will improve each time you return to the library. Something else will happen with multiple journeys there: your relationship with Thoth and Seshet will grow.

*Plate 1. Icon of Sekhmet in her fierce warrior aspect*
(Sekhmet the Eye of Ra *by master iconographer Ptahmassu Nofra-Uaa)*

*Plate 2. The eye of Ra*
*(Close-up of eye in the icon of Sekhmet by Ptahmassu Nofra-Uaa)*

*Plate 3. Approaching Karnak temple*
*(Photo by Tarek Lotfy)*

*Plate 4. Close-up of ram-headed sphinxes lining the approach to Karnak (Photo by Tarek Lotfy)*

*Plate 5. Main courtyard in Karnak (Photo by Nicole Haworth)*

*Plate 6. Entering the hypostyle hall between
pillars covered in hieroglyphs
(Photo by Nicole Haworth)*

*Plate 7. Exiting the hypostyle hall through a*
*small opening in the north wall*
*(Photo by Nicole Haworth)*

Plate 8. Approaching the entrance to the chapel of Sekhmet, Ptah, and Nefertum (Photo by Tarek Lotfy)

Plate 9. Ancient sycamore tree, sacred to the goddesses Sekhmet and Hathor, in front of the entrance to the chapel of Sekhmet, Ptah, and Nefertum in Karnak (Photo by Indigo Rønlov)

*Plate 10. Entrance to the inner courtyard of the chapel of Sekhmet, Ptah,
and Nefertum showing the stone altar within
(Photo by Nicki Scully)*

Plate 11. Raising of the djed, from the temple of Osiris at Abydos
(Photo by Nicole Haworth)

*Plate 12. Ankh, djed, and was scepter (Photo by Tarek Lotfy)*

*Plate 13. Wall in the inner courtyard of the chapel of Ptah, Sekhmet, and Nefertum. Central figure on left is Ptah with the djed ankh, and was staff. The figure to his right is Hathor/Sekhmet holding the ankh. (Photo by Nicole Haworth)*

*Plate 14. Statue of Ptah in his chapel at Karnak
(Photo by Nicole Haworth)*

*Plate 15. Statue of Sekhmet in her chapel sanctuary at Karnak*
*(Photo by Indigo Rønlov)*

Plate 16. The front entrance to the Temple of Man at Luxor (Photo by Jacob Cohl)

Plate 17. Wadjet with Khonsu at Karnak: The large winged serpent figures in this image represent Wadjet. The central figures, with the solar disk resting in the lunar crescent on their heads, represent the moon god Khonsu. (Photo by Jacob Cohl)

*Plate 18. Wepwawet (an aspect of Anubis)*
*(Photo by Nicole Haworth)*

Plate 19. *The White Desert*
*(Photo by Mickey Stelavatto)*

Plate 20. *Alabaster ankh with amethyst crystal ball represents the magnifying lens gift from Ptah (Photo by Indigo Rønlov)*

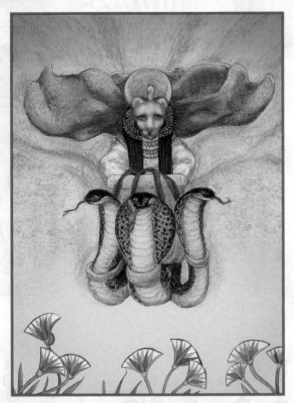

*Plate 21. Sekhmet and her chariot of cobras (Illustration by Kris Waldherr from* The Anubis Oracle*)*

*Plate 22. Kom Ombo Temple at night
(Photo by Tarek Lotfy)*

*Plate 23. Horus and Sobek pillars at Kom Ombo Temple*
*(Photo by Tarek Lotfy)*

They can help you explore the records and can teach you how to access your own higher self, which is a necessary skill when making changes that are needed for the future.

Regardless of the choice you made in this journey, you can see your direction more clearly now. There is a peacefulness that comes with this awareness. You know that you are not being given anything that you cannot do. You have all the tools you need, and what you don't have you will be given in time.

As you continue through the processes and rites in this book, if you decide to make a different choice while you are still in the belly of the goddess, you can return and do this journey a second time. This journey is also a stand-alone journey if you choose to take it outside of the context of this book. It must always be taken with great respect and recognition of the privilege of this exceptional access to the Akashic Records.

## SHARED VOICES

*As I wrote I saw Thoth's third eye illuminated, witnessing me writing. My heart/mind was illuminated, and then Ptah anointed my mouth.*

*As I retold all I'd seen to Sekhmet she smiled as she listened, and when I said I don't know how this will all happen she said, "The magic is in you. You are the end result, you are the alchemy. Everything is within you. You already are the end result." This felt like an important, powerful energy to embody.*

*I am just deeply open, and I surrender. When I went back in meditation I began to break down, and Sekhmet said, "Its okay, walk with me." I felt held.*

*I lay down all my blocks to love, all my barriers to love.*

*I claim my womb back to rewrite the legacy of conception, nurture, birth, raising children, love, love in the family—parent to child, child to parent, parent to parent. I claim my womb back with the script rewritten, with love at the bottom, top, middle, left, and right. I claim my rebirth.*

ELOISE JOSEPH

*Having spent my life and my career without the benefit of consistent clairvoyance, clairaudience, or clairsentience, I have often felt like I am living a challenge: I accepted to go through life as a seeker of higher consciousness without the benefit of "sight" and other modes of access. Being thus handicapped, it has been as if I were climbing a mountain with a blindfold and earplugs. This has been both an advantage and a disadvantage.*

*The advantage side relates to the dynamic of choosing to teach people how to see in order to become informed myself. That actually worked quite well for many years. However, it was often frustrating and difficult to validate what I experienced as a "knower," one who gets information directly rather than in pictures, sound, or other primary accessing modes. "Knowing" is the most difficult perception to validate; consequently I dealt with a higher level of insecurity about what I knew and didn't know than those with "sight," who had learned to discriminate and thereby discern the truth in their visions.*

*The benefits of my insecurity were subtle, yet quite powerful: Not only did I teach many people to see, but it was often those students who helped me to co-create the teachings that followed. And, because I required a "seer" to help me bring in the work, I could not own it; thus I learned the power and importance of co-creation and humility.*

*On the disadvantage side, it was extremely frustrating, particularly when taking classes from various teachers, to have others describe their experiences in vivid detail, whether because they saw images, heard thoughts, or felt distinctive feelings that they could interpret. I felt exuberant if I was shown a color. I remember a class back in the early '80s during which, after a guided journey, I reported seeing the color blue. I felt encouraged when someone responded that "it all comes out of the blue" anyway. (It's somewhat ironic that I was given the name Blue Eagle by the neteru during ceremonies in both Peru and Egypt, and I have always associated the color blue with Thoth.)*

*Back to the advantage side, I found my validation in the natural, physical world. Because I couldn't rely on sight (actually, since sight can* be manipulated and misinterpreted, it is less reliable than feeling, which cannot be manipulated or feigned), I was forced to trust at a level that required me to believe more fully in the process I was living—because it worked.

As a healer, when my teacher would tell me I could do something, often someone would appear within a day or two with a need for just that. I would attempt the work regardless of how inadequate I felt, and inevitably (and surprisingly) I was almost always successful. I became my teacher's protégé and her guinea pig, and also the person whom she first sent out into the world to teach. When I argued that I was not ready, she told me that I needed to teach what I needed to learn, and by doing that I would integrate the teachings at a deeper level. Although every person is different, that's what worked for me.

This journey helped me to clarify the choice I have no memory of making but that I surely did make at an earlier point in my soul's journey (apparently I made an agreement to come into this life with limited sight and imaginitive prowess, which constantly demanded validation from the "real" world), which has led me to this point and made it easier for me to make the right choice for this time in this journey—a conscious choice in this lifetime to re-member myself as a priestess/warrior for Ma'at and to bring forth and share the teachings and tools of healing that are so needed now on our planet.

NICKI SCULLY

# 12
## First, There Was the Word

You and Sekhmet return to the sycamore tree, where she stands and listens intently to the sound that emerges from the universe. The sound comes in as a wave.

If you drop a stone in water, the energy that hits the water is converted into waves of force that radiate out in concentric circles, ever expanding. In a standing wave the movement of the energy is reversed. As energy converges from all directions from the outside, concentric circles are generated that move inward, concentrating the energy in a smaller and smaller area. When the energy reaches the center, it has to have someplace to go, so it moves upward, creating a quivering pillar of water that is called a standing wave.

This is just like pulling out the end ball of a row of balls hanging from a string, then letting it fall back to hit the others. The energy is transferred from one to the other in stillness until it reaches the last ball. The energy has to continue moving, so it pushes the last ball out with the same amount of force that hit the first ball. Similarly, the energy in a standing wave needs to continue moving. That upward thrust creates an orb of water that rises above the wave, like a dot on an "i." As the wave falls back down, the drop is suspended for a fraction of a second. In that moment of suspension, energy becomes matter. In that moment, all things are possible—it's a moment outside of time and space where everything and nothing exist simultaneously. It is also a portal to other dimensions.

As Sekhmet hears the sound of the universe, it reverberates through her body, and therefore through you. The wave of sound comes in from every direction simultaneously. It oscillates and transfers energy and vibration through its peaks and valleys. When the wave hits the liquid inside the belly of Sekhmet, the sound waves translate into energy waves, circular waves that converge to the center, forming a standing wave that moves the energy upward.

The point at the tip of the standing wave is within Sekhmet. The materialization happens at the peak of the standing wave, both in Sekhmet and in you when you are within her. Things are shifting at the molecular level so that they become synchronized. If you are attentive, you will be aware of the fine-tuning as it occurs.

## ☀ MEDITATION ON THE STILL POINT BETWEEN ENERGY AND MATTER

[*As Sekhmet lies down under the dappled shade of the sycamore tree, take a couple of Heart Breaths and look within. . . . You now discover that you have been reduced to nothingness: the state between being soup and being reconstituted. This is a good time to meditate, directing your focus to the connection between energy and matter. . . .*]

You are held in Sekhmet in a wordless state of satori-like nothingness. You are at the point of nothing and everything, where all possibilities exist simultaneously. This is known to some as the void. Because this is the moment of power, the moment when you can help direct the outcome of who you will be, it is imperative that all thoughts are positive and directed at creating your highest potential as a fully realized human. It is during this time that a major portion of DNA repair happens. . . . [*Pause.*]

When you find yourself thinking, notice where the thoughts come from. You want to be certain that all thoughts that you allow to enter during this momentous opportunity are sourced in your higher self and in conjunction with the highest intelligence of the universe. . . . Hold your focus for as long as you are able to maintain your clear intention to support your transformation into the fully realized human that is the goal for this alchemy. . . . [*Pause.*]

When you feel complete and have expressed your gratitude, ground and center yourself, without coming back fully, and write in your journal. . . .

## THE ADVANCEMENT OF ONE CONTRIBUTES TO ALL

Consider for a moment that we humans, as a collective species, are coming to a place of little choice—shift or get off the pot. It's the same with this alchemy. At this point the potential is greatest, and it is up to you to keep your intention and your focus clear throughout the re-membering of yourself. From this point forward you are in the process of reconstruction, and you have plenty to say about how you re-create yourself.

As with the rest of the world, you are at a place where you are approaching an incredible opportunity to participate consciously in the potential for all humans to spontaneously evolve. The more people who are engaged in this or similar work to awaken to higher states of consciousness, the more likely we can make the quantum leap in consciousness and intelligence that is required of us. What happens on the planet is a reflection of the collective desires of our communal heart—including our thoughts, wishes, and prayers. Already, through the disintegration of the negative habit patterns and past harmful behaviors, there is an opportunity for our species to transform; as we make the most of this opportunity, what we do for ourselves we do for the collective as well.

For example, when I underwent my chemotherapy and radiation treatments for cancer back in 1992, my mantra was "mutate or die!" My husband and I decided to use our shamanic tools to observe the process of the chemotherapy, surgery, and radiation that I chose to undergo.* That made it possible for me to experience the mutation as it happened. It was both spontaneous and ceremonial and included *chanunpah* (sacred pipe), peyote and sun dance ceremonies, and other healing rituals with various shamans and Alchemical Healers, during which I often had visions and worked with various spirit allies that showed up for me. Each thing I did and each thing that happened, no matter how insignificant it seemed at the time, was an essential part of the healing process. When looked at through the lens of Ptah's ankh (I didn't have it at the time), each ceremony is revealed as part of a larger cycle of death, renewal, illumination, and rebirth, all of which I experienced during the treatment.

Work such as Alchemical Healing and Planetary Healing is especially important right now, because many of the tools and sensitivities that we activate are designed to affect the collective DNA as well as our personal mutations. The evolutionary process that we are attempting to speed up and achieve is not only for our immediate survival in this crazy world and this crazy time; we need to take it a step further and adapt until we can successfully embrace and become nurtured by the changes that are being foisted upon us.

Things are changing much more rapidly on the planet than we expected. We knew that climate change would be significant. We knew that the tremendous amount of toxicity that we have released onto our planet would cause major consequences. Because we are less prepared in many ways than we hoped to be, the mutations and changes required to survive during this time are essential, and often quite radical.

The alchemy in the belly of the goddess offers us some unique opportunities for healing that evolved during the writing of this book. I've been very excited about the work that I've been doing with

---

*My journal notes during my cancer treatment are published in *Planetary Healing: Spirit Medicine for Global Transformation*, coauthored with Mark Hallert, and on my website, ShamanicJourneys.com, in an article titled "Counting Coup on Cancer."

conscious evolution, adaptation, and mutation so that we can survive the expanding die-off and thrive in a world that is quite different from that into which we were born.

Sekhmet, as the quintessential healing goddess that she is, is offering to help us make great changes as we reconstruct our new bodies. As long as we are completely dissolved, safe in her belly, and beginning the reconstruction process, we might as well go for the most that we can co-create, and let her do her magic. Our attentiveness, intention, gratitude, and focus are all key aspects of what we contribute to becoming stronger and smarter human beings, with abilities that allow us more access to the intelligence that is available within and all around us.

The changes that we influence in this process can endure and will have a tremendous effect on how we move forward in our lives individually and collectively. During this part of the alchemy, it is time for you to embrace the emptiness—the dissolved nature of where you are in the process so that you can leave behind the last threads and shreds of anything that would hamper your capacity to reconstruct in the most positive way possible.

# CHECKING IN
# WITH THE NETERU

You are just about half way through this alchemical process, and it is time for a check-in with the neteru family. For some of you it will be the first time that you meet many of these deities, and for others it will be like a reunion. It is Sekhmet's hope that you will recognize that her family is also your family, and they exist within our DNA. What's most important, according to Ma'at, is that you realize that the entire pantheon stands as witness to what you do and how you weave your destiny into this world. The gods and goddesses of this pantheon are in all of us. They are our ancestors, and it is time to refresh the memory of the old ones so that those who have yet to come have a chance at the preciousness of life with its natural state of joy.

##  MEETING WITH THE PANTHEON

*[The next morning breaks warm and streaming with sunlight. You can feel the warmth of the amniotic flux in which only the tiny remaining particles of your being are still dissolving, and it's time to move toward your reconstitution in earnest. . . .]*

Sekhmet in her lioness form stretches, rises, and walks to the inner courtyard of her chapel at Karnak. The big wooden door to the sanctuaries is open, and there seems to be a casual council of neteru hanging out waiting for you. Ma'at is standing next to Ptah, on his left in his central room in the chapel. Ptah's statue appears as if in ancient times, brightly intact, including his blue-capped head. Ptah welcomes you. Sekhmet in her goddess form comes in from her sanctuary and stands to the right of Ptah, superimposed upon the lioness that is casually lounging there also. She is and has been watching over the entire process. As we seek to expose the truth of ourselves, we must always remember to be grateful for her truth.

Other neteru are also there, but you may not see them, and they don't need to be mentioned at this time. Acknowledge those whom you know. You become aware that other initiates who are going through this alchemy are also in attendance, although they may be invisible to you. It's up to you to show up and be present and to pay attention to everything, including what appears to be minutiae.

A number of Egyptian neteru are present and willing to assist you as you make the necessary changes. Listen carefully to what any of them might have to say to you at this time. Perhaps they are there to congratulate you on your progress so far. Perhaps they wish to remind you of abilities that you have not been using that would be helpful. This is an opportunity to receive talismanic gifts and further guidance from your Egyptian neteru family. You will receive one or two that are especially for you. Be sure to thank the appropriate neteru for their gifts and their encouragement and support. . . . *[Long pause.]*

Take some time to record the salient points from your meeting with the pantheon and to consider and integrate where you have come so far. It is dusk again when you return to the sycamore tree.

## SHARED VOICES

*I have taken this class many times, and each is more powerful than the last. During the First There Was the Word section, I found myself in a void space that felt like a huge cave. I was not sure whether it was made of physical material or the Sky itself, but it is a secure cave, and I'm really at home there. It's a safe place where anything and everything can happen. As I explore the cave it is as though Earth and Heaven are combined, and all things are included.*

*I noticed that at first my thoughts were just chatter, not really focused. Many things were happening at once, which created a lot of chaos. Then the thoughts started coming from inside, and it became more and more calm, until there were only a few thoughts. And then it was just being there in this heavenly cave—standing in the stillness of the cave.*

*Meeting with the pantheon: It is clear that I am in Sekhmet and she is the holder of this heavenly cave. I went into the chapel with her, and I am still inside the cave while I'm in Ptah's chapel. There are beings from the pantheon and also beings that I don't recognize. When I asked, I was told that they were star people.*

*The pantheon is standing there in a half circle, and I know most by name: Ptah, Sekhmet, Anubis, Bast, Wadjet, Jesus, Horus, Maat, Isis, and others and many more behind them. Behind the first row I see other, bigger beings that I don't recognize. I greet the ones I know, and then it's as though they make space, and I can see one of the bigger ones in the back more clearly. Thoth tells me they are beings from the stars and introduces them to me.*

*One of them spoke through Thoth and said they are from the stars and have come from a great distance. They are supporting first the pantheon (all pantheons) because they are connected to each other forever, but now we are showing up as well. The neteru are connected one to one, each to his* own star being, as they are another dimension of the pantheon. We have been here forever but only now are we showing ourselves, because it is time to make a net over the Earth. There are people like us (you and me) who are aware of the pantheons, and the pantheons are connected with the star beings, so there are three dimensions. The humans on this planet need to connect in this net with others who are aware of these three dimensions. I recall that two days after I first took these journeys, a friend had this same experience with a different pantheon. It doesn't matter which pantheon you are connected to; they are all connected with one another.

I asked, "How can we work with you? And how can we use these three dimensions?" It's always about the connection with the neteru, and we have to know now that when we call one of the deities we are also calling on this third dimension, and there will be new answers, new possibilities, faster speed and strength in manifestation. Also, the people who are aware of these three dimensions can connect with each other very easily.

Mother Earth and all the Earth beings and elements are also a pantheon. It makes our work with the elements stronger when we consciously have this connection and knowledge.

When Sekhmet began to move I was still in this heavenly cave in her body, so I knew it was time to go. I thanked the deities and the star beings as we backed out of the chapel, and I instantly found myself again with Sekhmet under the sycamore tree.

It's so real, so clear in my vision. Thank you for this journey. I know I can go back there anytime now.

PILIAKA CORINA PETER

# 13
## Akasha and the Elements

Akasha is usually considered the fifth element, yet it is the most important.* Akasha gives birth to all the unique elements that have separated out to become earth, air, fire, and water, as well as all the other elemental constituents of our three-dimensional reality. As the matrix of the intelligence of the universe, akasha is the first and most vital of the elements you will call on for your reconstruction. Among its many attributes, akasha is a universal solvent and a pain reliever. It can function as pure consciousness itself. Most importantly, it creates an intelligent window between time and other dimensions.

We call in akasha at this time because this etheric element functions as the network of dynamic relationships in which the one and the many are the same—the embodiment of existence and action in both the spiritual and physical worlds. The blueprint for your new body, including your DNA and any serious healing that you are ready to receive, is imprinted on the intelligent field that surrounds all the celestial bodies of the universe, including Earth.

There are two symbols that can be used as portals into the dimension of akasha. The first is a purple-black egg, flecked in gold. I have used the egg as a universal symbol of creativity and the gateway into

---

*See my book *Alchemical Healing,* chapter 15, for an in depth discussion of akasha and its use in healing.

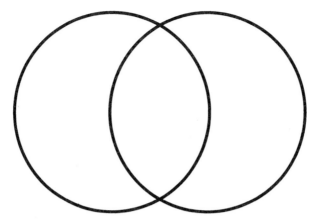

*Fig. 13.1. Vesica piscis: The vesica piscis is the shape that is formed by two circles of the same radius intersecting in such a way that the center of each circle lies on the perimeter of the other. (Illustration by Debbie Clarkin)*

other realms since my first book, *The Golden Cauldron,* published in 1991 and later reissued as *Power Animal Meditations.* The second equally potent symbol is the vesica piscis. If you were to draw two intersecting circles, the geometric shape that is at the center and shaped like a yoni and is called the vesica piscis, or "bladder of the fish." This particular sacred geometrical form famously decorates the cover of the sacred well at Glastonbury, in the UK. One circle represents spirit and the other matter, or above and below. The shape that is created by the intersection of above and below is the doorway through which you can connect to the element akasha. Both symbols are equally effective.

Because akasha is expansive and inclusive simultaneously, it is likely to make you sleepy until you get used to working with it. For many it takes practice to stay awake when infused with akasha.

## THE BELLY BREATH

Although the Heart Breath is one of the most important practices you can integrate into your life, there are times when you will want to change the focus of your breath from your heart to your abdomen, to the focal point from which *chi* or *qi,* the life-force energy, is sourced and expressed. It's located in the abdomen in various places depending upon what tradition you follow. For our purposes, find the spot about two finger widths beneath your belly button, in the center of your body in front of the spine. Here, in what in Japanese is termed the *hara* and in the Taoist tradition is known as the lower *dantien,* is the central foundation from which energy is sourced and generated in many traditional meditation and breathing techniques, from qigong, Daoist practices, Buddhism, and various martial arts to the Western magical tradition. By whatever name it is called, this central point is fundamental to the balance and gravity of the human body; it is within the cauldron that is your belly that Thoth stirs the principle ingredients that express your individual identity and your will.

The Belly Breath is very similar to the Heart Breath, with a simple redirection: You inhale from the heart of Earth directly to your lower abdomen instead of to your heart. Then you hold your breath as you observe the mixing of the inhaled breath with love that, as with the Heart Breath, you constantly pour into the cauldron in your belly (rather than directing it into your heart). When you exhale, direct your breath from your hara, or lower dantien, to whatever part of your body you are working on, or to whomever you wish to gift the power of your intention.

You can use the Earth part of the Belly Breath by itself when you need special grounding; however, you can also inhale from Earth and Sky simultaneously, as done with the Heart Breath, but to your belly instead of your heart, and then direct the breath as needed. The difference has to do with the intention for the direction of your breathing.

The Heart Breath connects us with the transpersonal shared space, and the Belly Breath brings that connection into the physical, three-dimensional realm. As above, so below; as without, so within—this breath is used to solidify this magical working.

As we move in to the reconstruction phase of this alchemical process, this new way to focus your breath will help ground your intention into the physical body that is being repaired as it is being reactivated.

## INTENTIONAL RECONSTRUCTION

At any time during the following journey or any other part of the process of reconstruction, you may wish to record in your journal the various things that you notice as parts of you begin to coalesce. It is also important to maintain the depth of your meditative state while doing this part of the work to deepen your connection to Sekhmet and the process while it is occurring. Eventually, and with practice, you will be able to pause to write about your experience without interrupting yourself and losing your place.

## ☀ RECONSTRUCTION BEGINS WITH AKASHA— AN ELEMENTAL JOURNEY

[*Sekhmet chooses to return to the courtyard at Luxor Temple to engage in the next part of the reconstruction. When you find yourself back in the courtyard, the cooing of the doves nestled in the capitals of the pillars are calling you to breathe; they remind you to add lots of love to your Heart Breaths. As you call on akasha, allow yourself to relax and feel completely at peace, safe in Sekhmet's belly. . . .*]

As you continue breathing the Heart Breath and feel the resonance with Sekhmet's heart, reach up above your head and draw two intersecting circles with your fingers, then reach through the portal in the design you have created with your fingers and draw down akasha with your intention, pulling it through the opening, while holding a clear understanding of your intention to allow akasha in to do its work on whatever is left of you. . . . [*Pause.*]

I cannot stress enough how important it is to keep your thoughts positive, clear, and focused when you are working with akasha. Because akasha empowers any manifestation process when used with clear intention, any confusion or doubt will distort the results.

As the akasha pours in through the portal you have created, you may sense a darkening, almost as though a squid just swam by and squirted its inky black mist all around you, obscuring your vision and perhaps attempting to put you to sleep. Try your best to stay conscious and clear. The black mist will disperse, and you will have called in the universal solvent to complete the task at hand. . . .

With each exhale of your Heart Breaths, allow yourself to let go of any shreds of detritus or other remnants that might be clinging to your old self and that could possibly hold you back—those last vestiges of anger or fear, shame, guilt, vulnerability—all the things that have come up as well as those that haven't come up during your preparations. . . . [*Pause.*]

Anything that has shadowed your perception, anything that may have caused moral weakness, needs to dissolve, now. . . . You want to leave behind any remaining static as you continue to pour the akashic medium through your hands and your breath. . . . Notice how you can feel a further dissolution of any binding threads and all the final bits of stuff that might still remain. You have been reduced to shadowy threads that become wispier with each breath, until they are gone. . . . [*Pause.*]

Pay close attention as you enter a place of darkness or emptiness, a void space, a no thing—nothing, emptiness where you are simply suspended in stasis and there's no weight to your essence. It may appear that you are surrounded in darkness. . . . Your vision and senses may become obscured. You might find it difficult to stay conscious. The total dissolution will happen regardless of your awareness, although it's better if you can stay alert enough to observe it. . . . [*Pause.*]

In this dissolved state the most essential spark of your being is reduced to a fine pinpoint of light, with just the smallest spark, small enough to pass through a tiny portal that is like the eye of a needle. As you focus on the spark in the midst of the darkness, you will perceive an eye coming out of the nothingness. Feel yourself drawn toward the pupil, as if the eye is focusing on you with such intensity that it is all there is in the entire emptiness of space. . . . Enter the pupil of the eye. . . . [*Pause.*]

You've crossed the threshold. . . . You've passed through, and you know that nothing is the same and yet everything seems as if it were. . . . Notice as you begin to become aware of the structure of creation starting to return. . . . [*Pause.*]

You feel the water first, and with the element water comes a heightened awareness of your sensitivity. . . . As the waters flow through you, it is as though your cells have been separated and all your molecules are miles apart from one another. The water passes between each as it nourishes, feeds, and pours intelligence into each molecule. . . . As the molecules begin finding each other once again, they bond together and begin to coalesce, reshaping themselves. . . . Ask for the continued sensitivity to be able to maintain your awareness regardless of what's going on around you with courage, compassion, and total comprehension. . . . [*Pause.*]

The earth element now enters; put your focus on a strong physical constitution. . . . As you feel the molecules coming together and taking form in your body, set your intention to invigorate the strength and sense of security that you've had an opportunity to experience, and are still experiencing, in the belly of the goddess. . . . Earth brings structure, solidity, and physical healing. It also enhances your awareness of our physical, natural world and our relation to the organism that is our precious planet. As you focus on earth, be aware that too much earth brings stubbornness, rigidity, and apathy. . . . [*Pause.*]

Take some time to pay close attention while you witness the harmonious reconstruction and contribute, with your will and desire, to this most important part of the alchemy. . . . All of this is being written into your DNA—it's being written into the programs that are entering into all the molecules and the cells of your being. The strength and the ordered structure is Ma'at, where all cosmic laws are in dynamic equilibrium within you as you come together in your physical body. . . . [*Pause.*]

As the water and earth elements continue to do their work, experience with as many senses as you can all the ways in which the reconstruction has begun. . . . There is no need to hurry. However, it is vital to keep your thoughts clear and positive and focused on witnessing each change and addition as it happens. . . . [*Long pause.*]

If you haven't already, you may wish to pause within your meditation to record in your journal the details of your reconstruction so far. . . . [*Pause.*]

This is also a good time to begin using the Belly Breath. Inhale the powers of Earth and Sky while you focus love into the cauldron that is both the belly of the goddess and the first stages of the body that is beginning to coalesce within her. Your breath will assist in the process of bringing the elements into physicality within. Take several Belly Breaths and feel the power of the individuation that is beginning to occur. Again, you are not in a hurry. . . . There are many opportunities for adding your divine will into the alchemy. . . . [*Pause.*]

You will know when it's time to call in the fire. It might feel like an ignition as the spirit awakens in all the cells and molecules that are coming together and reforming along with the will to live. The spirit is strong, bright, and animated. You may be able to discern a vague human shape filled with flame and spark. . . . You begin to feel energy flowing between the newly ignited synapses as they begin firing. Everything is turning on and awakening at a spiritual level within you as the life-force energy connects with the water and the earth. As they come together, you feel an infusion of courage and with it a strong sense of passion for life and for what you know in your heart to be your new journey starting to awaken within you. . . . [*Pause.*]

Keep your focus as you observe the elements, these basic elements of water, earth, and fire, dancing together in sacred geometric patterns that are coming into play and into shapes that are functional and harmonious. . . . The cooperation you sense within the community of cells in your body and in your being is how you know that cooperation and harmony are also being infused into your family, your inner circle of friends, your community, and beyond, into the medium of this petri dish that is planet Earth. . . .

From this vantage point, you realize that this order that you are perceiving taking shape in your own being is becoming part of the collective template for the possible, fully awakened human and that you are at the forefront of this part of human conscious evolution. Take a moment to consider the possibilities. You might want to look through the lens of the ankh that Ptah gave you so that you can better perceive the intricacies of the moment. Journaling what you see as you look through the lens will add power to the moment. . . . [*Pause.*]

Now take a conscious Heart Breath and invoke the element air. As you inhale this breath of life, it nourishes every cell of your being, every molecule, and all the new patterns that are taking form. It's like adding music, infusing joy, and experiencing pure pleasure as you sniff the air and the mind comes into light in the heart. . . . Your mind and your heart merge with Sekhmet's as the air moves through your body, nurturing this new template and all the new blueprints that are bringing you into perfect harmony and balance with all the elements of your being. . . . Let the breath flow through and nourish every aspect of the new possibility that is beginning to grow within the belly of the goddess. . . . [*Pause.*]

Take a moment to honor and express gratitude from your heart to each of the elements that is facilitating your renewal at this time. . . . [*Pause.*] Reassess how you are feeling at this moment. . . . Use your heightened awareness to perceive not only the new you that is being created but all the possibilities of the attributes you wish to include as well. . . . [*Pause.*]

If you can perceive them elementally, then also honor the elements as those qualities come into you. For example, structure, strength, and fortitude contribute to your physical health—these are aspects of the element earth. Your sensitivity, compassion, fluidity, and emotions—these are attributes of water. The energy and vitality, the life force that moves through you, the kundalini, the excitement, the quickness, creativity, courage, and passion—this is your fire. And the lightness, the joy, the capacity for pleasure, the mind, the music, the communion, and the ability to communicate and give voice—these are attributes of air. And, of course, akasha, the matrix, the whole multidimensional matrix from which these elements derive, is the glue (along with love) that holds it all together. Take a moment to give the whole creation an infusion of love and gratitude. . . . [*Pause.*]

Before we complete this part of the alchemy and this particular journey, take a moment to simply be in the stillness and allow that which we have not been wired to imagine to share something new with us. We are asking for divine intervention in our reconstruction—that which is beyond the abilities that we have in our consciousness thus far. . . . [*Pause.*]

When it is clear that all is in place and the elements are ready to begin the restructuring process, take a few minutes to breathe the Belly Breath, inhaling the powers of Earth and Sky, mixing them with the love that you are infusing into the cauldron, and exhale the alchemized breath into the mixture that is becoming the *prima materia* of the next phase of the alchemy. . . .

It's peaceful here, and it's been a long day. Sekhmet stretches and yawns, then slowly rises and walks back through the Temple of Man, back along the path between the sphinxes, and finally returns to her favorite place of rest under the sycamore tree in front of her chapel. As you comfortably rock back and forth and from side to side with the rhythm of her gait, you may simply fall asleep and dream of beauty, of possibility—a magical dream that is somehow connected with this process of alchemy. . . . [*Long pause.*]

When you awake and are grounded and centered, take time to scan your developing self and record everything that you can remember and notice in your journal.

## SHARED VOICES

*I am delighted to write about this particular journey, as I think it is important, not just for me, but for the world.*

*At first I perceived a lot of gold energy. There was gold in my hair like a crown, and when I entered the pupil of the eye, I felt like I was entering a galaxy. It occurs to me that akasha is cosmic spiritual force that transforms into reality. I can feel the structure of creation as it begins in my heart, where I feel a very high frequency.*

*When the water flows in, it feels as though I'm coming into a new world for the very first time. I feel raw. There is going to be a time for me to learn from everything in the nature around me, and the nature around me will be learning from me. It feels very new and raw, yet I feel like an adult, although an infant energy is coming into an adult's body. . . .*

*With the element earth I saw dinosaurs, and they represent those entities that came to Earth as vehicles to ground the energy of the Earth. I am filled with the emotion of gratitude here, for I have been entrusted with information, wisdom, and comprehension with the Law of One. . . .*

*I feel that I am a fetus form inside of Sekhmet. I am her creation, in her belly, a seed of potentiality that has not yet been born or delivered. This realization is really important. It opens consciousness to the full potential of imagination and who I can become. . . . At the same time, there is the understanding of where I came from, which is from the body of Sekhmet, who represents a specific aspect of the Law of the Universe.*

*The fire element is the element that activates the kundalini energy and governs the spine. It feels like it could take over if one does not know how to hold this energy. It's an element that can be misused easily, yet its signature is purification. Purification calls for discipline, vigilance, attentiveness, development, self-control, dedication, and sensitivity, as well as how they are related within my body. It was grounded in the physical blueprint when I breathed the Belly Breath. . . .*

*The element air brings with it an octagonal figure spinning around in the air. It is a sacred geometric device, technological, and full of potential. My physical body will become that new technological device. We are becoming that device. We are becoming something very new and advanced, and it is in our own body system from which we are and will be operating. It's a big opportunity that has not been seen before, as our previous frequency did not allow it until now. This is for those who are ready to take this evolutionary step. Anything is possible, as I am a creator now.*

*I offer gratitude to the elements. . . . This reconstruction and this redefining has to do with our DNA and the reclamation of the divine blueprint, the new template for our DNA that will help us to develop new ways to do things and a new quality of life.*

CRISTINA TRUJILLO

# 14

# Rebuilding Your Bones

We will now rebuild your skeleton. In this next meditation you will direct your mind's eye to the vast, unique landscape of the White Desert, not far from Egypt's current border with Libya (see color plate 19). Within this remarkably sculpted and desolate desert, you will find the source of your own original bones. It is important to remember that bones in living organisms are actually rich and dynamic, and skeletons are interconnected in complex interaction with ligaments, tendons, muscles, fascia, and other related tissues.

This journey (and all of the reconstruction that follows) provides a coherent activity that defines you as a living organism, completed only when its nested systems are in full relationship with each other and the surrounding ecology. As we continue your reconstruction, the many nutrients that enrich your anatomy result in a dynamic physiology, wet and vibrant, even when the prime material is ancient and presents itself as a dead, barren desert, made up of the fossils of ancient sea creatures.

Have the lens that Ptah gave you ready to use in the following meditation (see color plate 20).

The journey below was initially channeled from Sekhmet through Indigo Rønlov during a vision quest in the White Desert. Following is an excerpt from her journal entry on that day.

*What I sought in the desert was silence. What I found in the desert was a silence so profound that it brought me to an utter state of disintegration. I came to see that the bones become the bones become the bones again. As I sat as witness to the vastness contained within this place, I could recognize that the land formations were the result of millions of shells and bones from creatures long ago alive, who then died and sank to the ocean floor to accumulate and collect, until from the pressures above they compacted into a great white layer. Eventually the waters subsided, and the wind and the sand etched and carved the limestone like a skilled sculptor. I knew then that my bones will soon be dust, and throughout the ages other life-forms will be composed of the molecules that are now me.*

## ☀ JOURNEY TO RETRIEVE YOUR SKELETAL SYSTEM

*[Begin by breathing the Heart Breath and offer your exhales to Sekhmet as you contemplate the description of the White Desert in Egypt. . . .]*

Now imagine that you are in the belly of Sekhmet as a lioness that ranged the desert six or seven thousand years ago during a time when lions roamed along with antelope and grasses covered the savanna. . . . The climate is changing, the desert is encroaching, and the human population has been forced to leave their villages in search of water as the lakes are drying up. . . . The only other source of water is the Nile River, a long distance from the fantastically beautiful part of the Western Desert where you now find yourself. . . . *[Pause.]*

The lioness is now carrying you in current time; the fierce winds and sand storms have carved one of the most interesting, if barren, landscapes in our world. She climbs to the highest point at the top of a limestone escarpment that juts up from the desert floor. From here, you can look out in every direction, taking in the amazing, convoluted, yet apparently lifeless landscape that seems to go on forever. As dry and empty as this desert looks, however, there are many creatures that make their home here. This landscape is forever in motion. The sand constantly shifts under the winds that also create the unique and exquisite limestone shapes that stand as giant sculptures created for the amusement of God. Use your lens to look closely at the white limestone. See how it is composed of the eroded skeletal mass of sea creatures that lived in the ocean that was here eons ago. Envision this desert, covered with waters with myriad life forms living within. . . . [*Pause.*]

Now, when you telescope your vision, as though looking through a wide-angle lens, see the protrusions and mounds scattered across the desert floor. See the bones of your current body stretched across the land, expressing themselves in forms that jut up from the dunes like hips and ribs. . . . You can see the smaller pieces that make up the spine as well as the spaces between the vertebrae. The finest bones, those from hands, feet, and inner ear, are the last to come into view. . . . As the form of your body comes into shape there is an opportunity to see the places that have been weakened or injured. . . . [*Pause.*]

An abundance of nutrients appears scattered across the desert, many of which are useful to strengthen the weaker parts of your skeletal system. . . . The various minerals are spread out around the skeleton like a puzzle. You find pieces that fit in all the places where you've had injuries, breaks, inflammation, or degeneration. From skull to toes, you carefully rebuild your skeleton, including the adjoining related anatomical systems of your own body, piece by piece. . . . [*Long pause.*]

As you reconstruct your skeletal system in this way you also discover the associated places in the planetary body and comprehend that you are simultaneously fortifying Earth's skeletal body as well. Be open to a sense of wonder as the new form replaces the old, as what looks like it was left behind for thousands of years is actually being gathered and repurposed into a new body. . . . [*Pause.*]

Now telescope your vision a great deal more. . . . When you look through the magnifying glass at the end of the ankh, everything comes into perspective as you see your re-forming skeletal system in the belly of the goddess. . . . Your understanding becomes clearer as you reconstruct the skeleton in accordance with the way you and Sekhmet put your puzzle together. . . . Remember, you are not the only one who is creating here. You are in the body of Sekhmet, and she is paying close attention, so do not fear and, as always, be willing to ask for help when needed.

This is a good time to breathe the Belly Breath, drawing the powers of Earth and Sky into the cauldron that is your belly, holding your breath while it mixes with the love you are adding into the mix, and exhaling it into the regenerated anatomy of your skeletal system. . . . Notice how the repaired bones and associated parts solidify into their new and invigorated structure. Calcification run amok can become arthritis; now is the time to exert control—lay the joints perfectly smooth. . . [*Pause.*]

Even as you see the skeletal system strengthened and fortified in those areas that needed attention, it is essential to honor the fact that the bones will become the dust of the desert someday. We patch, fix, and mend, gathering the bones, including the minerals of the multitudes of sea creatures from the bottom of the ancient sea or lakebed, which over millennia shaped this desert.

As new bones are reconstructed from this ancient material, the newly formed molecules can be more complex, resilient, and new to this Earth. So it is from bones to bones and back to bones again; and so it is recycled. . . . Each time new bones are reconfigured from ancient materials, the newly formed molecules can be more complex and new to this Earth. You focus on this body because it is what you know, and yet someday your bones will be the minerals of the land formation that some other being will walk by. That's just the way of it, and your bones will be stronger with this knowledge.

Be sure to thank Sekhmet and all the creatures whose shells and bones have given you this gift of regeneration. . . . It is a good time to add a prayer for the waters of the world, that they may be distributed in a balanced way so that life can continue to flourish for all beings with whom we share this sacred planet. Take some time to fill in your journal, taking care to remember any details that you might have missed in the past few entries.

## SHARED VOICES

*I was in the desert with Sekhmet. I was walking along next to her and at the same time being carried within her. We stopped and sat awhile just looking at the desert. It is strange, but I did not feel the heat of it or any discomfort . . . probably because Sekhmet was holding me inside her.*

*We went to look at the formations. They were quite beautiful. I used my lens from Ptah; it was working like a pair of glasses. When I looked again at the same formation while wearing my glasses, the formation became alive—like an aquarium. It was full of water, and in the water were all kinds of sea creatures—fish, crabs, whales, sharks, creatures huge and very small. There was even a mermaid. All were swimming in this ancient sea, now a stone formation in a desert. I had a sense of vast time.*

*I saw my own bones laid out in large scale. I noticed my tailbone where I had broken it while cross-country skiing, and all the memories of that day came back to me—the day of being in the mountains in Wyoming, the deep snow, my skis, how cold it was, my then husband with me. And I had so many memories of being married and being happy. I wanted to patch up the break in my tailbone. I didn't know how to do it so Sekhmet urinated into the sand and told me to make a paste. Even her urine was full of ancient sea creatures, and I knew we were all being recycled over and over. I did not reexperience any pain. It was just a very vivid memory of what happened. I patched the tailbone and wonder if by patching these bones I am repairing other broken parts of that relationship and of me and my husband.*

*Then I moved on to my neck bones lying on the desert floor. My cervical bones were damaged from a motorcycle wreck, and I could see that damage in the desert bones. They were black and crumbly where the damage occurred. Again just by looking at those bones I remembered vividly the wreck . . . and I realized the bones hold all our memories in them. Sekhmet had me go to a place where the desert formations looked like an arch and they created a little shade. In that shade was a small pool of water—brackish, not drinkable—but perfect to use to mix with the sand and create a cast for the bones to help them fill out from degenerative arthritis and a loss of the cervical curve. I was aware of all the former life that made the sand—water creatures, camels, humans, plants, all kinds of life was compacted into the sand and now into the cast for my bones. While I was applying the cast I could sense that energy moving in to help reform and shape them and give me more support. . . .*

*Then Sekhmet and I just hung out in the desert resting and watching. She licked her leg and paw and as she did I could see through her fur and skin to her bones and see they were full of all the same sea creatures and, I knew, of her own memories as well, although I did not know what those memories were. . . .*

*Healing goes forward and backward in time, and this desert was clearly showing me that time is what we have a lot of—more than we realize, because our bones keep on going after the rest of us is dead and this keeps our memories a part of the Earth and Gaia forever.*

*I am joyful and grateful!*

KATHRYN RAVENWOOD

*The more I contemplate the White Desert, the more it evolves into a better metaphor for me and the becoming of me.*

*Where do I start? In the beginning, of course. The Big Bang.*

*Time didn't exist—and then it became an integral part, along with matter, of a universe that has been evolving until this moment. The element calcium didn't exist for the first many millions of years until the stars were formed and then died in spectacular events called novas. Let me reiterate: It took more than a humble death of a star back when the existing menu of molecules was shorter and less complex than today. It took a crucible (albeit short-lived) to make calcium. Eventually, when enough material gathered, including calcium, to create the stars and planets, moons and asteroids, and everything else a galaxy needs to come into existence, our Milky Way was formed. And then Earth was formed, and it included many of the new and complex molecules that are required to form and sustain the living beings that preceded us during the long march that brings us into this moment.*

*That brings me back to the White Desert and the history of it.*

*Life: A shallow sea will support a greater variety of life than a forest, and the longer said sea is in existence, the more evidence of that abundance will accumulate. A creature's soft tissue can leave an imprint in the muck, but those perfect conditions are rare compared to limestone deposits that can show the entire animal after the soft stuff is gone. And that's what the White Desert is made of. (Note: A "shallow sea" averages 200 meters deep, and fossils don't form when the depth is more than 300 meters. Sixty-five million years ago dates the shallow sea that became the White Desert, but the time leading up to, and coming from, that moment was great, and the limestone is deep.) Whether it swam, crawled, burrowed, or just sat there like coral, each living organism practiced a form of alchemy that turned calcium into another form of itself, mostly calcium carbonate. In addition, each of those organisms left behind a message for us, most of which still exist today. For example: The time it took for a vibrant, shallow sea to become a great deposit of bone, shale, coral, and more is me, now, as I percolate from soup to the bones and teeth needed at the end of this process. And, the alchemy that transformed liquid into hard structure, perfectly formed and engineered to do its job supporting me when I walk again in my new body, is evident in the crafted and sculpted forms found throughout this desert. As in the desert, something greater than a man has shown its hand during the formation of my wonderfully engineered skeleton.*

*And, finally, I see the similarity of keeping and placing that which is needed and finding ways of discarding that which is not.*

MARK HALLERT

# 15

# Reconstructing the
# Network of Body Systems

Three of the most important systems in our body that have a hard time dealing with the stress, the toxicity, and the chaos of life are the heart/circulatory system, the endocrine network, and especially the nervous system, all of which are interconnected. In the next empowerment, as we continue to reconstruct our physical body, we will devote our attention to the psycho-neuroendocrine-immune, or psychoneuroendocrine, networks, hereafter called PNI. My understanding of this view of how our body systems work together as a network comes from deep discussions with my naturopathic physician, Dr. Mitch Bebel Stargrove. He gave me some good book references, which you will find in the footnote below.* We all need the strengthening of these systems as we go forward, which is accomplished by direct transmissions from Sekhmet. As the feminine face of the sun, Sekhmet can shine her light—her power, her sekhem—into our bodies, particularly while we are inside of her, but also when we are not inside her belly.

Now that your skeletal system has been strengthened, Sekhmet is ready to assist you with the regeneration of other systems within your

---

*Craig Holdrege, ed., *The Dynamic Heart and Circulation;* Richard Grossinger, *Embryogenesis: Species, Gender, and Identity.* See also the work of the late Candace Pert, *Molecules of Emotion: The Science behind Mind-Body.*

body. We are going to start with the heart, and then you are going to receive direct transmissions from Sekhmet during which she will assist you in restoring coherent activity, the self-healing intelligence of some of your other major body functions, in particular the three coordinating glands in the brain: the pineal, the pituitary, and the hypothalamus.

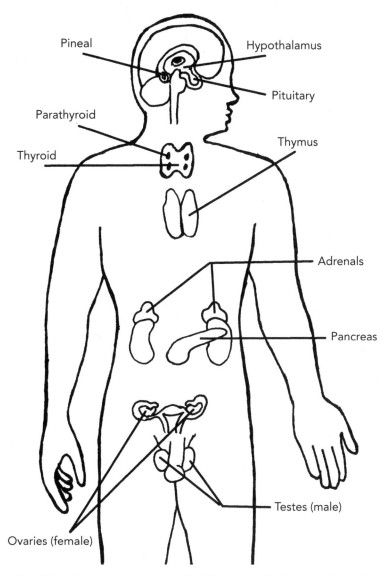

*Fig. 15.1. The endocrine network (Illustration by Debbie Clarkin)*

The PNI network is a non-hierarchical coordination and feedback system guided by the pituitary gland, which signals all of the other glands in the endocrine network and the hormones they secrete. Among its many activities, the pineal gland secretes melatonin, a substance with antioxidant properties, which induces the creative dream state, and, as a nutrient, can help some people with jet lag and some sleep disorders. The hypothalamus coordinates the autonomic nervous system functions. These include the things we don't have to think about as we go about our lives, such as our circadian rhythms, breathing, heartbeat, the cycles of eating when we are hungry, how our blood circulates, and how our temperature is controlled. These are all autonomic functions of the PNI network, which connects the circulatory system, heart, nervous system, brain, and spine. They are all ruled by the reptilian brain, which operates our primary response patterns.

During this journey, you will be asked to focus on numerous concepts simultaneously. This can take time and repetition as you become proficient with the practice and are subsequently able to receive as much as possible for your new body and all of the coordinated systems within it. Please look at color plate 21 before starting this journey.

## ☀ SEKHMET'S TRANSMISSION TO RESTORE YOUR BODY SYSTEMS

[*This is a long journey, so give yourself plenty of time to take it all in and do the work while the transmission from Sekhmet is happening. Throughout the journey it is important to maintain attention on the heart and to continue to breathe the Heart Breath. . . .*]

### ◉ Restoring Your Heart and Circulatory System

Begin by focusing on your heart. . . . Expand your focus to include the Heart Breath, noticing how the breath pulls in everything associated with Earth and Sky and how your attention expands as you recognize these gifts as they flow into you. From Earth there are minerals, magnetism, elements, and the forces of the core entering from below. From above, at the same time, comes a flood of intelligence, energies, and stardust from the eons that contain the entire history of our universe. . . . [*Pause.*]

Acknowledge all the allies that are here to witness and lend their assistance and the new ones that respond to your light and are coming to add their support. . . . Invite any new supportive beings that come into your mind, and greet them.

Continue breathing the Heart Breath. . . . The magnitude of this gift grows with time and attention. Every exhalation of this Heart Breath contains a record—similar to an echo—of all you have received and all the love you have added. This reciprocation radiates out in every direction and the in- and out-flow of the breath creates a resonance with each cell and molecule in your body. . . .

The heart is the first clear definition that is formed within the new body. Look up and out toward the desert. In the distance you will see Sekhmet riding in swiftly on her chariot of cobras. She arrives at the altars, both within her chapel at Karnak and the one you are using in our ordinary reality, dismounts her chariot, and looks at you with great depth and focus. . . . As she looks you in the eyes and you look back into her eyes, you see that her pupils are golden. They are shaped like the center of the vesica piscis, upright portals of pure sunshine. As her pupils dilate, you begin to feel the rays of her sunshine. . . . You feel it in your eyes, you feel it in your third eye, but mostly you feel it enter right in the midpoint between your brows; the laserlike beam goes straight to your pineal gland. As you are receiving this golden light transmission from Sekhmet, take in whatever message that she has for you at this time. . . . [*Pause.*]

Now Sekhmet turns her attention to your heart. Once again, you gaze into each other's eyes, and she speaks to you for a moment about your heart and how important it is to learn to see through your heart and the filter of the intelligence of your heart. . . . [*Pause.*] It is important for you to keep a strong connection between your heart and your vision as well as between your heart and your brain. Your personal free will is a precious gift; when your will is expressed through and from your heart, life for you and those around you becomes rich and rewarding. As the light reaches the cavern of your heart, your heart center fills with light, and the light begins to penetrate the pulsing rhythm of the entire organ. . . . [*Pause.*] Sekhmet's transmission continues. . . .

Once the heart is filled and has received its message directly from the goddess, the light begins to move through your circulatory system, out to your lungs and back to your heart, before it goes out through the arteries and all around your body. From your unique vantage point within the belly of the goddess, you can perceive the heart and the entire circulatory system with new eyes, particularly when you engage your magnifying lens. . . . Notice how the heart is a rhythm maker, like a drum that regulates the inherent momentum of the blood that pulses through the network of arteries, veins, and capillaries. You can perceive the vitality of the blood; it is vital, alive, and has, as part of its character, motion and rhythm. The heart functions as a guide like any good leader. . . . [*Pause.*]

Follow the course of the light with your mind, focused throughout every part of your body—all the way out to your fingertips, down to your toes, into and through all your organs and viscera, allowing yourself to receive the healing everywhere it touches. It may feel as though you are taking years off your life even while it is happening. . . . [*Long pause.*]

Open yourself to the ray of Sekhmet's light as it shines through to the arteries and veins and cleanses the platelets, the red blood cells, and the white blood cells, focusing on the cholesterol, oxygen, hormones, nutrients, stem cells, and everything else that's carried in your blood until it finally returns to your heart. . . . [*Pause.*] Notice how the electromagnetic field that now surrounds and generates outward from your heart has grown and radiates farther and farther out from your heart with each beat. . . . [*Pause.*]

Pay particular attention as the blood moves through all the blood vessels around your eyes and any places of weakness. Once you have circulated through your entire body, continue your eye-to-eye connection with Sekhmet. At this time, shift to alternating between your Heart Breath and your Belly Breath to give back to her. . . . Your reciprocation intensifies all that you are receiving. It also intensifies the connection between your heart and your solar plexus, and also your heart and your eyes. These connections strengthen your personal will and power and your identity; they help you to see, hear, and feel more fully from your heart. . . . [*Pause.*]

Notice how the blood circulates between your heart and circulatory system and Sekhmet's. Your blood is rhythmically resonant, strengthening the bond that has grown between you and is nourishing you both in the process. . . . [*Pause.*]

Again it's time for a journal break. Notice how it is useful to go in and out of the various states of consciousness that you are learning to perceive. The more you move back and forth, the more you learn to be in two or more dimensions simultaneously.

## Restoring Your Psychoneuroendocrine Network

Once again return to the Heart Breath. . . . Feel Sekhmet's transmission in your eyes and into your third eye, but mostly notice how it feels in the ray that goes directly to the pineal gland. . . . [*Pause.*] Sekhmet reaches in and places a glowing crystal pinecone so that it encompasses the three organizing glands that are part of the endocrine network: the pineal, the pituitary, and the hypothalamus. . . .

Gradually the light begins to spread. . . . It illuminates the pathways that connect the pineal and pituitary to every cell in your body, as this pure liquid gold light flows through channels already in the template of your developing body, through your entire endocrine network, pausing at each gland and filling it with light. . . . [*Pause.*]

As you feel more deeply into your experience of the illumination of the PNI network, notice the electromagnetic field of intercommunication that connects all aspects of this complex and important system. . . .

Notice that this pure sunshine from the feminine face of the sun carries intelligence beyond our imagining. Consequently, each gland is given new instructions, energy, and balance, along with whatever healing is needed in the moment. The light moves quickly, as the appropriate information is being given to all the glands simultaneously. . . . [*Pause.*]

## ◉ Restoring
### Your Nervous System

Sekhmet shifts her focus; now she brings her attention to the base of your brain at the medulla oblongata, the lowest part of the brain stem. There her fierce compassionate sunlight softens as she touches the hypothalamus, just above the brain stem. . . . It is through the pituitary that the hypothalamus connects the endocrine network's glands to one another. Sekhmet's soft, warm liquid sunlight activates and nourishes stem cells that will create new neurons that will develop synapses connecting them to networks of communication. . . . [*Pause.*]

Her light continues to move down from your brain stem into and through the inside of your spinal column. Take a moment to feel the light fill your third chakra and your solar plexus, revitalizing your personal power. . . . [*Pause.*] As the life force flows downward, it radiates outward through the vertebral foramina, the side openings between vertebrae, into major branches of your nervous system extending to every single nerve throughout your body. . . . [*Pause.*]

Sekhmet takes a deep breath and, as she exhales, her soft, healing light again moves through your body in every direction, down to the tip of your spine, out to the sides from between the vertebrae, and down through your limbs to your feet and toes. . . . It flows out from the thoracic spine and down through your arms to your fingertips, gently nourishing every part of your nervous system. . . . Wherever it comes to a place where the nerves have been pressed upon, cut, or broken, she includes stem cells with her intention to help create new neurons that will develop new neural pathways. Her light is also imbued with natural medicines that help reconnect the neurons; wherever implants have been inserted, such as new body parts, electrodes, plates, artificial knees or hips, they renew and rewire the nervous system, creating new pathways that circumvent the injured or missing ones. . . . [*Pause.*]

As your neural pathways grow and flow, take a moment to simply allow yourself to feel your nervous system as it relaxes and communicates smoothly and clearly. . . . If you happen to have any metal parts in your body, you might experience a field of sensation around any area associated with pain. As your nervous system fills with this soft liquid light, and interconnects and communicates with the rest of your PNI network, you may notice a lessening of any sense of distress as well as the reorganizing or rerouting of the nerves themselves. . . . Notice the calming and quieting effect that happens with the relaxation and the infusion of light. . . . [*Pause.*]

Offer your deepest gratitude to Sekhmet, then take a deep Heart Breath, offering it to her as she breaks the connection and steps away from you. . . . Feel the imprint of her eyes on your own. Once you have taken her transmission inside of you, you can use these eyes, these golden rays of sunshine in your new, redeveloping human body to heal others as well. Offer lavish gratitude to Sekhmet for this deep and potent healing transmission. . . . When you feel complete, it will be time for another longer break to write in your journal and to integrate the work of reconstruction and renewal with which you are currently engaged. . . . [*Long pause.*]

### SHARED VOICES

*I've been feeling peaceful and very grounded and happy since I entered Sekhmet's belly. Her lioness face just popped out at me from the shining circle on the little speaker on my desk. All this is magical and has transpired.*

*What is mind blowing for me and almost unbelievable is when we received new glands and you concentrated on the pituitary, hypothalamus, and pineal, you said that all our glands would be transformed and renewed. I could feel pain in my shrunken thyroid gland. I have had Hashimoto's disease since my early forties. It is an autoimmune disease that causes inflammation of the thyroid gland. I have been on synthroid for more than thirty years. Many times I've tried going off my medication, but if I miss one, I have no energy or am very weak.*

*We did the transformation on Thursday night. I found it phenomenal, but I was on overload and had to close my telephone after 10:30 p.m. and go right into bed. I felt out of it most of Friday. It was as if my brain was adjusting and all the wires were trying to get aligned and into balance. I went to tennis without my racket, tennis shoes, and hat. I never played. I was being rewired all day and had difficulty thinking clearly.*

*I woke up this morning and I knew that I had been TRANSFORMED! I was fully in my body and connected in both realms at the same time and totally happy. I finally wrote a review for a friend that was very long overdue. I was getting things accomplished like doing my homework for you. AND I DID NOT TAKE MY SYNTHROID PILL this a.m. I feel fabulous. I'm writing to you at 10:30 p.m. on Saturday full of energy, joy, love, and light.*

*P.S. It's Sunday at 11:30 p.m., and I did not take a synthroid today either and still raring to go.*

*PPS: October 18: I do believe in miracles. I actually felt this one happening. It is not just my thyroid gland. I have been off my synthroid for eleven days now. I have a requisition for a blood test. . . . My brain is more alive and alert. I'm getting more things accomplished. Not running* around myself as usual. There is also an improvement in my gallbladder, which has not been good for too long a time. It too is happy and healthy now.

Thank you, Nicki, for the NEW ME and for the gift of being able to let go, heal myself, and cross between both worlds and be there at the same time.

Thank you for being you and sharing your gifts.

BLESSINGS,
TRISH BLOCK

# 16

## Reconstructing the Brain

Kom Ombo is the only Egyptian temple that can be seen today that is known to be dedicated to two neteru triads, each with a primary god, Horus the Elder and Sobek, the crocodile god. The triads are: Sobek, Hathor, and their son, Khonsu; and Horus the Elder, Tasenetnofret (a form of Hathor), and their child, Horus, Lord of the Two Lands (Panebtawy). The temple at Kom Ombo is also famed for its walls that portray images of tools for surgery and was a place where pilgrims flocked to receive healing (see color plate 22).

Horus and Sobek, the two primary gods, could not be more opposite (see color plate 23). Horus the Elder in most mythological versions is the son of Nut and Geb and never fully incarnated, preferring to range the sky from horizon to horizon to be closer to his mother. His attributes include spirit and intellect. Sobek is an ancient fertility god said to be one of the lovers of Hathor, as is Horus. The seat of power for Sobek is the hypothalamus gland,* which is responsible for creating hormones that direct the autonomic functions of the body. It regulates the body systems that we tend to take for granted. Those include breathing, keeping the heart beating, the instinctual knowledge of when to eat, and all the things that keep us going that we don't have to think about. As we experienced in the previous chapter, these functions of the reptilian brain are vital to our

---

*Nicki Scully, *Power Animal Meditations,* 115.

*Fig. 16.1. Khonsu, the moon god, and Sobek, the crocodile god, at Kom Ombo Temple (Photo by Tarek Lotfy)*

survival. This ancient god is closely associated with the Earth and instinct.

The crocodilian species are so very ancient that they haven't changed or evolved in any great way since they crawled out of the sea as reptiles. We still have this ancient ancestor within us, and we can learn much from him. Because he was a dangerous menace living in the waters of the Nile, he was propitiated and honored as the powerful and often deadly being that he is; he was also seen as having the power to protect the people of Egypt.

Horus, the hawk, on the other hand, evolved when some of these dinosaurs learned how to fly and took to the sky. Horus, as the ruler that is personified by every pharaoh, represents the potential of higher intelligence that comes with the evolution of our neocortex, some 200,000 years ago. He is the embodied, integrated, and self-aware human—individuated consciousness or *Homo veritas,* the "true human" who has connected the three worlds (Heaven, human, and Earth) and is capable of achieving the potential of the fully realized human. Since then, our still developing self-aware minds have vastly increased our ability to communicate and express consciousness. We are only now discovering the enormous potential that the plasticity of the brain offers us, and we have yet to fully understand, let alone utilize, the vast potential within it.

Every pharaoh, starting with the early dynastic period, is called Horus, for once the young Horus mastered Set, after the lengthy battle to avenge the death of his father, Osiris, he became the new ruler. He had developed the wisdom to become an enlightened ruler such as his father had been. In pre-dynastic Egypt, what we now think of as pharaohs were called kings, and their retinues were called the *shem su Hor,* or "followers of Horus."*

When you study the Egyptian mysteries and learn about the development of Horus from his divine conception through his youth

---

*For one of the most masterful translations of the myth of Isis and Osiris, I again direct you to *Feasts of Light,* by Normandi Ellis.

*Fig 16.2. Horus the Elder with Tasenetnofret*
*(an aspect of Hathor) at Kom Ombo Temple*
*(Photo by Jacob Cohl)*

and impetuous warrior stages, and finally into the enlightened ruler that he becomes, you discover that his, like your own, is the hero's journey.

Kom Ombo is a good place to do shadow work—work that seeks to solve inner conflict. To help activate resolution, Sekhmet again shows up in her chariot made up of three powerful cobras that represent kundalini energy. You realize by now that you have given yourself to Sekhmet. She has consumed you and separated out what has been outworn and is no longer functional for you. She has strengthened herself with every useful part of your being and has brought great healing as she renewed your body and the incumbent emotions, feelings, and spiritual insights that come with each of those portions of the transformation.

With the following journey, as you realign the parts of your brain that have gone askew in one way or another, you will transmute unconscious reactive patterns and obsolete habits that, in some cases, predate your very birth. In cooperation with the magic of the mystery, you can now add new coding to your DNA, which will make you smarter and more capable of finding solutions to the vast array of choices that we face as individuals, in communities, and on the planet. The first layer of DNA reconstruction and repair started in the centrifuge when you first passed through the eye of the needle. It is the hope of this part of the process that you can regain your ability to reclaim responsibility as a steward of our precious world as you become aware of the great potential for new sensory capabilities within your brain and begin to use them to a higher and more effective advantage.

We are so much more than we think we are. It's important when you glance into the future that you are aware that the outlook contains many potentialities. You can become attached to what you perceive as reality rather than what is actually only one possible path of many. Some of the choices that you see may be truth, and some are more like a mirage. It could be a symbol to put you on a direction that will change the course of your life, or it may be your own informed intuition that could be wise council, which could only come to you now that you have been taken on this path.

This next journey includes bringing together the parts of the brain that in many of us have become somehow disconnected, confused, or whose thought processes are slowing down beyond the ordinary aging process. The brain is an incredibly complex organ, and new research is happening so fast that by the time this book is printed much more will be known and some longheld beliefs about it will have become outdated. Stay curious; keep up as our understanding of the brain continues to deepen and its potential expands with our understanding. Recent discoveries in neuroplasticity, the ability for the brain to create new neural pathways, even in adults, were unthinkable just a few decades ago, and there is still so much that we don't yet understand.

The brain is composed of three major parts, independent of one another, yet connected by countless neural pathways, allowing them to influence one another. As I mentioned earlier, the reptilian brain, associated with Sobek (one of the first deities sorted out in the earliest days of civilization along the Nile), is the oldest of the three parts of the brain. It controls the autonomic functions that we don't have to think about. It includes the main structures of the brain, the brain stem, and the cerebellum. The limbic brain, or midbrain, keeps track of our relations, experiences, memories, and emotions. It also influences our judgments and behavior. The limbic brain processes information and forms new memories. It helps us make decisions, such as distinguishing between right and wrong. The translation of smell into emotion is also a function of the limbic brain. For example, if you smell unexpected smoke, an emotion best described as alarm washes over you. When you are learning something new, the limbic system processes the information and then distributes it to the appropriate part of the brain. Just as the autonomic functions are controlled by the reptilian brain and identified with Sobek, the functions of the midbrain are associated with Thoth and the more sophisticated skill set that he brings to bear on the regulation of the limbic system. The neocortex came much later. It first appeared in the brains of primates and gave us the power to develop language, writing, and abstract thinking, each of which would also be considered part of Thoth's domain—or even to be gifts from Thoth. We have barely begun to utilize all of the functions, perspectives, and learning capabilities of the neocortex. It is also associated with Horus the Elder, who flies above time and space. His panoramic point of view and intelligence helps us to become self-aware human beings.

During the following journey you will be introduced to another goddess, Neith, considered by some to be the oldest goddess and one who has her own creation myth in which she reaches within herself and pulls out the whole of the universe. You can recognize Neith by her hieroglyph, a cobra, and/or the presence of one of her two symbols, two crossed arrows or a weaver's shuttle. Her symbol, the shuttle, appears on most of the cobra-goddess figures of the Nile Delta and is seen throughout Egypt, especially in the tombs, where she uplifts and protects the dead. Her name means "the Great Goddess," although she has many epithets. Pronounced *nt,* which means "n," for *net* or *neter,* with the "t" that makes it feminine, making it *netert,* or "goddess." A great female warrior, she strikes fear in her enemies and love and awe in those who call her mother, for she is the mother of every divine being, and she weaves the fates of all with her shuttle and loom as she casts her net across the universe. As the goddess Nut, she holds up the sun and other celestial bodies, creating the Milky Way, the river of light that divides the sky as the Nile divides Egypt.* I wonder if those dividing features of nature are similar to the medial longitudinal fissure that divides the two hemispheres of the brain, which Neith will be realigning in the next journey.

The Festival of Lights, one of the most important festivals in

---

*Normandi Ellis, *Feasts of Light,* 22–23 and 84–85.

ancient Egypt, was dedicated to Neith every autumnal equinox. People throughout the land lit candles and lamps in every corner of every building and upon the waters of the Nile in reverence to Her, reflecting the dazzling, star-studded belly of the goddess on the Earth below, uniting all with her light and love.* One year when the fall equinox came during our yearly Egyptian Mysteries retreat, we floated candles on our pond to mirror the glittering night sky in honor of Neith's reign in Heaven and on Earth. I hope you get the opportunity to do something like this wherever you are, to make a heartfelt connection with Neith as the candles burn.

*Fig. 16.3. Neith as she appears in the New Kingdom tomb of Ramses III
(Illustration by Karen Klein)*

*Normandi Ellis, *Feasts of Light*, 84–85.

#  BRAIN RECONSTRUCTION AND RECONCILIATION WITH HORUS AND SOBEK

*[Start with the Heart Breath, and be sure you are deeply connected when you start the journey. . . . In the light of the glow you create as you Heart Breathe, use your breath to invoke Horus and Sobek with the intention of reconciling the old with the new. . . .]*

At the temple of Kom Ombo, Sekhmet and Thoth are standing in the temple with Sobek and Horus. Thoth is holding an ornate silver tray. There are three jars on the tray, which he places on the altar. From one of the jars, Thoth takes the new limbic brain, your midbrain, and places it in the center of your head, where it wraps around the crystal pinecone that Sekhmet placed over the three central glands during the endocrine network activation. . . . You can feel the sensation of weight on the back of your head as it settles in. Thoth is doing some adjusting, making sure that it fits perfectly between the frontal lobe and the medulla oblongata, the reptilian brain. . . . He appears to be checking and fine-tuning the repurposed DNA. . . . He is working on the part of the brain that makes memories and registers emotions, adding the smart genes you requested. . . . [*Pause.*]

Sobek takes the reptilian brain out of the second jar and inserts it in the back of your head. It fits perfectly into the limbic brain that Thoth placed first, like a three-dimensional puzzle. . . . You can feel where your reptilian brain merges with the top of your spine at the base of your skull where it forms the spinal cord inside the vertebral column. This connection reaches down through your autonomic nervous system and touches all the associated parts of your body. Be as present as possible as you sort through the individual connections, although many connections happen simultaneously. . . [*Pause.*]

Horus now picks up his portion, the neocortex, from the remaining jar and wraps it around, covering the limbic and reptilian brains. . . . The

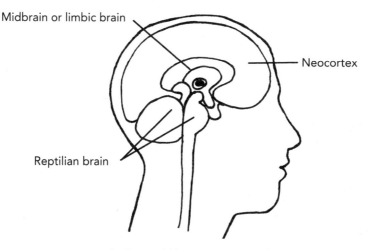

*Fig. 16.4. The brain (Illustration by Debbie Clarkin)*

neocortex includes the frontal lobe and the left and right hemispheres. Simply witness and feel (or see or know or experience in whatever way that works for you) as the connections are being made and the pieces put into place.... [*Pause.*]

## ◎ Restoring Right and Left Hemisphere Connections

Once the three main parts of the brain are received, the gift of the restructuring of the brain begins. Shift your breathing to include the Belly Breath, alternating Heart and Belly Breaths to help solidify the new parts of the brain as your physical body adjusts to them. This will also connect and balance the lower chakras with the higher chakras and the lower emotional and physical aspects of ourselves with our higher spiritual aspects... Simply witness and experience, and notice every nuance as the changes are shown to you.... It is very important to honor the old reptilian brain and how it helps us move through our days, fulfilling the functions that we don't have to think about, which allow for simple existence and survival... [*Pause.*]

Horus begins to look into the parts and folds of your new brain with a flashlight to show you the powerful potential connectors that until this point have lain dormant. . . . It is now time to awaken and ignite those connectors, including the stem cells that Sekhmet added to create new neurons, and rejuvenate those parts of the brain that have atrophied, or been underdeveloped, inactive, injured, or weakened for whatever reason. . . . [*Pause.*]

There comes a strong presence of the goddess Neith, the weaver. You can tell it is Neith because she wears a weaving shuttle on her head. She removes the shuttle to use it to weave the right and left hemispheres of the brain closer together to enhance communication between the two. . . . [*Pause.*]

When Horus and Sobek return to their positions and Neith commences weaving, a balancing of logic and creativity occurs as she reconnects the left and the right hemispheres, creating neural pathways between the two. This allows the two sides of our brain to communicate with each other more clearly. It also increases function. . . . It is the wiring of new, unprogrammed neurons that form new patterns. These are being created so that there's no more opposition between what we consider masculine and feminine, or intuitive and rational. There is a harmony in the new patterns as these new neural paths form. . . . Test your new cognitive abilities; try brain games and math.

Be sure to thank Thoth, Horus, Sobek, and Neith for their meticulous care in restructuring your brain. . . . As you write all the details of your experience in your journal, notice any changes or nuances in the way you communicate; this is the first opportunity you have to take your new brain for a spin. What has changed? . . .

## ◉ Restoring Clear Vision

Horus and Sobek, future and past, new and old, now face each other. . . . There is no conflict between them as Sobek reaches forward to Horus. Be present as a connection between the old and the new comes together in the midbrain.

Sobek (having made his connection with Horus) and Sekhmet each touch one of their eyes and then touch each of your eyes, open-

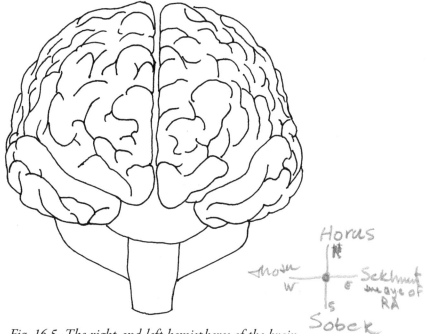

*Fig. 16.5. The right and left hemispheres of the brain*
*(Illustration by Debbie Clarkin)*

ing your left and right eyes. The left eye is associated with the moon and the lunar god, Thoth. The right eye is associated with the sun, and in this case the goddess Sekhmet. The right eye is also called "the eye of Horus" or "the eye of Ra." As they touch your eyes, a connection is formed between the visual and interpretive centers in the brain. You can feel it behind your eyes, on the bridge of your nose, at the back of the throat, and into your ears. All of these are connected through the tear ducts and the Eustachian tubes. Also connected to the brain are the ocular vision, the olfactory sense of smell, and the auricular, or hearing, system.

Once more turn your attention back to Sekhmet before you. She looks into your eyes and notices that some adjustments are needed. Carefully she reaches through until she finds the occipital nerve bundles and brings them forward and connects them to the receptors at the back of each eye. As this is completed, and you look into and through her eyes, your eyes and her eyes line up. Your vision changes as you look through Sekhmet's eyes. It is as though you are looking though the wide-angle lens of a high-quality camera or telescope. Her night vision is many times sharper than ours, and the colors, shapes, and focus are truer. As you look through her eyes, you see yourself. There may be many faces superimposed over your face, but one image is glowing. It is your true self. As you see your true self, you feel the unconditional love that Sekhmet has for you. You also feel a brightening happening in your solar plexus, your radiant nexus of power.

As the connection that has been made between your eyes, your heart, and your solar plexus is further strengthened, the foundation for the fierce power of Sekhmet within this inner circuit at your core is lit up within the mirroring of your true self. Take a few moments to allow your vision to adjust. When you separate your eyes from Sekhmet's, you experience a new clarity and depth of physical and subtle visual perception. . . . [*Pause.*]

### ◉ Restoring
### Brain System Connections

Horus, Sobek, and Thoth come together, almost as though they are nose to beak, joining the three parts of your brain. There is a spark that issues forth when the parts touch, and it ignites the new patterning formed in your midbrain. As they come together, all three parts—the limbic, the reptilian, and the neocortex—ignite in a flash that allows you to see that they are now all firing, creating a new sequential rhythm in accordance with the new patterns that have been created. It may feel like flashes of light or fireworks in your brain as new synapses and neurons awaken. You begin to feel an electric pulse from the ground beneath your feet. It moves up through your heels to the back of your body and up your spine. The electric pulse now moves in waves from the back to the frontal lobe of the brain, further sparking and igniting those connectors initially shown by Horus. As they ignite, they glow brightly with activity. . . . [*Pause.*]

The upward movement of energy from the base of the brain through the reptilian brain is important, as it enables us to draw upon the ability of the ancient wisdom to project into the new, higher wisdom and consciousness offered to us through evolution. All of this activity can be seen as you observe the activation. The reptilian brain has been energized and is sending messages throughout your body. The midbrain is making you more aware of what is going on around you, and your ability to describe it to yourself and others is sharp, agile, and fun! The perfect words come quickly, and your eyes and ears have become brighter and clearer. There is one other sense that has improved and it is amazing! Start exploring your surroundings with your nose. Smell the heat of the desert and then try some flowers. There is a pulsing coming from the neocortex as your connection to higher consciousness is fortified, alternating and moving left to right and right to left. There is also a connection with the neocortex as information is sent back and forth between the three main brain systems. The pinecone in the center is glowing. If you have brain injuries, now is the time to focus on where those injuries exist so that you can help to create new neural pathways and observe the healing that takes place as the new patterns solidify.

Now apply what you have gained to the reconciliation of self. Meet that head on, honoring who you are becoming. Pay homage to whatever you are finding within yourself. Draw upon the energy between Sobek and Horus, with you as Sekhmet coming forward to be the arbiter of reconciliation. By now, you are the fiercely compassionate activator of transformation.

Although you are still within Sekhmet, you are your own person. You are Sekhmet, riding the chariot, in full control of the cobras and the powerful energy that they represent. Like the mighty god or goddess awakening in you, you face all doubt and inner conflict with forgiveness, compassion, and discrimination, leaving no room for any continuing battle. All conflict dissolves in forgiveness and the love that you feel and generate.

## ◉ Restoring Your Connection to the Source

Horus in his hawk form picks you up in his talons and carries you up higher and higher until you transfigure into him. The feathers on your back are being ruffled from the astral realm of the ancestors in the stars. You are being held by the earthly winds that come up from beneath you. When you reach the altitude where you can see the curve of the Earth, you can perceive where each part of your forebrain that has been ignited has direct access to Source above.

Using newly awakened senses may be difficult to articulate, as they may be different from anything in your past experience. It is as if you were to see a color you had never seen before, or to hear a sound not of this world. Go ahead and fly with Horus, in him or as his companion, and look to the future. Soar above the cycles of day and night, of the seasons, of life and death, your eternal self beyond time, yet able to swoop back into time. . . . [*Long pause.*]

You are still connected to the Earth, suspended between Earth and the cosmos, spirit and matter. Anything is possible. You see what could be rather than what is. You can always wind up making a choice that has a different consequence or outcome. There are no mistakes, only opportunities. This is an opportunity to see the potential for yourself, for your community, and for the world.

Mut (the mother, protector, and alchemist) and the Elder Horus have called you; from your new vantage point in the sky above, as you look down, you can see yourself and you can see the bigger picture, including the connections between you and other people, and between the neteru. You can also see into the future as well as the past. The intelligence about what is happening in present time is coming from the mid- and limbic brains of your physical body, and the abilities to be aware in other dimensions including past and future time, and the wisdom of the higher consciousness of your higher self, conjoined with the universal mind, comes from above the horizon, hence the neocortex.

Mut says that when you temper the knowledge from the brain with the wisdom of the heart, that's where you find true wisdom. Offer gratitude to Horus and Sobek, Thoth, Neith, Mut, Horus the Elder, and any others who came together to assist in this adjustment of your brain. . . . [*Pause.*] Make a conscious prayer that you will use this new adjustment and knowledge to create the wisdom required to move forward with grace and ease.

Fly back to the temple at Kom Ombo and find yourself once again in the belly of Sekhmet. Take a few Belly Breaths to ground the experience of these transmissions and adjustments into your physical body. As Sekhmet saunters back to the sycamore tree in Karnak, you are no longer sloshing about within her—you can feel the weight and solidity of your newly reconstituted being. Write the details of your experience in your journal.

### SHARED VOICES

*I have been experiencing intense and powerful dreams. In the physical world I have been very emotional and seemed to have been faced with certain issues that have tested my old patterns. I have had fears that I thought I had eliminated reappear recently in my life (yes, more knots!). I feel Sekhmet's presence and courage in these situations and have found myself approaching them differently. I am experiencing such a roller coaster of emotions and change in such a short amount of time, and not in a negative way, but in a fully aware and conscious state of mind (if that makes sense!).*

*But the one experience I really want to share is the one that happened after we worked on the transformation through the body and the brain. This was by far the most powerful journey for me. As we worked through all of the systems, I felt every part, every cell, every gland, every nerve respond intensely. I had tiny points of sharp but quick pain hit certain areas of my body. My brain (not my head!)*

*tingled immensely, and I heard several times "pay attention" and "let go."*

*The day after I slept hard, had a ton of dreams, but can't seem to remember them even though I know they were very important. I woke up this morning and then went back into a very light sleep, not deep at all. And then almost immediately I felt like my brain (not my head!—not the outside!) was being massaged and worked on intensely but gently. I felt a presence next to me. I then felt as if my body was somewhat trying to astral project, my spirit leaving my body, but it was different, almost out of my control. There was a comforting tingling sensation, light vibrational feeling, as if my body was almost levitating off the bed. I felt my body arching as I reached into the comforting embrace of this experience. My head was still being worked on, pulsating sensation directly in my brain. I thought I was fully going to leave my body but I do not believe that was the intent. And then I was gently, quite in a loving and nurturing way, settled back fully into my body and consciousness. When I came fully to awareness, every inch of my body (from the inside), felt renewed and light. . . .*

DINA MARU

*Since the last class, I've noted the crystalline pinecone beaming. I've felt this with my heart (light) many times, but sometimes when I feel baffled, the cone illuminates my path with the feeling of a direction.*

*I felt past lives with injuries to my spine fall away with Thoth's work. It's strange, but I had very vivid memories of physical injuries from past lives. The emotion with Horus was intense. I felt the release of a great deal of trauma from my childhood.*

*(I watched my brother die for several years. He was institutionalized and lived for fifteen more years. But I saw his intelligence and physical coordination dwindle away from a genetic illness. I was four and he was six months old when it began.)*

*The exchanging of my dominant hand (left to right) combined with my parents' lives falling apart had merged as tissue and improperly connected synapses. This was changed and healed during the section on the neocortex and balancing of right and left brains.*

*It is interesting to note how my knots, which were mainly feelings, related to the emotional trauma, released during the class. (It made me see the importance of continuing to knot.)*

*Despite the tiredness, I love the class. I wish it would go on for months. Thank you so much. It's marvelous.*

BLESSINGS,
JULIA GRIFFIN

# 17

## Energizing the Meridians, Eyes, Ears, and Nose

Sekhmet has come to renew and reinvigorate the flow of life through your meridians. Meridians are pathways of qi (life activity) that flow within us, connecting all of the organs into a coherent, creative, and responsive living being, aligned and bright. As Sekhmet moves into the meridians and certain sensory organs, you will discover a personal connection with the Earth. Your personal meridian system will connect with Earth's corresponding network of subtle flows of life activity, the ley lines.

### ☼ JOURNEY TO ALIGN YOUR ENERGY WITH THE ENERGY OF THE EARTH

[*Begin by preparing for meditation and breathing the Heart Breath. . . . As you move into a deep and relaxing state, acknowledge and connect with Sekhmet and others who appear from the Egyptian pantheon and the spirit world. . . .*]

Once again you are under the sycamore tree in the belly of the goddess. Even though you are curled up in her belly, you are also standing before Sekhmet, who is carrying a painter's palette and holding very

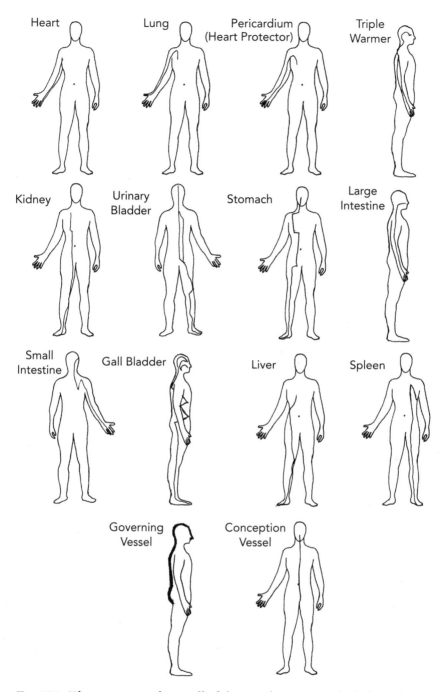

*Fig. 17.1. The energy meridians: all of the meridians run on both the right and left sides of the body with the exception of the Governing Vessel and Conception Vessel, which follow the center line of the body on the back and front.*

fine brushes. She examines you closely, going over all of the work you have already done together. . . .

She dips her finest brush onto her palette, drawing out liquid golden light. . . . Starting with the heart meridian, she begins to paint with soft golden light the various meridians that carry coherent activity between all of your organs. As each line is drawn on your skin, you can feel the qi, the living, coherent communication in motion as the robust channels course through your body like little rivers or streams that bring your many living systems into perfect balance and alignment. . . . [*Pause.*]

As these renewed meridian lines continue to vibrate through your body, front and back and on both sides, they create a continuous loop of qi. You can perceive this richly nuanced system with its wide spectrum of density as it cascades through the subtle bodies into manifest physicality along with the movement of Sekhmet's brush. . . . [*Pause.*]

## ◉ Renewing Your Hearing

By now, you are almost covered in radiant, golden sunshine light. . . . She looks into your ears. She has what looks like a tiny seashell, perfectly sculpted and balanced. . . . She places it in your ear canal behind the drum. It fits perfectly. As one is dropped into each ear, the nerves attach that will carry the signals of sound as it reverberates through the tiny new eardrum that Sekhmet places within the ear as well. . . . [*Pause.*] She whispers your name, and you hear it clearly. . . . Take the next few moments to use this new hearing to listen deeply to whatever sounds are around you, both inside and outside of Sekhmet's belly. Notice how clear and sharp they are with these new implements and how easy it is to hear with greater range than you are accustomed to. . . . [*Pause.*]

Offer your gratitude to Sekhmet and then take a moment to add key points to your journal. . . . [*Pause.*]

##  Renewing Your Senses of Smell and Taste

Sekhmet begins to sniff you with her great big muzzle and you can detect the tickle of her whiskers. As she breathes up into your nose, her breath activates the inside of your nose in such a way that you can feel it all the way up through all your sinus cavities. . . . It may feel as though there are a billion little Sekhmets traveling up through your nasal system, awakening in you her keen sense of smell. Notice as it connects with the olfactory nerve, which is innervated by her breath. . . . Your nose flares out and feels like a cat's muzzle, black and moist with whiskers. Pay attention to how the whiskers inform you. . . . What is different? Observe how your sense of taste is also increased through this activation. . . . Sniff, smell, and taste the air and catch whatever messages come in during this transmission. . . . [*Pause.*]

Give gratitude to Sekhmet for all the gifts that your olfactory and aural systems convey. . . . Now do some Belly Breaths to set this renewal into physicality, then ground and center yourself. . . . [*Pause.*] It's again time to take a break from your meditation while you fill in your journal with the details of your experience so far. . . . [*Long pause.*]

Some of you may discover that your nasal organ is a primary way of discerning energy for you. There are people that can literally smell cancer and death, as well as be informed of many subtle things. Odors, particularly the smoke from pure resins and certain plants when they are burned, or the scent of pure oils, or even certain foods, will bring back the memory of past events. Certain scents act as catalysts for memory, such as rosemary, juniper, or sage. Often in Egypt, or even in my home temple, I've noticed that when certain fine incense or oils are burned or heated, people will have flashbacks, even as far back as past lives in antiquity, and can remember specific rituals or other experiences.

Back to the meditation. . . .

## ⦿ Renewing Your Energetic Connection to the Earth

Next, bring your attention to the pads of your feet. Sekhmet gathers the ends of the meridians that reach down to your feet and twists them to create a rope. She then gives them three short shakes to further activate them and strengthen the flow of qi. She reaches down into the Earth with this rope, and each thread opens out and connects to a ley line (an invisible line that creates alignment between significant or sacred places of power) within the Earth. Feel your connection to the ley lines and how your consciousness can follow any pathway where these flow patterns move within the Earth. . . . [*Pause.*]

A ley line glows to attract your attention and you follow it. . . . You find yourself at the Sphinx, the Earth altar that keeps the Akashic Records of our planet and all the creatures that dwell upon her. It is time to update or refresh your personal record in the great hall of records. . . . Take a moment to feel the Sphinx absorbing the blueprint of your new body, mind, and spirit and the potential for the sacred purpose that you have been given. . . . [*Pause.*]

When this process feels complete, be sure to thank Sekhmet. Thank the Earth. Thank the Sphinx, and thank yourself. When you are ready, become aware of your body. Belly Breathe deeply and become grounded. Then write the details of your experience in your journal. . . .

Now that your inner meridians are connected to ley lines in the Earth, practice walking barefoot and focus on the meridians beneath the surface of Earth. You will be able, especially when you are out in nature, to follow the lines to different power places in the world. Sekhmet will teach you the work that goes with this activation. You will learn how you are informed and how you can communicate with people on the other side of the Earth. You will also be able to use medicines and minerals from faraway places. Whatever you need

*Fig. 17.2. The Great Sphinx guardian of the Giza Necropolis
(Photo by Nicki Scully)*

to support the work that you are doing will become accessible. The more you work with your meridians and the Earth's ley lines, and the more harmonious those connections feel, the more aware you will become. As more and more connections become apparent, additional teachings will come.

### SHARED VOICES

*In the summer of 2015, I was assisting Nicki with the Transformation in the Belly of the Goddess retreat in Eugene. While we were on a short break, she had asked me to find her notes from a previous version of the class for an empowerment based on the body's meridians.*

*I found the notes easily enough, but it took me awhile to open them in the new, updated program. After several attempts, I finally got them to open and print, and I was quickly reading them and preparing to go back to class. It didn't feel right; the notes were a little disorganized and some of the information was wrong. I was getting a little panicked; I was due back in class, and I was to lead the participants on this journey. I didn't know what I was going to do.*

*That was when I very clearly heard, "You don't need these notes. I will lead you through it." I trusted Sekhmet implicitly. I took a deep Heart Breath to ground and center myself and headed back to the temple where the retreat was being held. As I was walking, Sekhmet appeared before me in her beautiful goddess form holding a painter's palette with gold paint on it. I shifted my consciousness so that I was in both worlds again, and this amazing journey began.*

*Using a very fine brush Sekhmet began painting the meridians on my body with the gold paint, each line glowing and shimmering with light. With each brush stroke, I could feel the energy moving along the meridians clearing blockages and opening the pathways. I stayed in this altered, fully energized state as I returned to the class.*

*After a brief introduction to the meridians, Sekhmet and I began to lead the class on this new journey. As I described what she was doing she painted the meridians with her gold paint. It was incredible to watch each person begin to glow as the energy moved through their meridians. When she finished painting the lines on us she gathered threads from each glowing line and brought them down into the Earth, connecting them to the ley lines beneath us.*

*I saw that the ley lines of the Earth are the same as the meridians in our bodies. Each carrying the energy through and around us, balancing the flow and bringing it to where it is needed. Each line was dependent on the others to feed and nourish the whole system. These radiant lines correspondingly connected me to the Earth and the Earth to the universe and to creation. By bringing my attention to a specific place I was able use the pathways to travel there, and I could feel the energy of the ley lines to receive information.*

*Even now, just by focusing on the golden lines that Sekhmet painted on my body, I can feel the energy flowing along them, clearing the pathways and nourishing my entire being. I can also feel the connections to the ley lines beneath my feet whereever I walk. When I am traveling, I no longer feel the need to connect and ground to the new location as I am already linked to the lines that run through it.*

*I hope that when you do the amazing work in this book Sekhmet will bring to you the love, strength, and joy that working with her has brought to me.*

MANY BLESSINGS, LOVE, AND LIGHT,
DEBBIE CLARKIN

*Discovering and exploring the Akashic Records is something I was introduced to in the mid 1980s. I have frequently returned since then, but you never forget the first time.*

*I am always learning—sometimes my lessons are pertinent and about the quest that brought me there, but sometimes the teachings are about me, the work I need to focus on, or sometimes it is about the Great Hall itself.*

*I wish I could say it is always open and easy to access, but it is not. Sometimes I can imagine it based on previous visits. At other times I feel gauzelike curtains interfering with my ability to negotiate my way or even read what has been placed before me. But then, when I have all but given up, it becomes clear and inspiring. It was on this journey, working with the Sphinx and Sekhmet, that I finally felt the ley lines. I have a lot of work to do—I need to map and compare with some traditional sources, but it sounds like fun to me, a lot like my first visit to the Akashic Records.*

MARK HALLERT

# 18
## Khnum's Temple at Elephantine

Khnum is the ram-headed creator god who fashions the bodies of all the creatures of this Earth on his potter's wheel. He is distinguished from the creator god Amun by his horns, which move outward like DNA spirals or waves on the river, whereas the horns of Amun circle around the sides of his head like the ones on the sphinxes at Karnak. Khnum's current main temple is located on Elephantine Island, a beautiful island surrounded by great boulders in the Nile River just above the first cataract (now hidden by the older dam), which was considered the source of the Nile by the ancient Egyptians. There is a lovely garden on this island and many layers upon layers of excavations that show temples built upon older temples and villages on top of one another. Of all the places I've been in Egypt, Elephantine Island most reveals the layered ages upon ages of history hidden beneath the sands throughout Egypt. As a fertility god, Khnum had many consorts. His temple at Elephantine is dedicated to the triad of Khnum, his wife, Satet (Satis), huntress, archer, and goddess of the Nile, and their daughter, Anuket. He also shares a temple at Esna with Neith, with whom he fathered Ra, and Heket, the ancient frog goddess of childbirth and magic. I have a strong personal connection with Khnum, whom I both respect and trust, as his skill has brought healing to

*Fig. 18.1. Khnum at Elephantine Island*
*(Photo by K. Indigo Rønlov)*

many people during our ceremonies at Elephantine and through journeys previously published in *Shamanic Mysteries of Egypt* and *The Union of Isis and Thoth.*

Toward the end of this journey to Khnum's temple, you will be introduced to Khepera, the scarab beetle god. Khepera represents an aspect of the sun, the morning sun that warms and nourishes without blistering. He is also a master of the cycles of life and a protector of Earth and the beings of Earth. He wraps his wings around Earth's atmosphere as a filter to keep out hard radiation and other space toxins from above. Small faience (glazed pottery) scarab beetles, usually associated with Khepera, were placed on specific parts of bodies during mummification for the protection of the deceased. These amulets became quite popular during the Middle Kingdom and continue to this day as talismans and for jewelry.

*Fig. 18.2. Khepera, the scarab beetle god*
*(Illustration by Kris Waldherr*
*from* The Anubis Oracle)

During this journey, you will be connected with your ka, which, as mentioned earlier, is each being's etheric double and connection to his or her ancestral spiritual line. When we are consciously connected to our spiritual ancestral line, we are constantly feeding and nourishing one another. It is a reciprocal arrangement. In ancient times, it was generally believed that only the pharaoh was consciously connected to his ka, and it was he who held the reins of the empire. At death, all regular people's kas returned to that of the pharaoh. Thus the pharaoh was the connector between Heaven and Earth for the whole of the empire's collectivity, acting as a wise seer, guide, and steward of the people and the land as a whole.

In this age of awakening, this redefining moment of renewed awareness, there are no more pharaohs, and the position of "charismatic leader" is no longer given without question. Rather, each of us must step up to the plate of full conscious awareness, which includes that of our ka. At this time in history each person is called to realize their full potential as a human in a harmonious dance with all life, and by so doing, each becomes as the pharaoh, connecting Heaven and Earth.

*Fig. 18.3. Ka image from statue at the Cairo Museum, with the hieroglyph of arms extended out from headless shoulders and raised ninety degrees at the elbows (Illustration by Debbie Clarkin)*

Don't be surprised when you meet your ka and discover that it is the opposite gender from the one with which you identify.

You are approaching the completion of your reconstruction, so be sure to give yourself plenty of time and space so that you will not be interrupted in this major initiatory meditation. This is also a long journey, with a number of powerful activations.

## ☀ JOURNEY TO COMPLETE THE CREATION OF YOUR NEW BODY

[*Prepare as you would for any journey, setting your space and breathing the Heart Breath. . . . Continue until you have full focus of yourself in the belly of the goddess in her lioness form, back in the shade of the sycamore tree.*]

Sekhmet, the lioness, enters her temple at Karnak and merges with her statue. You now experience the familiar schism as you are taken within the belly of the goddess to Elephantine Island, where you find yourself in Khnum's studio in the garden next to the temple of Khnum. . . . [*Pause.*] Continue Heart Breathing as you enter the temple. Offer your breath to Ptah, Sekhmet, Khnum, and Thoth. There are others there to witness and support this important rite, and they too need to be greeted with respect. . . . [*Pause.*]

Khnum and his ka body are sitting at his potter's wheel. Although you are still in the belly of Sekhmet, you experience yourself as though you are standing and facing them. There are two wheels next to each other, and it appears as though Khnum is preparing to work on both wheels simultaneously. Khnum will create your human vessel, and Khnum's spiritual ka body will create your ka body on the second wheel.

Ptah is on Khnum's right, and Sekhmet is on his left. Thoth is directly behind him, observing and recording everything that happens. Khnum looks at you and can see you, although you are still in the process of reconstruction. He can see you as you have been and as you will be when his work is done. He knows you completely. Offer him your next Heart Breath as you hold the intention for him to bring all his skill to this moment of creation. . . . [*Pause.*]

Khnum exudes confidence as he reaches down to take a ball of clay that has been specially prepared for you and places it in the center of the wheel that is directly in front of him. Although Sekhmet has consumed and incorporated most of the twine and knots that you had tied, she did save some special strands for this purpose and is now untying those remaining knots. As she unravels the knots, the twine transforms into filaments of gold that are being infused into the clump of clay at the center of the wheel.

Watch Khnum at his wheel as he looks at the clump of clay and at you. You are still within Sekhmet and yet also in Khnum's studio. Khnum invites you to step onto the wheel. . . . He then adjusts you so that you are at the precise center. Ptah begins whispering words that you cannot quite hear. These words, as your new hearing sharpens and you begin to understand what they are, merge with the threads of gold. These are the prayers and gratitude that you put into the knots of twine. . . . [*Pause.*]

Khnum begins to turn the wheel using the kick wheel; as it starts to turn, he dips his hands into water and drizzles it onto the clay. The clay comes into perfect center underneath his skilled hands. . . . The wheel begins to spin faster and faster, although you feel centered and quite at ease, watching the long fingers of his graceful, skillful hands as they begin to work the clay. . . . Both wheels are being spun simultaneously, and you are still unsure of whether you are experiencing the creation of your new physical self or your ka. Soon you realize that you are experiencing this act of creation from two places simultaneously. . . .

Khnum deftly starts shaping your body, beginning with your feet. . . . As your outer shell begins to take form, and the threads continue to weave into the clay, the material begins to glow with the golden light from the threads and the words of prayer and gratitude. The words that Ptah continues to speak into the threads are written on the outside of your skin along with this new, golden energy that is becoming your shell. Khnum works his way all the way up your body almost to the top of your head, where he leaves an opening at your crown. . . . [*Pause.*]

As your body is being completed you become aware of new capacities of the visionary, the shaman, the healer, or whatever it is that you are becoming. This does not necessarily come as a vision, but rather as an ancient memory of the visionary that you have always been and forgotten, or perhaps your visionary abilities have been strengthened through this alchemical process. . . . [*Pause.*] As the golden glowing clay surrounds you, you feel a sense of safety and confidence as your new potential self enters your new skin. The role you perceive as your sacred purpose becomes clearer. . . . [*Pause.*]

Thoth watches closely, witnessing, inspecting, and scribing with his stylus into the stone tile that he is holding. . . . The you on the wheel in front of Khnum is radiating as the golden energy of Sekhmet is infused into you. . . . The words from Ptah are translucent and glowing, written all over your skin in light. You might notice a very soft, gentle, yet cool tingle that is warm and light at the same time. . . . Khnum has almost completed your new body's skin, but he is still waiting for whatever fills the space at the top of your head.

Allow yourself to become aware of your personal and planetary vision for the future and your sacred purpose. . . . You can now begin to see how this work helps to weave together your dreams and their manifestations and how your new capacities for visioning and creating new ideas and solutions are assisting you to see the potential future that you wish to bring into your life. . . . [*Pause.*]

Ma'at appears, holding a single feather above your head. There's a palpable feeling as though someone is breathing into you. Sometimes it is Ma'at, and sometimes it is Sekhmet. Perhaps they are taking turns, as their mingled breath enters and moves down through your crown, filling your new vessel. Notice how you feel as you are held within Ma'at's sense of perfection in all things and how this brings balance into your body. With each breath you become more centered, accompanied by a growing sense of self-confidence and ability to trust that you can bring forth the sacred purpose that is growing inside you. . . . Your entire being expands with the breath as you come into perfect balance and harmony with yourself and with the world. . . . Allow yourself to feel more deeply the fullness of this embodiment so that you can express it back to the world, and so that you can be in the flow with the perfection of all things. . . . [*Pause.*]

As Ma'at now places her feather upon the top of your head, feel the tip of the quill at your crown. . . . Notice how you can now feel all the nuanced energies that the feather detects as they flow around you. This feather of truth not only conveys your new level of connection with Ma'at, but it is also a tool that you can use to comprehend the finest details in any situation, thus helping you make choices.

Anubis appears and advises you to focus on your heart. . . . Your heartbeat has been one with Sekhmet until this moment. Now you feel the separation, yet there remains a sense of togetherness and rhythmic harmony, a kind of syncopation between your hearts. . . . There is also an intense heart connection between you and Anubis. As you focus on your heart, it expands and fills to overflowing with unconditional love and joy, the joy that is the natural state of being when all is in perfect harmony. . . . The joy, accompanied with increased compassion, creates an intense heart connection with everything and everyone around you. It is this joy and compassion that you will express in the world to help create and maintain the balance and perfection of life and the human condition. You receive a glimpse of what that will look like as you move forward in your life. . . . [*Pause.*]

Khnum and his ka double continue the work that is being done to refashion your body and your ka body to make them strong and solid. . . .

Now turn and face your ka body. Hold your hands upward in the position of the ka (see fig. 18.3 on p. 181). Offer a Heart Breath to your ka. Feel it come from the depth of your being and enter into the depths of your ancestral lineage. Your ka responds, and you feel the energy return to you, entering your body through the palms of your hands. It then circulates through your body and exits through your heart and back to your ka. Notice how this mutual exchange of nurturing energy and support creates the shape of an infinity sign as it continues to move back and forth between you and your ka body. . . . [*Pause.*]

Relish the next few moments as you scan your new body and feel the power that continues to rise within you as it moves back and forth between your physical body and your ka body. . . . [*Pause.*] Now it is time to step off the wheel. Khepera, the beetle, comes to assist you. He places a perfect spiral from a shell at the base of the wheel. Intentionally step onto the shell and descend from the wheel as if you are descending a spiral staircase or following the yellow brick road. Honor the ebb and flow of life's cycles and the process of continuous transformation with each step. Thoth and Sekhmet are waiting for you when you reach the ground. As you move forward on your path, Khepera will be a strong guide and supporter to help you dance through the rough places.

Sekhmet stands before you holding up a mirror so that you can see yourself. . . . [*Pause.*] Notice how you look in the mirror as you see two reflections looking back at you. One has your face and the other is Sekhmet. As you observe, the two reflections move together and become one. At the same time, you feel your material, physical body merge with your ka body, including all the energy of your spiritual ancestral line. Use all your heightened sensitivities to experience the wholeness of your new being. . . . [*Pause.*]

Thoth asks, "Are you ready to go forward with the power of

Sekhmet and the balance, truth, and justice of Ma'at, and to take what you have learned out into the world?" Speak your appreciation and verbally state your intention and commitment regarding what you want to do as your sacred purpose or simply your work in life. Where will you go from here? Your answer is scribed, carved into the tablet along with whatever important changes Thoth sees in you at this time.

Offer your gratitude to Khnum, Thoth, Sekhmet, Ma'at, Khepera, Ptah, Anubis, and any others who have been supporting this creation of your new body and its connection to your spiritual roots. When you are ready, take a few steps down from the garden studio at Khnum's temple and find yourself back at the sycamore tree at Karnak. There you are, still in Sekhmet's body lying under the tree. Although you might be able to feel your special bond with Sekhmet, the feeling of separation continues as your readiness to emerge becomes apparent. You are still wrapped in Sekhmet's body, yet you can feel her sense of completion with the regeneration that you have been working with her to achieve.

Practice Belly Breathing to ground and center yourself in your new, very much more physical body, still within Sekhmet's. . . . Be sure to capture all the details from this journey with Khnum in your journal before they slip away.

Your re-crafted, stronger body is capable of carrying forth your joyful, compassionate heart into and through the world, no matter how chaotic it gets, for you are presently in the perfection and balance of Ma'at. The key is presence. You will be able to sustain this state of consciousness for longer and longer periods of time without burnout or other distractions as long as you stay present.

As you contemplate the changes you have made and the process that you've experienced, it is important to remember that it is gratitude that brings complete acceptance of this transformation. Once you recognize and fully engage in gratitude, you will be able

*Fig. 18.4. Ma'at*
*(Photo by Mickey Stelavatto)*

to embrace who you are, and you no longer have to repeat the same lessons over and over again. When you actually become grateful for the experiences you've had, no matter how difficult or tragic, great resilience and fortitude is gained.

## SHARED VOICES

*The weeks since our retreat have been wonderfully engaging and transformative. As you know, Angela and I had to leave you a bit early, and so that weekend, we carried ourselves fully through the rebirth and completion in a beautiful ritual, journey, and meal. We burned our twine outside in the twilight and then we each made a list of commitments that we declared aloud to our new self and to Sekhmet. We celebrated every commitment with a delectable bite of our chosen Celebratory Pleasure (dessert).*

*I am finding myself organically moving into alignment with those commitments with little effort, and a surprising amount of support from the universe.*

*June 6 marked my nine-year rebirth and anniversary of coming back from my trauma. That day I felt called to seek out a statuette of both Sekhmet and Bast, and the store I went to had just happened to get in one of each, both the same size and perfect. They now watch over me as I sleep, in sacred space on my bedroom altar.*

*One thing I am truly beginning to understand about this process is that when we shift the energy, some ailments may simply vanish. Others—we see the blocks keeping them present unwind and dissolve. And the information, resources, and ability to address and shift them become present. It has been such with my struggles with hearing loss, tinnitus, and my body's memory of suffering.*

*Since the retreat, life has carried me through powerful epiphanies, and I have been led step-by-step into research and resources that have allowed me to connect the dots on what my underlying problems may be. In a nutshell: my body and nervous system seem to be stuck in fight-or-flight mode, and the "warning bells" are literally always ringing.*

*I am finding a wonderful network of healers, scientists, and energetically aware doctors to help me calm my body; run diagnostics on my brain, heart, and blood; and to heal my ears and other difficulties. I am also naturally drawn to exercising more and eating healthier and healthier. All commitments I had made to myself I have naturally kept to. No willpower needed. It's been amazing.*

JAIME MINTUN

# 19

# Divine Intervention

There is a gestation time in every alchemical process, a time when patience is required and when you simply wait and hold space for that which is beyond your current brain wiring and imagination to happen. In some ways, this is the most important part of the work, as you are allowing time for the mystery, the unfathomable magic that takes co-creation with spirit over the top, so to speak.

When you engage in holding space for the mystery, take as long as you need and pay close attention to all signs or messages, in both the spirit and physical worlds. Try keeping your mind open, notice how you feel, and keep your focus on gratitude and on the ultimate goal of your work: the transformation on all levels that you desire.

## ☀ ACCEPTING BLESSINGS
## FROM THE COSMOS

[*Take a few Heart Breaths and bring yourself once again fully into present time and into your present location. Your consciousness is easily able to split between the temple and your home or wherever you're reading.*]

Recognize yourself curled up in Sekhmet's belly at the entrance to Sekhmet and Ptah's chapel, by the sycamore tree. As you continue to breathe the Heart Breath, take a few minutes to contemplate what you've been through during the time it has taken to get this far in the book. As you consider what has changed for you, consciously allow space for another level of divine intervention: consider the possibility of intelligence beyond that of Sekhmet and the deities we have been blessed to work with thus far. Compared to the cosmic scale of the sun or the galaxy, we are but the tiniest filament of gold, such as that strand of gratitude that Sekhmet wove into the clay of your new body. Simply be, without thought or desire, an empty field upon which only divine intervention itself can add or change any aspect of the work that has been done. . . . [Long pause.]

As you open your heart and your mind to new, unexpected possibilities, become aware of a gathering of Egyptian neteru and other allies quietly coming into Karnak and approaching the temple. They have come to witness a special blessing that is being given to you from a source beyond naming or even description, although you may have your own personal vision at this time. Simply be still, quiet, and aware for the next few moments. . . . [Pause.]

When the energy shifts again, turn your attention toward gratitude and all the things you have to be thankful for as well as all the beings, plants, and other allies who have helped and supported you along the way. . . . [Long pause.]

As you complete the expression of your thankfulness for all the beings, from both the spirit and physical worlds, who have witnessed and supported you throughout your time in the belly of the goddess, be sure to write a complete account of your most recent experiences in your journal.

You might feel a mixture of joy and anticipation, as it has been quite some time since you were devoured, digested, and have been gestating your renewed and reconstructed self. For many of you it has become remarkably comfortable to be consciously aware of your intimate relationship with Sekhmet and the perspective you have gained from living within her body. For others, you may be chafing at the bit to be out and on your own once again. Regardless of how you feel at this moment, this round of "Transformation in the belly of the goddess" is almost over, and the love that has been created between you and Sekhmet will last; yet it will be some time before you have fully integrated the transformation that has occurred within you.

## SHARED VOICES

*First of all I have always felt sorry for spirits that have not moved on but never knew how to help them and didn't have the courage to in case something went wrong and things became worse. So as you know during this class I saw someone get killed in the temple while visiting Nefertem, and because of this class, with the help of Sekhmet, Anubis, Ptah, and Osiris, I found the courage to go back to the temple and help this spirit move on. It was an amazing experience, one that I will I never forget. So from this class I discovered that Sekhmet and the other deities will not just take care of our problems, but they will also be here to support and protect us if we have the courage to face our fears and try to help ourselves.*

*Since this class I have had to live through some really trying times, and I have found that I can calm down and think through things and work on solutions without drinking or going into complete depression. The change has been a miracle, because I am not a calm person; I have always reacted first to difficult and hurtful situations without considering the consequences of my actions, and I usually made things worse.*

*Also, I have found the courage to express my beliefs, in a nice way, and to share my beliefs about my spiritual life without worrying whether others would accept me. I feel I have grown and am still growing every day into the person I was meant to be.*

*Thank you for a wonderful, life-changing class.*

DEBBIE CROSTHWAIT

*Ma'at (Photo by K. Indigo Rønlov)*

This has been an amazing class. The journey I had on the eve of the 3/21/2018 was the entire class work. I was able to connect to the light pathways of my body to the light pathways of my earth, and to feel myself from the Netherrealm, from my own on my side, maybe Sekhmet on both my connect to the wild Pathways allowed me access to everything, all worlds all times, all places that summoned me :)

PART IV

❧ ❦ ❧

*Transformation*

# 20

## Emerging

As you rest in Sekhmet's lioness body under the tree, there is a sense of completeness in your new body. You are aware as your new akashic blueprint takes shape and consistency as it fuses with and fills the body created by Khnum. You find yourself in between meditating and participating in your physical experience.

### ☀ MEDITATION ON THE REGENERATION OF YOUR NEW SELF

[*Take a few Heart Breaths and allow yourself to enter into a deeper state of presence with the spirit world. . . .*]

Sekhmet twitches her tail as she paces back and forth. She crouches down, rolls in the sand, and tumbles around, and you can feel yourself being jostled about in the fluids of her belly . . . You can also hear her heart beating. Listen to her heartbeat and feel its rhythm pulse through you as your new body takes in the final nourishment of this gestation time, this magical time in the belly of the goddess. . . . [*Pause.*]

As you scan yourself, notice the most obvious changes: more clarity, more awareness. . . . Notice the firmness of your skeleton, and perhaps a lessening or lack of pain or tension and greater mobility where you might have sustained past injuries. . . . [*Pause.*]

Although Sekhmet's heart continues beating quite strongly, she has calmed considerably and stopped her pacing and rolling. . . . Her belly ripples. . . . She stands still and strikes a pose, such that her haunches are slightly down and her front legs stiffen. . . .

From within her belly you can feel Sekhmet inhale a mighty breath. When she reaches the top of her breath she pauses. . . . You can feel yourself being lifted as you rise up and out of her body as she exhales with a giant ROAR. . . . [*Long pause.*]

Most often you land standing, but if you're folded up, unfold yourself so that you can be standing as quickly as possible. . . .

Reach up and start pulling all the mucous coating off yourself, digging it out of your mouth and your nose. . . . Use both your hands to pull the veil from your eyes and clear your ears. . . . Notice the texture of your skin as it toughens and changes from soft wet pink to the firm consistency of the strong adult body that you are. . . . [*Pause.*]

Even if you are experiencing this journey sitting or lying down, you see yourself naturally upright, as though you are ready for anything. One foot is slightly in front of the other. Your knees are slightly bent, your shoulders back and your head held high. . . . Taste the air. Look around you. Listen. . . . See your renewed self as the powerful being that you are. Notice how you receive information clearly and without bias through your heightened senses. Notice the healthy hunger growing within you for knowledge and sustenance, and the realization and confidence that everything you need is within your reach. . . . [*Pause.*]

As you tune in to your surroundings, there is a sense of harmony and resonance, as though you are not only in tune with your surroundings, but you are also the master of your universe.

Allow yourself to move into your natural state of being, where you now experience at least two worlds simultaneously, if you choose. As you become more and more aware of the new clarity of your experience, you can now release yourself from the meditation, yet stay in the clarity of the meditative state while you consider the following:

No longer will you be fooled by people's lies or illusions as long as you maintain this state of being. You can and will act with wisdom. You have strength and courage, and with all the qualities that you recognize in yourself there's also a natural welling up of the desire to help, to guide, to council, and to do the right thing moment by moment. You receive information constantly, and with that information you make decisions that will be of benefit for yourself, for others in your family, for your workplace, for your community, and your tribe.

You might notice that you have even more of a sense of protectiveness with regard to the youth and children of future generations. Wherever you are, wherever you stand, you are in the center of your power. And because of this, and because of the perfection that you have achieved with this ritual and ceremony, from now forward, your job is simply maintenance. Remember, you can always call on Sekhmet to help you if you begin to falter; awareness of her presence is never more than a breath away.

You are in control of your body and your mind, including your hunger. You choose what you eat because you know that you are what you eat. You choose how to respond and what to do because you can see in a moment the results of your actions. You can feel a new sensation around the choices you make—and it feels like wisdom. You know the difference between what you can control or change and what you cannot. . . . [*Pause.*]

You also know that you're not given more than you can handle, regardless of what's happening around you. You are spirit inhabiting a body; you are whole and in balance. Your next steps are now crystal clear. Affirm this knowledge and your commitment to it out loud, speaking your intention and your will with true conviction, and observe how your voice grounds and anchors your statement and your new body. . . . [*Long pause.*]

Take some time now to bring your journal up to date and record your intention and your will, even as you know that Thoth is scribing them. Remember the ankh with the magnifying glass that Ptah gave you. Use it and all the other tools in your life as well as those you've been given in this alchemical process.

Whenever you feel yourself start to falter or forget, just breathe in the realization that the goddess Sekhmet lives in you, as you live in her. She informs every cell of your being. You can choose to block it, but why would you? The more conscious you can be, the more consciousness you can sustain, until it just takes over and becomes the way it is. Staying aware and remembering that you are in control of yourself is up to you from this moment forward. Sekhmet, like any good mother, is always there to help you work it out. All you need is to remember that with this new level of presence and awareness, knowledge and healing will spontaneously come to you. . . . [*Pause.*]

You have the capacity to be informed as needed in every moment. Once you see your next steps, you'll know with confidence and certainty where you're going. When that happens, the most important thing to know is that you already have the tools that you need. They're not just the tools that you received in this process; you've spent a lifetime amassing and collecting experience and knowledge. What you don't have yourself, you know from whom and where to go to get it. From now forward, get out that medicine chest, dust it off, and use your tools to make whatever you need happen. Now that you know how to access the Akashic Records, there's a good chance that you will find what you need there. Quite likely others before you have found themselves working through the same problem that you are stuck in, and your answer is waiting there for you to find.

Meanwhile, while you've been experiencing and discovering the regeneration of your new self, the lioness has returned to the temple. Be sure to take time to offer gratitude to Sekhmet for all she has done for you. . . . [*Pause.*]

Walk through the colonnade to Sekhmet's chapel. Sekhmet greets you at the door in her goddess form. As you meet each other once again, eye-to-eye and heart-to-heart, give your gratitude to Sekhmet and receive your final benediction along with her gratitude for the work that you have done to co-create the possibility for achieving that sacred purpose for which you came onto our precious planet at this time. . . . [*Long pause.*]

### SHARED VOICES

*I love this class and have taken it several times, even though I had to get up in the middle of the night to listen to it live. Here is what I remember about emerging:*

*The roar of Sekhmet was like breathing new life breath into me—Sekhmet's breath was my new life breath. It was giving me life and allowing me to disconnect from being inside of Sekhmet and to begin to move my body on its own again, like a baby chick hatching from its egg. The roar of Sekhmet was the most important and powerful moment. Her breath from the roar also felt like it was giving me the possibility to grow into my highest potential. The feeling was as though her breath was inflating a balloon (my potential) so that it could become as large as it can be.*

*The connection for grounding this potential physically with the Earth is much stronger now that it is more evident that each and every cell of my new body is in direct relationship with the environment that surrounds me. This correlation exists with all that I have learned, not only with my heart, but with every cell in my body.*

*Once again, thank you!*

PILIAKA CORINA PETER

This next report came from Gloria Taylor Brown, a student/colleague/friend who has been working with me since the early 1980s. She took the first Sekhmet class that I taught in the United States, in Port Townsend, Washington, probably back in the late 1990s. At that time we were working only with rage and how to transform it. Following is some of what she remembers.

*My relationship with Sekhmet has always been tangled with my own issues around anger and rage. After a seven-year hiatus in my studies with you, I was SENT to the class on Sekhmet, because it was there that I would receive my new mission. . . .That training was without a doubt THE most POWERFUL training I have ever been in with you—I just hope that the book has an nth degree of that power for its readers. . . .*

*I became a midwife for the birthing process, helping each person to remove the globules of fluid from his or her nose and mouth, helping them stand, and become adults again. I became a midwife to the course of creation for the neteru, as they imbued each being with a new sense of self, a new connection with Spirit.*

*As the other students were reborn, I found myself reborn as well. I was asked as I stepped forward, did I still need that wellspring of rage, bubbling like a volcano, about to erupt, for my new journey. "No, not at this time," I replied. I could see that I could access the energy, without the corrosive rage component. I could create, and not destroy. I also knew that I could always reach back for that energy if it was necessary to defend those that I loved.*

*My new mission was to go into the world of women and learn how to relate to them, how to find the empowerment, within and without, as we moved forward. Thus began a new journey, working with the Women of Wisdom Conference, creating programs with that group, which culminated with my becoming president of the board of trustees, some nine years later. Sekhmet never left me during that time—and she still looks over my shoulder, as I write this. She has much to say, and wants to make sure that her thoughts are correctly delivered and understood. She will have many new voices as this book goes out into the world. Listen to her well. She has a message for each reader.*

*Her message for me is that rage is a tool, just as love is. It can be used negatively or positively. It all comes from the place of power. And power can bring you great joy or great grief. It all depends on how you use it. Use the tools you are given wisely.*

AHO.

GLORIA TAYLOR BROWN

# 21
# Completion

## FOUR PRINCIPLES
## OF ALCHEMICAL HEALING

As we move into creating your final ceremony, it is a good time to review the four principles upon which Alchemical Healing is based, for they are the principles that make co-creation work.

First are the skills that you have brought to the table of this alchemical process, including your intentionality and your skill in observation, discernment, and focus as well as everything you've learned in your life until now.

The second principle has to do with your relationships with Spirit. You've connected with Spirit on many levels to follow the instructions that allow the magic to happen. None of us can do this work alone. You accomplished your transformation with the help of Sekhmet and others from the family of the Egyptian neteru, as well as others that contributed, such as Medicine Buddha and the elements. You worked with the elements, honoring and relating to them, and were informed by them, taught by them, and guided by them. It is through these nurtured relationships that the second principle in this Alchemical Healing process is honored.

Divine intervention is at the heart of the third principle, which has to do with magic and miracles. You have held space and allowed for that which you could not imagine to happen. Some of that magic has already revealed itself in the wondrous process that has taken place over the course of your working through this book. Some of it has yet to be revealed and will unfold as a result of your continuing to hold space for this magic to happen as you move forward with your intended sacred purpose.

The fourth principle is gratitude and appreciation. Throughout this process, you have expressed your gratitude to the different beings and elements that have come forward to assist you. Now that the process nears its end, let the tangible feeling of gratitude flow through your body and shine like the sun.

## ☀ YOUR COMPLETION CEREMONY

Your completion ceremony can be simple, yet profound. Hopefully, there is some place outdoors where you can build a sacred fire. Or maybe you have a fireplace. If not and if you can't be out in nature, you can use a barbecue brazier or woodstove. You have to build a fire strong and hot enough to completely reduce the twine (or whatever medium you used) into ash. In that process is the actual consummation of this alchemy. You will wish to save the ash, as it is strong medicine in itself. Use it sparingly as you are guided.

When you are doing a ceremony of this nature you want every aspect of it to come with a level of respect and sacredness that honors what you are doing. Even the gathering of the paper, twigs, or whatever you use to create the fire should be done with a sense of sacredness and respect. Honor the wood that is going to transform itself for you. If you are going to split it, make that a sacred process—honor that process. If you live in an urban area, most hardware stores carry a natural product, pine heartwood that is saturated with the tree's pitch. It's sold as "fire starter." Smudge all of your implements. Express your gratitude for everything and every being that supports you.

Even though you have completed all the initiations and rites in the book, you might feel that you need more time. You may want to go over some of these journeys and rites again. Or maybe you realize some things you might have forgotten that you want to let go of or that you want to add to your reconstruction. If you can already see that more work is needed, do the work *before* you go ahead with your ceremony of completion. Then burn the twine to complete this round, with the understanding that there is no end to our growing and learning about ourselves—there is no end to our becoming. Be sure to collect the ashes when the fire has cooled. Then give yourself considerable time to integrate and truly learn where you have come to when you have completed the alchemy. Use your introspection and your intuition, and especially your practices, to fully discover what you have received before you go for more and start over again.

Your ball of twine (or wax or . . .) contains the whole process in it. Briefly review the thoughts and emotions that went into the knots; salute them for what they were—an integral part of who you have been before you accepted your own power and responsibility. Nothing has been lost except for your weakness and the blindness that caused you to occasionally stumble throughout your life. It is the act of burning that completes the transformation, so be sure that you create your own unique ceremony. Make it a memorable experience, one that informs the integration process and anchors the transformation with magic, respect, and gratitude. Give it the time and intention that befits the result you want in your life. Be sure to invite Sekhmet, Thoth, Anubis, and all your guides and ancestors to witness, and feel free to call on them for inspiration. It does not have to be a long ceremony.

Continue to develop your relationship with Sekhmet until you realize that you have access to her at all times, and have the discernment to know when you need to call on her. If you feel that you have to repeat the alchemy, you have to start all over again, which you can always do at any time. That's part of the beauty of this process—you now have an alchemical formula and allies in Sekhmet, Anubis, Ptah, and others to assist you. In the future, when you are confronted with aspects of yourself that need to be worked on or if you uncover a trauma that has been hiding, forgotten, yet still has a hand in your thoughts and decisions (yes, some things were so bad we forgot them in order to survive)—when you realize that you've gotten to a new layer that needs to be transformed, you can repeat the process. It might not take as long the second time, and once you really understand the way it works, you can make it fit into your life, knowing what you are getting in to.

You have enough knowledge and experience to design your own alchemy or process. You can then return to the temple and offer a new ball of twine along with your prayers and gratitude so that you can regenerate yet again. There will come a time when you realize that you can work on a specific troublesome characteristic, creating a much simpler and shorter alchemy that will bring about the transformation you need in less time. You can also choose to journey just to the land of lost hopes and dreams to retrieve aspects of your life or character that you may have lost. Even simply spending time with Sekhmet under the sycamore tree will give you an opportunity to receive clarity regarding something that you are working on in your life.

Meanwhile, take the time you need to review all the parts of this transformation between now and when you build your fire and complete your ceremony. In the end, it's important to once again pay your respects and offer appreciation to Sekhmet and all the elements and beings that have supported and assisted you. Be sure to carry that gratitude into your final ceremony and completion when it is all said and done and burned.

Sa Sekhem Sahu.*

---

*The mantra Sa Sekhem Sahu comes from *The Goddess Sekhmet: Psycho-Spiritual Exercises of the Fifth Way,* by Robert Masters, and means "the breath of life, the might, the realized human."

## SHARED VOICES

*It is the job of the shaman to shake people out of their ordinary, habitual states of mind and to reawaken latent faculties so that healing can take place. This can be a world-shattering, soul-quaking experience. It can be painful.*

*There is a vast reservoir of knowledge in such pain, and shamans are the ones seeking it out and imaginatively and courageously transforming it into soul, into art, into new knowledge. The kind of knowledge gained is a bone-knowledge, a marrow-deep wisdom, a soul-caliber comprehension.*

*Through the armor of Sekhmet's own belly we all passed through the alchemical fire, were digested into our physiological parts and reborn anew once more. The golden light of healing energy illuminated and purified us as Sekhmet carried us through the journeys that re-formed our bodies, hearts, and minds. Sekhmet, as a brilliant vehicle, carried us with compassion to shield us from the fear of the openhearted brokenness that egoless experience creates.*

*As with all of your work, Nicki, this teleclass was masterfully created and delivered. As with all the journeys that I have experienced with you, I usually perceive the next vision before you describe it. I am not alone in such experiences. Many students have made similar observations when discussing their experiences.*

*After the class ended and I burned my knotted cord to ash, I noticed that both sides of my brain were active and that I could feel the activity. I continue to experience my life as bi-planar—I experience on two planes at the same time. The class refueled my perception and cleared the cobwebs from my ability to "see."*

MERLIN HINDLEY

# Acknowledgments

Bern, Switzerland, January, 1997—Sekhmet spoke up. It was time, and her teachings would no longer wait. Dr. Christine Fehling, Jungian psychiatrist, lineage sister, and a teaching partner for many years, stepped comfortably in to her role for those first lessons, and the conversations began. In the years that followed, many others partook in the co-creation that has become this book, while a growing hunger for Sekhmet's teachings has become a flood that empowers students and teachers alike.

Another growth I've witnessed over the years is the number of Sekhmet priests and priestesses who have stepped in to the magic as the words and phrases waited for harvest. There are others, more than I can put a number to, who knew when to pick up the phone, fade into the dream, and flow through the mists with me. When the teachings came and the words were put into the manuscript that morphed into this book, they became available for generations to come.

It is at this moment—when a list is emerging as some of the co-creators whom I have turned to so often are like a parade before my eyes while the cheers of the ancients fill my ears and Sekhmet's banner flows over them—that I would like to present my gratitude to all of those without whom this book would never have been written.

Over the years, and in response to what I perceived as a growing need for Sekhmet's teachings to become more available, I continued to share the work, each time observing it expand and grow. Eventually I started keeping track of those with whom I worked to bring in new journeys to add to the alchemy. I apologize to anyone whom I may have forgotten, as all of her teachings are co-creations, delivered through trusted visionaries, fellow students, and Sekhmet priests and priestesses.

Those without whom this book would not have come to fruition, and upon whom I shower deep and abiding gratitude, include:

Debbie Clarkin, dear friend, colleague, lineage sister, and teacher of Alchemical Healing who spent countless hours on the phone with me from her home in Canada, three teleclasses, two retreats that were devoted to Sekhmet's work, and three tours to Egypt (so far) supporting me and Sekhmet's work. Debbie deepened the teachings with new journeys, including "Merging with Sekhmet," "Fierce Compassion," "The Land of False Hopes and Broken Dreams," "In the Soup with Wadjet," "The Oasis," "First, There Was the Word," as well as Nefertum's bubbles, the meridian chapter, and more. She patiently answered my endless questions, researched many of the things that I didn't fully understand, practiced Alchemical Healing on me when I hurt, and all the while kept me upbeat and on track. In addition, Debbie drew six of the illustrations and provided several photographs that are included in this book.

Indigo Rønlov, soul sister friend, who showed up again and again, whenever needed. Her vision quest in the White Desert yielded the journey to retrieve and strengthen our skeletal systems, and she contributed the bundle at the Sphinx while coleading with me during an Egypt tour devoted to Sekhmet's work. Indigo influenced Khnum's journey and almost every other journey in the book. She generously gave constant support and friendship. She was always available to listen to my changes, take the journeys, and give me intelligent feedback. She also did many Alchemical Healings and even typed for me when my back wouldn't allow me to do it myself. Indigo is also a great photographer who contributed a number of fine photographs to help illustrate this book.

The beautiful foreword that Normandi Ellis wrote captures the essence of what this book is attempting to convey, and, as with everything she writes, she managed to pleasantly surprise me on many levels, especially with the story of her healing from Sekhmet that parallels this work. Normandi was always accessible to answer my many questions, translate hieroglyphics as needed, and offer opinions that greatly influenced the content of this book.

Through a series of magical synchronicities and genuine surprises, Hank Wesselman's foreword appeared at the very last moment, eloquently completing the articulation that describes Sekhmet in a way that bridges the gap between science and shamanism. The story of his encounter with Sekhmet offers readers a sensitive demonstration of our ability to commune with spirit in a way that can alter a lifetime of deeply felt beliefs in a momentary flash of comprehension.

Mitch Bebel Stargrove, N.D., went over the manuscript with great care and helped me to understand the network of systems that work together to interconnect our bodies, minds, emotions, and spirits and make us human beings. Thank you for saving me from the embarrassment of my ignorance. Lori Stargrove, N.D., helped me to understand her husband and lent her unique perspective to the process throughout. The Stargroves also made many trips to Eugene from Portland with their healing magic to make sure that I was physically and mentally capable of completing the book, a project that took several years, even after Inner Traditions • Bear & Company agreed to publish it.

Kathryn Ravenwood, Gloria Taylor Brown, Jeya Aeronson, Indigo Rønlov, Debbie Clarkin, and Lois Stopple spent many hours and many phone calls going over the manuscript and tweaking it in ways that only their clear eyes and strong relationship with Sekhmet could achieve as they meticulously read and contributed considerable improvements to the rough drafts. These longtime visionary sisters have always had my back, and they always show up either just before or when I need them.

Amanda Starlight and Jacqueline Mullen, along with Indigo, added inspiration with their group visioning of the brain regeneration, as did my husband, Mark Hallert, and Debbie Clarkin. In

Egypt, Debbie, Jacqueline, and Indigo helped to envision Khnum's re-creation of the body and ka.

A special shout of gratitude to those students who took the time to write about their experiences, helping to shed light for those who are reading and will read this book, especially Cristina Trujillo, who took extensive notes on her experiences during the teleclass journeys, and especially those areas that were confusing, so that I could repair them. (See their signatures at the end of the Shared Voices letters, which appear at the end of each chapter.)

Safia Suboohi, Marjorie Bridges, Heidi Mason, Ellis Ganley, and Ashley Drowatzsky kept the office, garden, and home together to give me the time I needed to complete this project. For that I am forever grateful.

Kat Lunoe's oil painting, which graces the cover, is an exquisite portrait of Sekhmet portrayed in her aspect as the compassionate healer. Thank you for your beautifully rendered interpretation of the statue that lives in Sekhmet's chapel, where it all began and where an endless stream of pilgrims discover why they were called to Egypt and to this book.

I had not heard of nor understood iconography until I connected with Ptahmassu Nofra-Uaa, whose skill and commitment brought forth his magnificent icon of Sekhmet, the gift of which I am privileged to have as the first color plate in this book.

Tarek Lotfy, Indigo Rønlov, Nicole Haworth, Hank Wesselman, Jacob Cohl, Debbie Clarkin, and Mickey Stelavatto contributed many of the photographs that allow readers to see where they are at any given time during certain journeys. Their generosity and skill are greatly appreciated, as are the illustrations of Debbie Clarkin, Erin Alaina Schroth, Lauren Raine, and Karen Klein, who permitted me to use their beautiful images, some of which came from *The Union of Isis and Thoth*.

A huge thank you to Emil Shaker, my friend and Egyptologyst who is also our Anubis—our guardian and guide. Emil has accompanied me and my groups through countless pilgrimages to Egypt and has been a great support in the writing of this book. He tirelessly answers all my questions and, because he hails from Luxor, offers special tidbits of folklore and access to Sekhmet at Karnak, even when her chapel was closed to the public during restoration. When I was first sharing this work in Egypt some years ago, Emil recognized the ritual as authentic, and when he realized that it was becoming a book, he offered me access 24/7 so that he could contact the chief archaeologists at all the temples in Upper Egypt to answer my questions and make sure that I had all my historical facts correct. Blessings and gratitude, Emil; I love you too!

Without the constant support from Mohamed Nazmy, this book could never have been written. Mohamed's company, Quest Travel, makes magic happen and doors open for us as we sail the Nile on the *Dahabeya Afandina,* a magnificent luxury sailing yacht that was designed and built to our specifications. He also gives me and my cohorts spacious and comfortable apartments in which we can rest and write between tours. Mohamed provides for our needs above and beyond, and beyond the beyond . . . Thank you!

From conception to birth of this book, the folks at Inner Traditions • Bear & Company have been there for me. Yet before Bear & Company was bought by Inner Traditions in 2000, it was owned by Gerry and Barbara Hand Clow. In 1989 I was magically guided to consult with Barbara as an astrologer regarding some unrelated issues in my life. Although she had retired from doing personal readings, she followed her inner guidance and agreed to do one for me, letting me know that in no way would she *ever* use a reading to choose an author for her company. Many months later I received a message: "Where will you be day after tomorrow? I want to send you a tape of your reading." The tape arrived at exactly the same time as the great San Francisco earthquake of that year. I opened it with trepidation and discovered with joyous surprise that Barbara and I had a deeper connection than I could have imagined; if I could write the book that she was told I could,

I would have the backing of Bear & Company and the book would be illustrated by Angela Werneke (*Medicine Cards*). Barbara has had my back ever since. She did the blessing for Mark and me during our wedding. She sat with me for days while I was flat on my back from chemotherapy, refusing to leave until we discovered how and why I'd gotten breast cancer. I was diagnosed just a few weeks after my first book, *The Golden Caldron,* now *Power Animal Meditations,* was published. She did a benefit for me to help us get by. We are soul sisters, separated only by time and distance and the weighty circumstances of our ridiculously busy lives. In truth, I could never have written this or any of my other books without Barbara Hand Clow. My love and gratitude also encompass her husband, Gerry, who believed so much in me that he personally edited that first book, going over it with me line by line on the telephone—hours and hours of long-distance phone calls. Barbara and Gerry also joined me on my company's second tour to Egypt. It is safe to say that they were the first contributors to this book and for all the above reasons and more, I send my deepest gratitude to both of them.

At Inner Traditions I send my gratitude first to Jon Graham and Ehud Sperling for recognizing its importance and for waiting patiently for me to get it together. More thanks to Jeanie Levitan and her fine editorial staff, especially her assistant, Patricia Rydle, who was consistent in her ongoing encouragement and help, and for my brilliant editors, Laura Schlivek (the best of the best) and Nancy Yeilding, who showed magical perception as they reworked the manuscript with remarkable skill and care and suggested and implemented editing changes that improved this book beyond my imagining. And ongoing gratitude for the rest of the ITI staff who always make me feel like I belong to a family of people who want the best for this book and for me, including Erica Robinson and Nicki Champion for their work on cover text and design, and Manzanita Carpenter, Shannon Walker, and others who continue to help me get the word out after it goes to print.

It's difficult to express all the ways in which my beloved husband, Mark Hallert, supported me and contributed to this book. Not only did he go over every word, and had the last word on the final manuscript, but he was always aware when it was crunch time and there were many mornings when I didn't realize I'd forgotten to eat until he placed a plate of food in front of me, or the same with dinner and washing dishes and running errands. It probably would have taken another two years if Mark hadn't stepped up! Besides, he's put up with me for thirty-one years as of this writing . . .

And then there is the spirit world, inclusive of all the beings, totems, ancestors, and spirit allies from all spaces and dimensions who showed up to support the writing of this book and who will be there for the people who read it. Thank you for enriching this work with your presence and support.

I send my everlasting gratitude to Medicine Buddha—your magic catalyzed the vision that conceived this book. Your continued presence is appreciated more than words can tell.

Thoth, Anubis, Ma'at, Ptah, Wadjet, Khnum, Mut, Sobek, Horus, and the many others from my Egyptian neteru family who called forth the energy and focus required to make this book happen, I thank you. Like Mark and so many of my friends, you continued to believe in me even when I didn't believe in myself. Thank you for the privilege of writing this book for you, and for the world.

And finally, and most importantly, to Sekhmet: Thank you for choosing me to create this book—it has been a joyful honor. Along with my immense and overflowing appreciation for your trust, as one of your most devoted cubs I pray that my efforts please you and that I and my cadre of accomplices bring joy to you and your pride, and bring healing to the world. Hail to you and to all the warriors and guardians of Ma'at. Sa Sekhem Sahu.

WITH DEEPEST LOVE AND GRATITUDE,
NICKI SCULLY, BLUE EAGLE

# Glossary

**Abydos:** The village in Upper Egypt where the temples dedicated to Osiris are located. These include the temples of Seti I and Ramses II, which were added to the Osirion, the most ancient of the currently extant temples in Egypt. Called Abdju in ancient Egyptian language.

**adept:** An initiated person who is proficient at the esoteric and magical arts.

**akasha:** A Sanskrit word for the all-pervading subtle field wherein past and future events are recorded. In some systems considered the fifth element, the matrix from which the four fundamental elements—earth, water, fire, and air—are derived and through which they form a living system, an interconnected network.

**Akashic Records:** The subtle field that contains all the past, present, and potential future events.

**Alchemical Healing:** A comprehensive healing form created by Nicki Scully and published in the modern guide *Alchemical Healing: A Guide to Spiritual, Physical, and Transformational Medicine,* which is part of a trilogy that includes *Power Animal Meditations* and *Planetary Healing: Spirit Medicine for Global Transformation,* by Nicki Scully and Mark Hallert.

**alchemy:** The art of transforming base material into alchemical gold, the universal medicine or philosophers' stone, and accomplished through spiritual enlightenment. Also considered laboratory chemistry and mythopoetic psychology—a magical initiatory process, or a weaving of all.

**Amun:** Ram-headed creator god (horns curled around ears) to whom the main temple at Karnak is dedicated. Represents the sun as it sets and journeys through the night.

**ankh:** Ancient Egyptian hieroglyphic symbol for the key of life.

**Anubis:** Jackal-headed god of the underworld, Opener of the Way, who guides the dead on their journey back to the light. A dependable guardian, guide, teacher, and shaman. Anpu in ancient Egyptian language.

**arcane:** Esoteric mystery teaching, usually of a philosophical, mythic, or poetic nature; not generally available.

**autonomic nervous system:** Those bodily functions that we generally don't consciously manage or control, such as breathing, heartbeat, and other rhythmic cycles that we engage in more or less automatically.

**Bast:** Fertility goddess with the head, or head and body, of a cat. Originally a local goddess of Bubastis, in Lower Egypt, she became closely identified with Hathor and Sekhmet.

**calcination:** The first of seven steps of alchemy; involves purification by heat, breaking down and decomposing the prime material.

**cauldron:** a pot or vessel used for cooking or serving, meant here to describe the belly as the vessel within which the alchemy of transformation occurs, as in cooking.

**centrifuge:** A device (usually a vessel) that rotates an object around a fixed axis, thus activating or accelerating the principles of sedimentation. Denser matter will move out and away from the axis while less dense objects or matter will become displaced and travel toward the center of the spin.

**dantien (dantian):** Important physiological centers of activity and storage in the human body, with differing names, in several traditions. Of the three locations in the body, the lower dantien, located in the belly below and behind the belly button, is the most useful place to consolidate gathered life force.

**diadem:** An emblematic headband or crown that symbolizes sovereignty.

**dissolution:** the second step in alchemy, dissolving the base material within the subconscious mind.

**djed:** A pillarlike symbol with four crosses that represents the four planes of reality: physical, astral, mental, and spiritual. It is associated with the backbone of Osiris and signifies stability.

**Djehuti:** Egyptian name for Thoth, which is a later Greek name. Later appearing in Europe initiatic traditions as Thoth Hermes Trismegistus.

**eczema:** An itchy skin rash that appears most anywhere on the body, common in babies and less often in adults.

**endocrine network:** A network of glands that secrete hormones, chemicals that direct and organize bodily functions and response patterns; functionally inseparable from neurological, immune, and mental/emotional/psychological systems.

**epithet:** A word or phrase that is descriptive of the character or specific attribute of a person.

**faience:** A ceramic glaze used in ancient Egypt to make scarab beads and amulets and other talismans. Usually a pale blue-green color, although other colors are also used.

**foramina/foramen:** An opening in bone to allow passage of nerves and other aspects of the network of systems along the spine.

**Geb:** The brother and husband of the goddess Nut (Nuit), son of Tefnut and Shu. He is god of the Earth and his symbol is the goose.

**hara:** Place of activity in the abdomen or belly, just beneath the belly button, that is the vital storage place of will, qi, and power; lower dantien.

**Hathor:** Goddess of love, joy, celebration, beauty, music, dance, inebriation, sexuality; this beloved goddess is inextricably linked with Sekhmet. They are like the flip sides of the same coin. Hathor is considered by some to be, along with Thoth, the oldest of the neteru. Her name means "House of Horus" (*hat-hor*). She is associated with the sky goddess Nut. As the cow goddess, her milk is the Milky Way, and her totemic animal is the water buffalo. She was the golden calf that caused the kerfuffle in the Sinai when Moses came down from the mountain with the Ten Commandments and found his followers partying and worshipping Hathor, the sacred golden calf.

**Hatshepsut:** The daughter of Thutmoses II who became a notable leader as one of the few women pharaohs. She had a key role in bringing Karnak to its full magnificence.

**hieroglyphics:** The oldest sacred, pictorial writing system of ancient Egypt; only used in magico-religious contexts.

**ho'oponopono:** Hawaiian forgiveness ritual based on restoring and cultivating respectful relationships.

**Horus:** The son of Isis and Osiris, his is an ever-evolving story involving generations in god-time as well as throughout the civilization of Egypt. Although his stories and various forms are well documented throughout the temples and in Egyptian literature and mythology, his story also evolved with every pharaoh, for every pharaoh was called Horus to honor the living deity he embodied as the bridge between Heaven and Earth, the cosmos and the people of Khem; one who took the hero's journey and evolved from birth as a vulnerable infant to an impetuous warrior and ultimately to the true enlightened ruler that each earthly pharaoh was meant to embody. Usually refers to Horus the Younger in his many forms, rather than Horus the Elder.

**Horus the Elder:** The son of Nut and Geb, never fully incarnated so that he could soar high to be closer to his mother. He was the brother of Isis and Osiris, for whom their son was named.

**Huna:** The magical lineages and mystical traditions of Hawai'i.

**Hyksos:** An ethnic group from western Asia who ruled Egypt during the fifteenth century BCE. They were said to have built Jerusalem after they were expelled from Egypt. They introduced horses and chariots and other new weaponry when they successfully invaded Egypt.

**hypostyle hall:** A large interior hall with many pillars, found extensively in ancient Egyptian temples.

**hypothalamus:** A complex gland in the limbic system of the brain that releases hormones that control many autonomic and other bodily functions. It also connects the nervous system with the endocrine system through its interconnection with the pituitary gland. The relationship between these glands ensures that the body maintains balance. Roughly the size of an almond, it directly holds sway over many, if not most of the glands that divvy up the tasks and make a human tick. Hormonal secretions are controlled much like a puppet master with more hands than Medusa has hair, only the neurosecretory cells are the puppeteer's hands and the infundibular stalks that reach into the pituitary gland are its arms. Even though it is small, cone shaped, and dense (it can weigh as much as 1.73 ounces), it controls much of our optic and olfactory nerves via our endocrine network.

**in situ:** In its original place.

**Isis:** Goddess of nature and magic, wife of Osiris and mother of Horus. Ancient Egyptians knew her as Aset or Iset; her name means "Throne," as seen in her headdress.

**ka:** One of the higher subtle bodies in ancient Egyptian mythology, representing the etheric double that is each person's connection to their spiritual lineage.

**Karnak:** An ancient Egyptian complex of temples, primarily dedicated to the triad of Amon, Mut, and their son, Khonsu.

**khamaseen:** Blinding hot windstorms in Egypt, usually during late March or April. Because of the sands of the desert, visibility is often reduced to zero, although the storms usually last for only several hours.

**Khem:** The name of ancient Egypt as used by those who lived there. Khem refers to the inhabitable and arable "black land" enriched by the flooding of the Nile. Al-Khem is the likely root of "alchemy." "Egypt" is from the Greek word *Aigyptos,* referring to Thebes (Wasat).

**Khepera:** The god represented by the scarab beetle, considered self-created. He represents the sun as it is rising. Small scarab icons were placed within the tombs of the deceased for protection.

**Khnum:** The ram-headed potter god who is said to create all the bodies (and kas) of all creatures of the Earth on his potter's wheel. He is distinguished from Amun because his horns spiral outward like waves, or DNA.

**Khonsu:** Most often the son of Amon and Mut, also seen in Esna (Iunyt) as the son of Hathor and Khnum. He is a moon god, protector of travelers and foreigners; his name means "the wanderer." In the "Cannibal Hymns" from the Old Kingdom texts in the pyramid of Unis, he was interpreted as a bloodthirsty eater of the gods. We have since learned that this is a literalist misinterpretation; rather, he consumed the other gods, thus becoming them. After all, we are what we eat. . . . He was also a healer who was said to have healed a granddaughter of Ramses II from possession by honoring and creating a feast for the demon, after which the demon went away happy.

**Kom Ombo:** A town in Upper Egypt that is the home of the temple of Sobek and Horus; called Nubt in ancient Egypt. It was also the recipient of many of the Nubians who were displaced when their villages near Aswan were flooded when the Aswan High Dam was constructed (after eleven years, construction was completed July 21, 1970).

**kundalini:** The Sanskrit word for "coiled one," referring here to the snakelike life force that rises and integrates the aware and embodied human; considered feminine in nature and personified as an aspect of Shakti. Experientially parallel to the *sekhem* generated by Sekhmet and her initiates.

**ley lines:** Invisible lines that create alignments between significant or sacred places of power on Earth.

**limbic brain:** Located beneath the cerebrum and above the medulla oblongata, this midsection of the three main parts of the brain has complex attributes that are associated with emotional responses to memories, pain, and other senses. Some of its higher functions include learning, creating memories, and the organization of motor behavior. More formally known as the limbic system.

**Luxor:** Originally the capital of Upper Egypt, then called Thebes.

**Ma'at:** Both a goddess and a concept—the principle that we all serve—truth, justice, order, balance, morality, and law (cosmic law, not people's law). She is a winged goddess, usually shown wearing a single feather on her head, who embodies respectful relationships. She is the dynamic equilibrium within living systems.

**mantra:** A word, phrase, or sound that is vibrated aloud in a repetitive way to transform consciousness.

**Medicine Buddha:** Bhaiṣajyaguru, the Buddha of healing, the blue Buddha of Mahayana or Vajrayana represents the physician who cures suffering or the healer within. His mantra and visualization, with or without the traditional empowerments, are said to relieve suffering and increase self-healing and health.

**medulla oblongata:** Physically located at the lowest part of the brain, it is continuous with the spinal cord as well as the brain stem. At this intersection, abutting the pineal gland, it controls some of the involuntary vital functions, including the functions of the heart and lungs.

**melatonin:** A hormone secreted by the pineal gland that is stimulated by natural changes in light, as from dusk to dark.

**Memphis:** Old Kingdom first capital city of Egypt (3100–2258 BCE), founded by Menes when the Two Lands were united. The triad of Memphis is Ptah, Sekhmet, and their son, Nefertum. In ancient Egypt it was known as Inbu-Hedj, referring to its white walls.

**meridians:** A term for invisible lines used in charting various fields. Chinese medicine posits that qi flows through *jīngluò* (or channels) in the human body. Mapmakers use a system of meridians that go from the North and South Poles, crossing the equator perpendicularly.

**Middle Kingdom:** Pharaoh Mentuhotep II reunified Upper and Lower Egypt during the 11th Dynasty, heralding a renaissance of art and culture in Egypt, and paving the way for Thebes (now Luxor) to become the capital of Egypt during that time. According to which source you use, the middle Kingdom lasted approximately from 2030 BCE to 1640 BCE.

**Mut:** Associated with the vulture and Nekhbet, she is the nurturing mother goddess, wife of Amun and mother of Khonsu. Usually seen as a woman wearing the vulture headdress.

**Neith:** One of the oldest, most complex goddesses and known for her ability to have created herself without a partner, yet she is considered the mother of many of the gods. She wears the red crown and is a protector of the royal house in her cobra/Wadjet form. Associated with archery and weaving; often shown with a shuttle on her head.

**Nekhbet:** Initially a local predynastic vulture goddess of Upper Egypt, she, along with Wadjet (the cobra goddess from Lower Egypt), became one of the "two ladies," guardians of the pharaoh and the entire empire of Egypt. She is often seen flying in the corners of the walls of temples, carrying the *shen,* the symbol of eternal protection. Egypt's oldest known oracle was at the shrine of Nekhbet at Nekheb.

**neocortex:** The most recent adaptation of the evolving brain, allowing for higher brain function such as learning. Brain research is opening vast new avenues of knowledge about the plasticity of the brain and its ability to create new patterns of learning, even in adults. The neocortex governs sensory capabilities, balance, movement, cognitive responses, and higher mental functions.

**Nephthys:** Twin sister of Isis, mother of Anubis (with Osiris), wife of Set, and member of the Great Enead of Heliopolis. Although she has long been considered the nebulous or passive one, she is becoming more known as high priestess (see *Shamanic Mysteries of Egypt* and *Anubis Oracle*) and as the main nurse of every pharaoh, with extremely protective attributes. The ancient Egyptians called her Nebet-het or Nebt-het, "Lady of the [Temple] Enclosure."

**nervous system:** A complex network within the body that transmits signals to coordinate functionality in different parts of the body; interconnected with the endocrine, immune, and mental/emotional/psychological systems.

**neter, netert, neteru:** The Egyptian word for the deities of their pantheon. *Neter* is masculine, *netert* is feminine, and *neteru* is plural. It became *netcher* to the Copts, and finally *nature* in English. The ancient gods of Egypt are principles of nature.

**neuron:** Electrically excitable cells, most of which are found in the central nervous system, including the brain and spinal cord. Neurotransmission between these cells is accomplished by chemical and electrical means, and some of these cells have been measured to be longer than one yard in humans.

**neuroplasticity:** Refers to everything from remapping the brain to causing a change in an individual neuron. The ability to rewire an adult brain, once believed to be impossible, is an exciting new frontier in neurobiology today.

**New Kingdom:** Known as the Egyptian Empire, the New Kingdom included the eighteenth, nineteenth, and twentieth dynasties and lasted from 1570 BCE to 1069 BCE. The Golden Empire, as it's also known, included some of the most famous pharaohs: Akhenaten, several Thutmoses, Queen Hatshepsut, Amenhotep III, Tutankhamun, and a number of Ramses, including Ramses II, known as Ramses the Great, to name a few of the most well-known.

**Nut (pronounced "noot," also spelled Nuit):** This Egyptian sky goddess, daughter of Shu and Tefnut, and mother of Isis, Osiris, Set, Nephthys, and Horus, consort of the earth god Geb, is often featured on temple and tomb ceilings, her starlit body arching across the sky and within whose body the sun travels through the night to be reborn each morning. Each being is a star in her body.

**Old Kingdom:** The first peak of the great Egyptian civilization, from dynasties III to VI, ca. 2686 BCE–ca. 2181 BCE, during which Memphis was the capital and the high arts and pyramid building developed, starting with the

Saqqâra step pyramid. Tombs and temples from that era were notable for their rich paintings and other art forms depicting the life of the time and the natural world in which the people lived.

**olfactory:** That which relates to the sense of smell.

**oscillations:** Rhythmic fluctuations that create vibrations.

**Osirion:** An ancient, currently underground temple dedicated to Osiris, and some say where his head is buried. It is also where the mysterious "Flower of Life" images were found on one of its huge stone pillars, the source of which is unknown.

**Osiris:** First born of Nut and Geb, husband of Isis. Murdered by his brother Set, he rose as the Lord of the Underworld. Known in ancient Egypt as Ausar or Ausir.

**pantheon:** A Greek word for any family of deities such as the Egyptian neteru.

**pineal gland:** Named for the pinecone that it resembles, its main function is to secrete melatonin.

**pituitary gland:** Secretes a number of hormones that regulate many of the body's systems, including metabolism (stimulates the thyroid gland), lactation, sexual functions, blood pressure, growth, temperature regulation, and other important body functions.

**prima materia:** The prime matter in alchemy; that which is to be transformed in the process.

**psycho-neuroendocrine-immune or psychoneuroendocrine (PNI) network:** A non-hierarchical coordination and feedback system guided by the pituitary gland, which signals all of the other glands in the endocrine network and the hormones they secrete. It connects the circulatory system amd nervous system.

**psychopomp:** One who guides lost souls through the afterworld.

**Ptah:** The great creator god, consort of Sekhmet. With his blue head in the sky and his mummified feet in the innerworld, he owns all the space in between. Some say the world is the creation of a happy thought of Ptah, brought into manifestation by the Word. He is the patron of artists, craftsmen, architects, and builders.

**qi:** The life force or, more accurately, the activity of living.

**qigong (chi kung):** Pronounced "chee gung," qigong is a martial art, the skillful manipulation of qi through postures, movement, and focused intention for the purpose of gaining and maintaining physical and spiritual health, balance, strength, and vitality. *Gong* refers to the intentional and disciplined self-cultivation practice that confers skill, transforms character, and enhances healthy function.

**Ra, Re:** Great creator god associated with the sun at midday. Becomes Amun-Ra during the journey through the night and is known as Ra-Horakhty when later merged with Horus.

**reptilian brain:** The oldest of the three complexes of brain functions (limbic, neocortex, and reptilian), it controls primitive and instinctive as well as coping and memory mechanisms and lays the foundation of the many layers of sophistication that have been added to our brains over millions of years. Breathing, heart rate, and basic survival needs are ruled by the reptilian brain. It includes the brain stem and the cerebellum, which make up the current brains in reptiles.

**Sa Sekhem Sahu:** A powerful Egyptian mantra: *Sa* is "the breath of life." *Sekhem* is "power or might." *Sahu* is "the fully realized human," living with embodied awareness in all of their subtle and dense bodies. (See Robert Masters, *The Goddess Sekhmet: Psycho-Spiritual Exercises of the Fifth Way.*)

**Saqqâra (Sakkara):** The necropolis of Memphis.

**scarab:** A carving of the dung beetle, representing the god Khepera. As amulets, they were carried for protection and placed in the mummy wrappings and sarcophagi of the deceased to ensure resurrection. Rebirth and self-creation are associated with winged scarabs.

**sekhem:** Egyptian word for power, vitality, life force; parallel to kundalini.

**Seshet (Seshat):** Goddess of writing, keeper of the libraries (including the Akashic Records), feminine counterpart of Thoth. She is also the one who instructs temple building, lays the original seed stones for the temples, and determines the temple boundaries. She wears a seven-pointed star or flower atop a pillar on her head and is said to be related to the seven sisters (the Pleiades).

**shuttle:** Weaving tool often worn on the head of Neith or the chest of a cobra goddess representing Neith.

**smudge:** A form of purification and clearing of a place, situation, or person of harmful presences, smudging is a Native American tradition that uses the smoke of sage, juniper, cedar, or other sacred herbs. In ancient Egypt highly valued plant extracts such as frankincense and myrrh were used.

**Sobek:** Crocodiles were common in the Nile River before they were poached out of existence just in the past several decades. This powerful crocodile god was feared as well as respected and required propitiation to keep the people safe. Eventually he became known as a fertility god and became fused with Ra, as Sobek-Ra.

**standing waves:** The result of two waves meeting one another in the same medium. The resulting interference creates a new wave pattern called a standing wave.

**sycamore tree** (*Ficus sycomorus*)**:** The sycamore fig is the largest evergreen tree native to Egypt and one of several trees considered sacred. One of Hathor's names is Lady of the Sycamore. The sticky, milky white substance beneath the bark was and still is used as medicine by Upper Egyptians for skin and other disorders, especially eczema.

**Tahuti:** An Egyptian name for Thoth.

**Taoism (Daoism):** Ancient Chinese tradition inclusive of various models, concepts, and contemplative practices that lead to a perfected, healthy life by aligning with nature. One common translation of Tao is "The Way."

**Tasenetnofret:** An aspect of Hathor known as the "good sister," who married Horus the Elder; the mother of Panebtawy.

**thangka painting:** Exquisitely detailed Tibetan Vajrayana Buddhist religious paintings on cloth, usually kept rolled up when not gracing an altar or monastery wall.

**Thebes:** Ancient capital of Upper Egypt, now called Luxor.

**Thoth:** Lunar Egyptian deity of wisdom, language, communications, medicine, architecture, science, and more. He is the scribe of the gods and teacher of teachers. Known as Hermes to the Greeks and Mercury to the Romans, he is most often seen in Egyptian art as a man with the head of an ibis or a baboon. His role is to bring the unmanifest into manifestation though articulation with sound and symbols and to maintain the universe. He is associated with the arbitration of godly disputes, the magical arts, the system of writing, the development of science, the storing of knowledge and maturation of knowledge into wisdom, and the judgment of the dead. His feminine counterpart is Seshet, and his wife is Ma'at.

**transpersonal:** Beyond the realms of personal identification.

**universal life force:** Whether called qi, ki, reiki, sekhem, or by any other name from any and all traditions, the universal life force is the infinite animating force field emanating from Source. Anyone can learn to connect with and direct this force for healing and to amplify intention.

**uraeus:** Circular crown emblematic of the serpent power worn by deities and high initiates of ancient Egypt. The ancient Egyptian word was *iaret* (*j'r.t*).

**vesica piscis:** Literally, fish bladder. A geometrical pointed oval symbol created by the overlapping of two circles, the meaning of which can depend upon the intention for the meaning of each circle, such as above and below, spirit and matter, male and female, and so on. In Alchemical Healing, it is a symbol used as a doorway to access the element akasha.

**void:** The absence of anything, the ultimate vacuum. All energy, mass, and persona do not and cannot exist in a void.

**wadi:** An Arabic word that describes a dry riverbed or valley that fills with water only in times of intense rain. This usually dry riverbed can, over the eons, create a subsurface aquifer.

**Wadjet:** The cobra goddess originating in Lower Egypt who sits on the uraeus crown and the dais of Sekhmet. A protector of Egypt and the pharaoh. Also the name of the healing eye of Horus.

**was staff or uas scepter:** A staff with the head of an unknown animal at the top and a curved bottom end usually carried by the gods, like a tuning fork; it carries the ability to have dominion over chaos. The symbol of Set's authority as held by the pharaoh.

# Bibliography

Corcoran, Sandra. *Shamanic Awakening: My Journey between the Dark and the Daylight*. Rochester, Vt.: Bear & Company, 2014.

Ellis, Normandi. *Feasts of Light: Celebrations for the Seasons of Life Based on the Egyptian Goddess Mysteries*. Wheaton, Ill.: Quest Books, 1999.

———. *Imagining the World into Existence: An Ancient Egyptian Manual of Consciousness*. Rochester, Vt.: Bear & Company, 2012.

Ellis, Normandi, and Gloria Taylor Brown. *Invoking the Scribes of Ancient Egypt: The Initiatory Path of Spiritual Journeying*. Rochester, Vt.: Bear & Company, 2011.

Forrest, M. Isidora. *Isis Magic: Cultivating a Relationship with the Goddess of 10,000 Names*. St. Paul, Minn.: Llewellyn Publications, 2001.

Georgitsis, Tina, ed., *Daughter of the Sun: A Devotional Anthology in Honor of Sekhmet*. Australia: Bibliotheca Alexandrina, 2016.

Grossinger, Richard. *Embryogenesis: Species, Gender, and Identity*. Berkeley, Calif.: North Atlantic Books, 2000.

Hildago, Sharlyn. *Nazmy: Love Is My Religion, Egypt, Travel, and a Quest for Peace*. New York: Phoenix Rising Publishing, 2014.

Hoffman, Danielle Rama. *The Tablets of Light: The Teachings of Thoth on Unity Consciousness*. Rochester, Vt.: Bear & Company, 2017.

Holdrege, Craig, ed. *The Dynamic Heart and Circulation*. Fair Oaks, Calif.: AWSNA Publications, 2002.

Ingerman, Sandra, and Llyn Roberts. *Speaking with Nature: Awakening to the Deep Wisdom of the Earth*. Rochester, Vt.: Bear & Company, 2015.

Ingerman, Sandra, and Hank Wesselman. *Awakening to the Spirit World: The Shamanic Path of Direct Revelation*. Louisville, Colo.: Sounds True, 2010.

Kant, Candace C., and Anne Key, eds. *Heart of the Sun: An Anthology in Exaltation of Sekhmet*. Universe.com, 2011.

Lipton, Bruce. *The Biology of Belief,* 10th anniversary ed. Carlsbad, Calif.: Hay House, 2016.

Lubicz, R. A. Schwaller de. *The Temple of Man: Sacred Architecture and the Perfect Man.* Rochester, Vt.: Inner Traditions, 1998.

Masters, Robert E. L. *The Goddess Sekhmet: The Way of the Five Bodies.* Amity, N.Y.: Amity House, 1968.

Mulders, Evelyn. *Western Herbs for Eastern Meridians and the Five Element Theory.* Lake Country, B.C., Canada: Sound Essence, 2006.

Naydler, Jeremy. *Shamanic Wisdom of the Pyramid Texts: The Mystical Tradition of Ancient Egypt.* Rochester, Vt.: Inner Traditions, 2005.

———. *Temple of the Cosmos: The Ancient Egyptian Experience of the Sacred.* Rochester, Vt.: Inner Traditions, 1996.

Pert, Candace. *Molecules of Emotion: The Science behind Mind-Body Medicine.* New York: Simon & Schuster, 1999.

Scully, Nicki. *Alchemical Healing: A Guide to Spiritual, Physical, and Transformational Medicine.* Rochester, Vt.: Bear & Company, 2003.

———, and Linda Star Wolf. *Shamanic Mysteries of Egypt: Awakening the Healing Power of the Heart.* Rochester, Vt.: Bear & Company, 2007.

———, Linda Star Wolf, and Kris Waldherr. *The Anubis Oracle: A Journey into the Shamanic Mysteries of Egypt.* Rochester, Vt.: Bear & Company, 2008.

———, and Mark Hallert. *Planetary Healing: Spirit Medicine for Global Transformation.* Rochester, Vt.: Bear & Company, 2011.

———, and Normandi Ellis. *The Union of Isis and Thoth.* Rochester, Vt.: Bear & Company, 2015.

Thành, Minh, and P. D. Leigh, trans. "Sutra of the Medicine Buddha." BuddhaNet: Buddha Darma Education Association, Inc. www .worldwidehealingcircle.net/medicine_buddha_mantra.htm.

Wesselman, Hank. *The Re-Enchantment: A Shamanic Path to a Life of Wonder.* Louisville, Colo.: Sounds True, 2016.

# Index

Note: *Italic* page numbers indicate photos or illustrations.

# About the Author

Nicki Scully has been teaching Alchemical Healing, shamanic arts, and the Egyptian Mysteries since 1983. Techniques from her Alchemical Healing form are used internationally by thousands of practitioners.

She is a lineage holder in the Hermetic Tradition of Thoth and maintains the Lyceum of Shamanic Egypt through the Fellowship of Isis. She is ordained as a priestess of Hathor by Lady Olivia Robertson, cofounder of the Fellowship of Isis. During her first visit to Egypt with the Grateful Dead in 1978, Nicki experienced an epiphany on the top of the great pyramid and soon realized that her purpose in this life was to bring forth the hidden shamanic and healing arts of Egypt. In the late 1980s, Nicki founded Shamanic Journeys, Ltd., and, after leading more than sixty tours, she continues to guide inner journeys and organize spiritual pilgrimages to Egypt.

Nicki lives in Eugene, Oregon, with her husband, Mark Hallert. She maintains a comprehensive healing, mentoring, and shamanic consulting practice and welcomes you to study with her at her beautiful garden center or via phone or video conferencing. Please visit her websites:

**www.ShamanicJourneys.com**
**www.HathorsMirror.com**
**www.TheAnubisOracle.com**
**www.BecomingAnOracle.com**
**www.PlanetaryHealingBook.com**

# ALSO BY NICKI SCULLY

**The Union of Isis and Thoth** (2015)
*Magic and Initiatory Practices of Ancient Egypt*
Cowritten with Normandi Ellis

**Planetary Healing** (2011)
*Spirit Medicine for Global Transformation*
Includes a guided journey CD, *Making Spirit Medicine*
Cowritten with Mark Hallert

**Becoming an Oracle** (2009)
*Connecting to the Divine Source for Information and Healing*
A 7-CD audio learning course in 19 guided Oracular Journeys
For a sample journey visit www.BecomingAnOracle.com

**The Anubis Oracle** (2008)
*A Journey into the Shamanic Mysteries of Egypt*
Book with 35-card deck
Cowritten with Linda Star Wolf, illustrated by Kris Waldherr

**Shamanic Mysteries of Egypt** (2007)
*Awakening the Healing Power of the Heart*
Cowritten with Linda Star Wolf

**Alchemical Healing** (2003)
*A Guide to Spiritual, Physical, and Transformational Medicine*

**Power Animal Meditations** (2001)
*Shamanic Journeys with Your Spirit Allies*
Illustrated by Angela Werneke